MICROSOFT® OFFICE EXCEL® 2010
QuickSteps

JOHN CRONAN

New York Chicago San Francisco
Lisbon London Madrid Mexico City
Milan New Delhi San Juan
Seoul Singapore Sydney Toronto

MICROSOFT® OFFICE EXCEL® 2010 QUICKSTEPS

34567890   QVS QVS   10987654

ISBN   978-0-07-163489-2
MHID   0-07-163489-4

SPONSORING EDITOR / Roger Stewart

EDITORIAL SUPERVISOR / Jody McKenzie

PROJECT MANAGER / Vasundhara Sawhney, Glyph International

ACQUISITIONS COORDINATOR / Joya Anthony

TECHNICAL EDITOR / Marty Matthews

COPY EDITOR / Lisa McCoy

PROOFREADER / Paul Tyler

INDEXER / Valeria Perry

PRODUCTION SUPERVISOR / George Anderson

COMPOSITION / Glyph International

ILLUSTRATION / Glyph International

ART DIRECTOR, COVER / Jeff Weeks

COVER DESIGNER / Pattie Lee

SERIES CREATORS / Marty and Carole Matthews

SERIES DESIGN / Bailey Cunningham

Contents at a Glance

1 2 3 4 5 6 7 8 9 10

Contents

Chapter 5 Viewing and Printing Data 113

Chapter 6 Charting Data 137

Chapter 9 **Analyzing and Sharing Data**............................ 219

Chapter 10 **Extending Excel**.. 251

To Tony, Pinar, and Sinan...

...far away you may be, but always close in our thoughts and prayers

—John & Mom

About the Author

John Cronan has more than 30 years of computer experience and has been writing and editing computer-related books for over 18 years. His recent books include *eBay QuickSteps Second Edition, Microsoft Office Excel 2007 QuickSteps, Microsoft Office Access 2007 QuickSteps,* and *Dynamic Web Programming: A Beginner's Guide.* John and his wife Faye (and cat Little Buddy) reside in Everett, Washington.

Acknowledgments

Marty Matthews, technical editor, whose attention to detail caught several errors and omissions, and whose experience provided much appreciated counsel, as always.

Lisa McCoy, copy editor, ensured a cohesive and consistent voice, as well as correcting many grammatical and technical errors.

Valerie Perry, indexer, provided a thorough index to assist the reader in quickly locating the information they seek.

Joya Anthony, acquisitions coordinator, provided the "gentle" nudging to keep me on task and schedule.

Jody McKenzie, editorial supervisor, and **Vasundhara Sawhney**, project manager, brought all the pieces together to produce a fine deliverable.

Roger Stewart, sponsoring editor, for championing Excel and the other books in the QuickSteps series.

Introduction

QuickSteps books are recipe books for computer users. They answer the question, "How do I...?" by providing quick sets of steps to accomplish the most common tasks in a particular program. The sets of steps are the central focus of the book. QuickSteps sidebars show you how to quickly do many small functions or tasks that support the primary functions. Notes, Tips, and Cautions augment the steps, yet they are presented in such a manner as to not interrupt the flow of the steps. The brief introductions are minimal rather than narrative, and numerous illustrations and figures, many with callouts, support the steps.

QuickSteps books are organized by function and the tasks needed to perform that function. Each function is a chapter. Each task, or "How To," contains the steps needed for accomplishing the function along with relevant Notes, Tips, Cautions, and screenshots. Tasks will be easy to find through:

- The Table of Contents, which lists the functional areas (chapters) and tasks in the order they are presented

- A How To list of tasks on the opening page of each chapter

- The index with its alphabetical list of terms used in describing the functions and tasks

- Color-coded tabs for each chapter or functional area with an index to the tabs just before the Table of Contents

Conventions Used in This Book

Microsoft Office Excel 2010 QuickSteps uses several conventions designed to make the book easier for you to follow:

- A 🌐 or a 🖉 in the Table of Contents or the How To list in each chapter references a QuickSteps or a QuickFacts sidebar in a chapter.

- **Bold type** is used for words on the screen that you are to do something with, such as click **Save As** or click **File**.

- *Italic type* is used for a word or phrase that is being defined or otherwise deserves special emphasis.

- <u>Underlined type</u> is used for text that you are to type from the keyboard.

- SMALL CAPITAL LETTERS are used for keys on the keyboard such as ENTER and SHIFT.

- When you are expected to enter a command, you are told to press the key(s). If you are to enter text or numbers, you are told to type them. Specific letters or numbers to be entered will be underlined.

- Tools are identified on the ribbon by (1) the tab they fall under, (2) if applicable, the contextual tool family from which they come, (3) the group of tools in which they are located, and (4) the tool's name. For example: "In the Format tab (Chart Tools) Labels group, click **Chart Title**."

How to...

Chapter 1
Stepping into Excel

Excel 2010 is Microsoft's premier spreadsheet program. While maintaining the core features and functionality of Excel from years past, this version continues the evolution of Office products from a menu-driven user interface (the collection of screen elements that allows you to use and navigate the program) to that of a customizable *ribbon*, an organizational scheme to better connect tools to tasks. Along with these and other infrastructure enhancements, Excel 2010 adds several new ease-of-use features, such as a *paste preview* so you can see the results of a change before you make it, and this version improves on many functional features, such as new *sparklines*, which provide mini-charts to track trends that fit within a cell. While preserving the simple elegance of a spreadsheet to handle arithmetic calculation of data, Microsoft continues to find ways to make that task less onerous and adds features

QUICKSTEPS

OPENING EXCEL

Excel can be started by several methods. The method you choose depends on convenience, personal style, and the appearance of your desktop.

USE THE START MENU TO START EXCEL

Normally, the surest way to start Excel is to use the Start menu.

1 Start your computer, if it is not running, and log on to Windows, if necessary.

2. Click **Start**. The Start menu opens.

3. Click **All Programs**, if needed, scroll down the menu by clicking in the bar on the right of the menu, click **Microsoft Office**, and click **Microsoft Office Excel 2010**, as shown in Figure 1-1.

LOAD EXCEL FROM THE KEYBOARD

1. Press the **Windows flag** key ▦ (between the **CTRL** and **ALT** keys on most keyboards), or press **CTRL+ESC**.

2. Press the **UP ARROW** key to select **All Programs**; press the **RIGHT ARROW** key to open it.

3. Press the **UP ARROW** or **DOWN ARROW** key until **Microsoft Office** is selected; press **RIGHT ARROW** to display the list of programs.

4. Press **DOWN ARROW** until **Microsoft Office Excel 2010** is selected; press **ENTER** to start it.

CREATE A SHORTCUT TO START EXCEL

An alternative way to start Excel is to create a shortcut icon and use it to start the program. To create the shortcut, click **Start**, click **All Programs**, click **Microsoft Office**,

Continued . . .

that allow you to use and distribute information in more meaningful ways. In this vein, Excel 2010 does not disappoint.

This chapter explains how to open Excel, use and customize the ribbon, and then set it up to meet your own needs. You will learn how to open existing workbooks (the core Excel file), change the appearance of new ones, and save your changes. When you need further assistance, getting help, online or offline, is explained. Finally, you'll learn how to end an Excel session.

Figure 1-1: *The classic way to start Excel is from All Programs.*

OPENING EXCEL *(Continued)*

and right-click **Microsoft Office Excel 2010**. From the context menu, select one of the following:

- Click **Pin To Start Menu** to add a shortcut to the top, or permanent, area of the Start menu.
- Click **Pin To Taskbar** to include an icon on the taskbar next to Start.
- Click **Send To** and click **Desktop (Create Shortcut)** to add a shortcut on your desktop.

Open
Troubleshoot compatibility
Pin to Taskbar
Pin to Start Menu
Restore previous versions
Send to ▸
Cut
Copy
Delete
Rename
Properties

To use the shortcut to start Excel, use whichever of the following fits your shortcut:

- On the Start menu, click **Start** and click the Excel shortcut.
- On the taskbar, click the Excel shortcut.
- On the desktop, double-click the Excel shortcut.

You can see that the taskbar option is the simplest and most direct.

NOTE

The terms *worksheet*, *sheet*, and *spreadsheet* all refer to the same row-and-column matrix that comprises the working area of Excel. These terms are used interchangeably throughout this book.

Explore the Excel Window

The Excel window has many features to aid you in performing calculations, adding visual objects, and formatting your work, as well as performing file management tasks such as saving, printing, and customizing how you want Excel to work for you. These tools (also referred to as commands and tasks) are organized within the ribbon and File menu and support the work you do in the *worksheet*, the working area of an Excel file (see Figure 1-2), or *workbook* (workbooks are further described in "Using Workbooks," later in this chapter). The principal features of the Excel window are introduced in Table 1-1 and are described further in this and other chapters of this book.

Become Familiar with the Ribbon

The original menu and toolbar structure used in Office products from the late 1980s and early 1990s (File, Edit, Format, Window, Help, and other menus) was designed in an era of fewer tasks and features and has simply outgrown its usefulness. Microsoft's solution (starting with Office 2007) to the increased number of feature enhancements is the *ribbon*, the container at the top of Office program windows for the tools and features you are most likely to use to accomplish the task at hand (see Figure 1-3). The ribbon collects tools you are likely to use in *groups*. For example, the Font group provides the tools to work with text. Groups are organized into *tabs*, which bring together the tools to work on broader tasks. For example, the Insert tab contains groups that allow you to add components, such as tables, links, and charts, to your spreadsheet (or slide presentation or document).

Each Office program has a default set of tabs and additional tabs that become available as the context of your work changes. For example, when working on a picture, a Picture Tools-Format tab displays. The ribbon provides more screen real estate so that each of the tools (or commands) in the groups has a labeled button you can click. Depending on the tool, you are then presented with

Quick Access toolbar
Formula bar
Title bar and workbook name
Minimize and restore the ribbon
Minimize, maximize, and restore the Excel window
Close Excel
Control menu
File tab
Close the workbook
Minimize, maximize, and restore the worksheet window
Task pane
Excel Help
Mouse pointer
Worksheet window and grid
Sheet navigator
Status bar
Sizing handle
Scroll bar
Workbook views
Live zoom
Book1 - Microsoft Excel
File
Home
Insert
Page Layout
Formulas
Data
Review
View
Clip Art

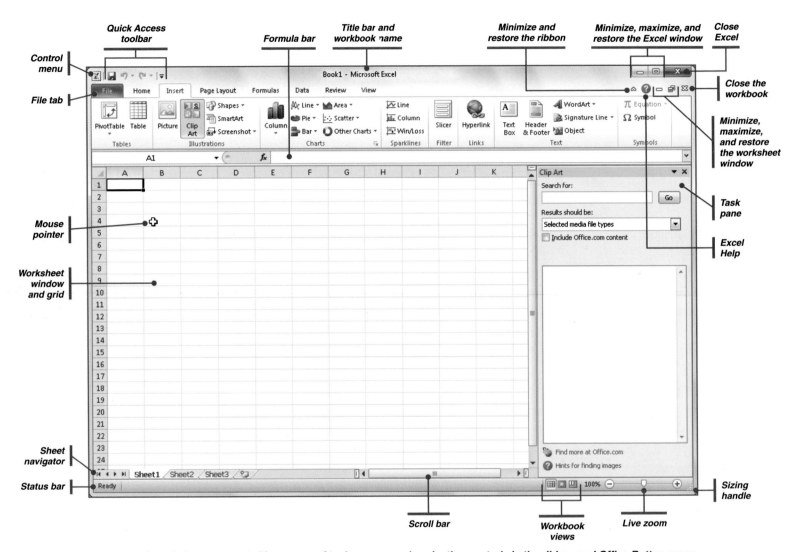

Figure 1-2: ***A worksheet, supported by groups of tools, panes, and navigation controls in the ribbon and Office Button menu, is the main focus of an Excel workbook.***

FEATURE	DESCRIPTION
Title bar and workbook name	Displays the workbook file name and can be dragged to move the window
Control menu	Provides windows movement and sizing commands
Office Button	Opens the Backstage view that displays essential tasks you perform with a workbook, such as Save, Open, Print, and Close, as well as exit Excel
Quick Access toolbar	Provides easy access to favorite tools
Ribbon	Container for available tools
Tabs	Organize groups of tools into areas of use
Groups	Contain tools with common functionalities
Dialog Box Launcher	Opens a dialog box that provides further options
Help	Opens the Excel Help window, the gateway to online and offline assistance
Minimize, maximize, and restore the Excel window	Minimizes the Excel window to an icon on the Windows taskbar, maximizes the window to full screen, or restores the window to its previous size
Close Excel	Prompts you to save any unsaved work, exits Excel, and closes the window
Minimize, maximize, and restore the workbook window	Minimizes the workbook window to an icon at the bottom of the Excel window, maximizes the window to full size, or restores the window to its previous size
Minimize and restore the ribbon	Minimizes the ribbon so only the tab names show
Formula bar	Displays a cell's contents and contains features for working with formulas and functions
Gallery	Displays visual examples of available options
Live preview	Displays results of options on a worksheet as you select or point to them
Worksheet grid	Provides the row-and-column structure where text, formulas, data, and supporting objects are added
Worksheet navigator	Allows easy access to all worksheets in a workbook
Scroll bars	Move the contents of the window in the direction they are clicked or dragged
Task pane	Contains controls for certain features in a pane that can be dragged around your screen and remain on top or "floating" on other screen elements
Status bar	Displays information on several workbook parameters, such as the sum of selected numbers, page numbers, and whether your SCROLL LOCK key is enabled
Workbook views	Provides shortcuts for Normal, Page Layout, and Page Break Preview views
Live zoom	Displays the current zoom level and interactively changes the magnification of the worksheet as you click the plus or minus button or drag the slider
Sizing handle	Sizes the window by dragging in one or two dimensions
Mouse pointer	Changes appearance to perform specific tasks. Used to select, size, and move cells; edit, select, and insert text; point to commands and tools; and draw shapes.

Table 1-1: Principal Features of the Excel Window

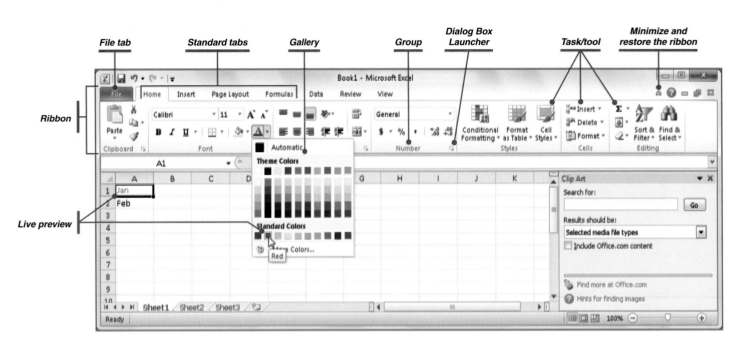

Figure 1-3: *The ribbon, containing groups of the most common tools, replaces the pre-Office 2007 menu and toolbar structure.*

TIP

The ribbon adapts to the size of your Excel window and your screen resolution, changing the size and shape of buttons and labels. See for yourself by maximizing the Excel window and noticing how the ribbon appears, and then clicking the Restore button on the title bar. Drag the right border of the Excel window toward the left, and see how the ribbon changes to reflect its decreasing real estate.

additional options in the form of a list of commands, a dialog box or task pane, or galleries of choices that reflect what you'll see in your work. Groups that contain several more tools than there is room for in the ribbon include a *Dialog Box Launcher* icon that takes you directly to these other choices.

The ribbon provides several interesting features, including a live preview of many potential changes (for example, you can select text and see the text change color as you point to various colors in the Font Color gallery). Co-located with the ribbon are the File tab and the Quick Access toolbar. The File tab provides access to the File view, which lets you work *with* your document (such as saving it), as opposed to the ribbon, which centers on working *in* your document (such as editing and formatting). The Quick Access toolbar is similar to the Quick Launch toolbar on the taskbar (pre-Windows 7) or *pinning* a program to the taskbar (Windows 7), providing an always-available location for your favorite tools.

The Quick Access toolbar starts out with a default set of tools, but you can add to it. See the accompanying sections and figures for more information on the ribbon and the other elements of the Excel window.

Work with File View

Excel 2010 shares with the other Office 2010 programs an improved way that you can easily access the tasks that affect a document, such as opening, closing, printing, and saving from one screen, avoiding the need to open several dialog boxes. This all-encompassing screen is called the File view (which makes sense, seeing as it handles background tasks not directly related to working in the spreadsheet), an example of which is shown in Figure 1-4.

To display the File view:

1. Open Excel using one of the methods described in the "Opening Excel" Quicksteps.

2. Click the **File** tab, and then click one of the areas of interest on the left of the window. For example, clicking Print displays the view shown in Figure 1-4 and provides a document preview and options for printing your work.

3. When finished, click the **File** tab to return to the Excel window.

Customize the Ribbon

The default ribbon consists of seven standard tabs (and the special File tab), as shown in Figure 1-3, with each standard tab containing several groups and sub-groups that combine related tasks. While Excel strives to provide a logical hierarchy to all the tasks available to you, it also recognizes that not everyone

NOTE

You'll see three types of tabs on the ribbon. The standard tabs appear when you open a workbook and contain a generalized set of tools. Tool tabs appear when you are working with certain Excel features, such as charts and pictures, and contain specific tools for working with these features. And, there is the special File tab.

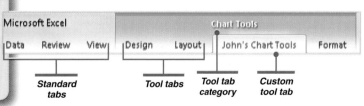

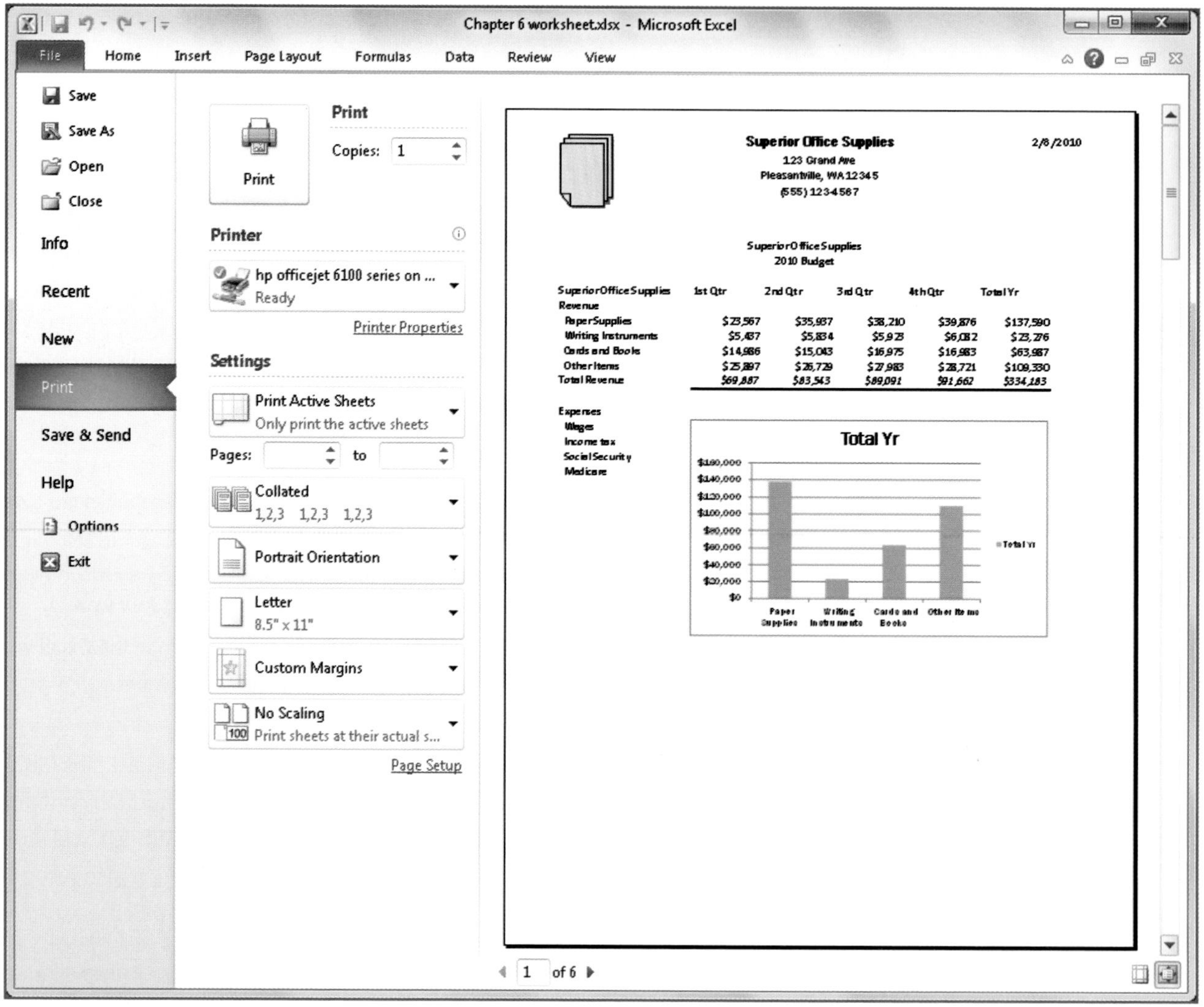

Figure 1-4: *File view provides a one-stop view of related document tasks.*

finds this way of thinking to be the most convenient and offers you the ability to change how things are organized. You can remove groups from the existing standard tabs, create new tabs and groups, and populate your new groups from a plethora of available commands/tasks.

To customize the ribbon:

Click the **File** tab, and in the left pane, click **Options**. In the Excel Options dialog box, also in the left pane, click **Customize Ribbon**.

–Or–

Right-click any tool on the ribbon, and click **Customize The Ribbon**.

In either case, the Customize The Ribbon view, shown in Figure 1-5, displays the list of available commands/tasks/tools on the left and a hierarchy of tabs and groups on the right.

REARRANGE TABS AND GROUPS

You can easily change the order in which your tabs and groups appear on the ribbon.

1. On the Customize The Ribbon view, click the **Customize The Ribbon** down arrow, and select the type of tabs that contain the groups you want to work with.

2. To rearrange tabs, select the tab whose position on the ribbon you want to change, and click the **Move Up** and **Move Down** arrows on the right side of the tabs list to reposition the tab. (The topmost items in the list appear as the leftmost on the ribbon.)

3. To rearrange groups, click the plus sign next to the tab name to display its groups, and then click the **Move Up** and **Move Down** arrows to the side of the tabs list to reposition the group.

4. When finished, click **OK** to close the Excel Options dialog box.

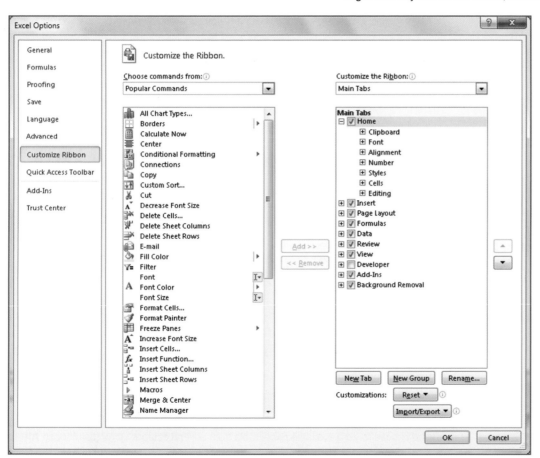

*Figure 1-5: **You can easily modify tabs and groups on the ribbon and assign tools where you want them.***

CREATE NEW TABS AND GROUPS

You can create new tabs and groups to collocate your most often used tools.

To add a new tab:

1. Click **New Tab** at the bottom of the tabs list. A new custom tab and group is added to the list.

2. Move the tab where you want it (see the previous section, "Rearrange Tabs and Groups").

3. Rename the new tab and new group by selecting the item and clicking **Rename** at the bottom of the tabs list.

   –Or–

   Right-click the tab or group, and click **Rename**.

   In either case, type a new name and click **OK**.

To add a new group:

1. Select the tab where you want to add a new group, and then click **New Group** at the bottom of the tabs list. The list of all groups in that tab appears with a new custom group at its bottom.

2. Rename and rearrange the group within the tab as previously described.

3. When finished, click **OK** to close the Excel Options dialog box.

ADD OR REMOVE COMMANDS/TOOLS

Once you have the tabs and groups created, named, and organized, you can add the tools you want to your custom groups.

1. On the Customize The Ribbon view, click the **Choose Commands From** down arrow, and choose to view available Excel tools from several categories (or just choose **All Commands** to see the full list). Select (highlight the tool by clicking it) the first tool you want to add to a custom group.

2. In the tabs list, select the custom group to which you want to add the tool.

3. Click **Add** between the lists of commands and tabs. The command/tool is added under your group.

TIP

Don't be afraid to experiment with your ribbon by adding tabs and groups. You can always revert back to the default Excel ribbon layout by clicking **Reset** under the tabs list and then choosing to restore either a selected tab or all tabs.

Customizations: Reset ▼

Reset only selected Ribbon tab

Reset all customizations

TIP

You can create a file that captures your customizations to the ribbon and the Quick Access toolbar so that you can use it on other computers running Excel 2010. In the Excel Options dialog box, click either **Customize The Ribbon** or **Quick Access Toolbar**, click **Import/Export** in either view, and then click **Export All Customizations**. To use a previously created customization file, click **Import/Export** and then click **Import Customization File**. Depending on whether you're creating or importing a customization file, a File Save or File Open dialog box appears that allows you to either store a new file or find an existing one, respectively.

4. Repeat steps 1 through 3 to populate your groups with all the tools you want.

5. If you make a mistake, remove a tool from a custom group by selecting the tool and clicking **Remove**.

6. Use the **Move Up** and **Move Down** arrows to the right of the tabs list to organize the added tools within your groups, and click **OK** when finished.

Customize the Quick Access Toolbar

You can provide one-click access to your favorite Excel tools by adding them to the Quick Access toolbar, which, by default, is above the File tab. The starter kit of tools includes Save, Undo, and Repeat.

ADD OR REMOVE TOOLS FROM A LIST

1. Click the down arrow to the right of the Quick Access toolbar, and select one of the commands on the drop-drop menu.

   –Or–

   Click the Quick Access toolbar down arrow, and click **More Commands** to view a more expansive list of Excel tools. The Excel Options dialog box appears with the Quick Access toolbar customization options displayed, as shown in Figure 1-6.

2. Click the **Choose Commands From** down arrow, and click the category of options from which you want to choose the tool you are looking for.

3. Click the tool to select it, and click **Add** in the middle of the right pane. The tool appears in the list of current toolbar tools to the right.

4. To remove a tool from the toolbar, select it from the list on the right, and click **Remove**.

5. Click **OK** when finished.

ADD OR REMOVE TOOLS DIRECTLY ON THE TOOLBAR

- To add a tool to the Quick Access toolbar, right-click a tool on the *ribbon*, and click **Add To Quick Access Toolbar**.

- To remove a tool from the Quick Access toolbar, right-click the tool and click **Remove From Quick Access Toolbar**.

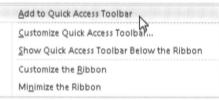

2

3

4

5

6

7

8

9

10

Select tools from
tabs and lists

Available tools in a
selected list or tab

Add and
remove tools

Customize for all
workbooks or just
the current one

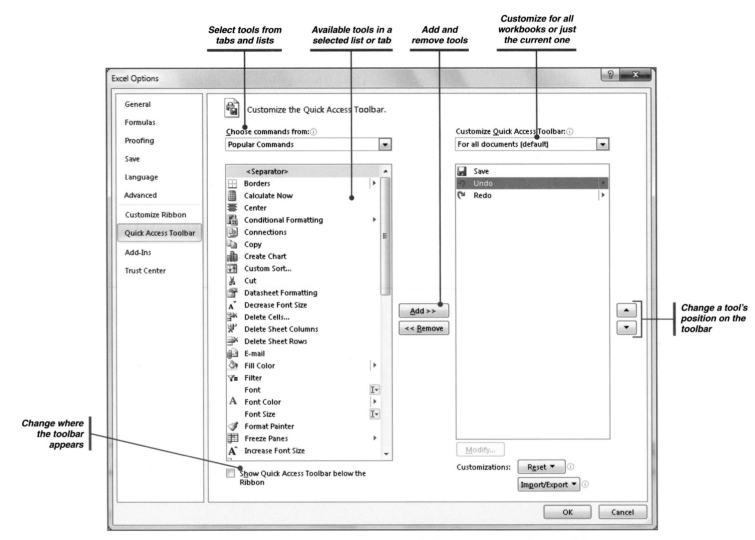

Change where
the toolbar
appears

Change a tool's
position on the
toolbar

Figure 1-6: *Any command or tool in Excel can be placed on the Quick Access toolbar for one-click access.*

RELOCATE THE QUICK ACCESS TOOLBAR

You can display the Quick Access toolbar at its default position (above the ribbon) or directly below the ribbon using one of the following methods:

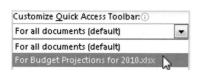

Right-click a tool on the Quick Access toolbar or on the ribbon, and click **Show Quick Access Toolbar Below The Ribbon** (once located below the ribbon, you can move it above the ribbon in the same manner).

–Or–

In the Customize The Ribbon pane (right-click a tool and click **Customize Quick Access Toolbar**), click the **Show Quick Access Toolbar Below The Ribbon** check box, and click **OK** (to return the toolbar above the ribbon, open the pane and clear the check box).

CUSTOMIZE THE QUICK ACCESS TOOLBAR FOR A WORKBOOK

By default, changes made to the Quick Access toolbar are applicable to all workbooks. You can create a toolbar that only applies to the workbook you currently have open.

1. In the Customize The Quick Access Toolbar pane, click the **Customize Quick Access Toolbar** down arrow.

2. Click the option that identifies the workbook the toolbar will apply to.

3. Click **OK** when finished.

REARRANGE TOOLS ON THE QUICK ACCESS TOOLBAR

You can change the order in which tools appear on the Quick Access toolbar.

1. In the Customize The Quick Access Toolbar pane, select the tool in the list on the right whose position you want to change.

2. Click the **Move Up** or **Move Down** arrow to the right of the list to move the tool. Moving the tool up moves it to the left in the on-screen toolbar; moving it down the list moves it to the right in the on-screen toolbar.

3. Click **OK** when finished.

TIP

You can hide tools on the ribbon and show only the list of tabs, thereby providing more "real estate" within the Excel window for the worksheet. Click the **Minimize The Ribbon** up arrow ⌃ to the left of the Help icon or double-click the selected tab name to minimize the ribbon; repeat the actions to restore it.

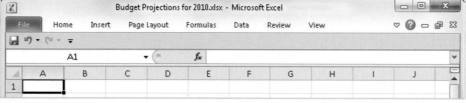

Toolbar   Search text
box   Content pane

Customize
toolbar

Connection and
filtering options

Status bar

Figure 1-7: *The Excel Help window allows you to search online and offline articles and topics using tools similar to those in a Web browser.*

Get Help

Microsoft provides a vast amount of assistance to Excel users. If you have Internet access, you can automatically access the greater breadth of information available at the Microsoft Web site. When offline, information is limited to what is stored on your computer. Also, "super" tooltips provide detailed explanatory information about tools when the mouse pointer is hovered over them.

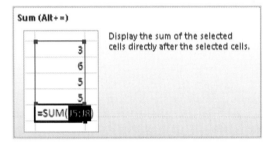

Open Help

You are never far from help on Excel. Access it using one of these techniques:

Click the **Microsoft Excel Help** question mark icon 🛈 above the rightmost end of the ribbon.

–Or–

Press **F1**.

In either case, the Excel Help window opens, as shown in Figure 1-7.

Use the Excel Help Window

The Excel Help window provides a simple, no-nonsense gateway to volumes of topics, demos, and lessons on using Excel. The main focus of the window is a search box, supported by a collection of handy tools.

TIP

The first time you open the Excel Help window, it opens to a default position and size. You can reposition and resize the window, and Excel will remember your changes the next time you open Help.

SEARCH FOR INFORMATION

1. Open the Excel Help window by clicking the **Microsoft Excel Help** icon or pressing **F1**.

2. In the text box below the toolbar, type keywords that are relevant to the information you are seeking.

3. Click the **Search** down arrow to view the following connection and filtering options for the search:

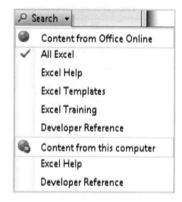

- **Connection options** allow you to choose between options from online (Content From Office.com) or offline (Content From This Computer) information. If you have an active Internet connection, Help automatically assumes you want online content each time you open the Help window.

- **Filtering options** let you limit your search to categories of information. For example, if you only want a template to create a family budget, click **Excel Templates** instead of All Excel (the default). Your search results will only display results from the chosen option.

4. Click the **Search** button when you are ready for Excel to search for your keywords.

TIP

You can have the list of top-level Help headings displayed in the initial Help page always available to you in the Help window. Click **Show Table Of Contents** on the toolbar. A Table Of Contents pane displays to the left of the content pane.

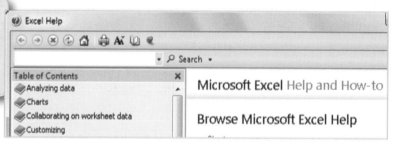

BROWSE FOR HELP

The initial Help window (shown in Figure 1-7) displays a list of Help categories similar to a table of contents. Click any of the headings to display a list of available topics and articles and/or subcategories of information. Continue following the links to drill down to the information you seek.

USE HELP TOOLS

Several tools are available to assist you in using Excel Help. The first collection of buttons contains standard Web browser tools. Table 1-2 describes these and the other Excel Help tools.

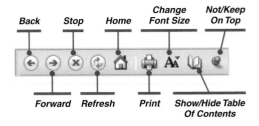

TIP

Once you start down a path to locate information, you can easily lose track of where you are in the Help system. Instead of backing out of your current location, page by page, you can directly hop to the level from where you want to resume your search. Below the Search text box, a navigation bar indicates where you are in the Help hierarchy. Each level is a link that you can click to take a shortcut to the level you want.

NOTE

The Keep On Top tool only works in relationship to Office programs. If you are multitasking with non-Office programs, they will move to the forefront (on top) when active.

TIP

You can check for new updates for Office, attempt to repair problems, contact Microsoft, and view your activation and product status from one handy location (see Figure 1-8). Click the **File** tab, click **Help**, and click the button next to the service you want.

TOOL	DESCRIPTION
Back and Forward	Allows you to move from the current Help page, one page at a time, in the respective direction
Stop	Halts the current attempt at loading a Help page (useful when loading an online demo if you have a slow connection speed)
Refresh	Reloads the current page to provide the most recent information
Home	Displays the Excel Help home page
Print	Opens a Print dialog box from which you can choose common printing options
Change Font Size	Opens a menu that lets you increase or decrease the size of text displayed in Help pages
Show/Hide Table Of Contents	Displays or removes a pane showing the list of highest-level Help categories
Not/Keep On Top	Keeps the Help window on top of the Excel (and other Office programs) window or allows it to move to the background when switching to the program

*Table 1-2: **Tools to Enhance Your Search for Excel Help***

Figure 1-8: *You can get assistance from Microsoft on Excel and other Office products.*

QUICK**FACTS**

UNDERSTANDING VERSIONS OF OFFICE 2010

Office 2010 has a newly expanded set of versions and platforms upon which Office will run. Office is now available on three separate platforms:

- Office 2010, as a resident program running on the user's desktop or laptop computer, has been available for many years, and is generally referred to as the "desktop platform"

- Office Web Apps, accessed through a Web browser such as Microsoft Internet Explorer or Mozilla Firefox, is a newly available platform

Continued . . .

Using Workbooks

The container for Excel worksheets—the grid where numbers, text, inserted objects, and formulas reside and calculations are performed—is a file called a workbook with a default file name of Book1 (see the QuickFacts "Understanding Excel File Compatibility" and "Understanding Excel's XML File Formats" for more information on file formats and extensions). When Excel is started, an existing workbook displays or a new workbook is created and displays a blank worksheet, as was shown in Figure 1-2.

Create a New Workbook

When Excel is started, you can just start typing on the first sheet of the workbook that is displayed, or you can create a workbook from one of several *templates*.

UNDERSTANDING VERSIONS OF OFFICE 2010 *(Continued)*

- Office Mobile, accessed through a mobile device such as a smart phone, is another newly available platform

Office 2010 on the desktop platform is available in four versions:

- **Office Starter 2010** is only available preinstalled on a new computer, has reduced functionally, and is advertised as being supported. It can be directly upgraded to one of the following three full versions of Office 2010 through a product key card purchased through a retail outlet.

- **Office Home & Student 2010** is available to be installed from a DVD or via Click-To-Run over the Internet, and contains the full version of Microsoft Word, Microsoft PowerPoint, and Microsoft OneNote.

- **Office Home & Business 2010** is available to be installed from a DVD or via Click-To-Run over the Internet, contains all the features of Office Home & Student, and adds Microsoft Outlook.

- **Office Professional 2010** is available to be installed from a DVD or via Click-To-Run over the Internet, contains all the features of Office Home & Business, and adds Microsoft Access and Microsoft Publisher.

There are also two enterprise editions available only through a volume license. Office Standard adds Publisher to Office Home & Business, and Office Professional Plus adds SharePoint Workspace and InfoPath to Office Professional.

This book, which covers the full version of Excel 2010, is applicable to all the editions with a full version of Excel and, to a limited extent, those features that are included in Office Starter and Office Web Apps.

Templates provide a framework that you can modify as needed to suit your needs, saving you much redundant work. (Even a blank workbook is a template, however so stark.)

1. Open Excel using one of the methods described previously in the "Opening Excel" QuickSteps.

2. Click the **File** tab, and click **New**. Two panes are displayed: Available Templates and a preview pane, as shown in Figure 1-9.

3. Click any of the categories of templates displayed. Depending on your choice, you may be presented with folders organizing the templates within a category. Continue navigating through the choices until you see a template that approximates your needs.

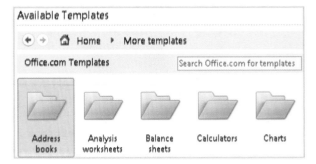

4. Click the template and view a preview in the right pane of the window.

5. Depending on where the template is located, click the **Create** or **Download** button below the preview (see Figure 1-9) in order to open the template in Excel.

6. If you don't initially find a template that meets your needs, click the tools on the toolbar to navigate back through your choices.

–Or–

Type search keywords in the Search Office.com For Templates search box, and click the **Start Searching** arrow to do a more exhaustive search in Microsoft's online inventory.

7. To keep a permanent copy of the template, you will need to save it as an Excel workbook (see "Save a Workbook" later in this chapter).

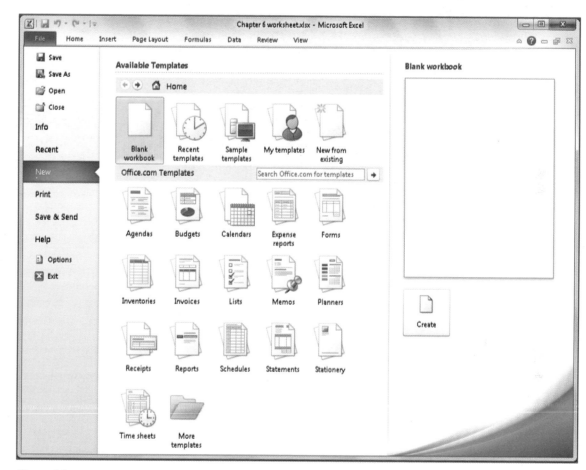

Figure 1-9: *The New view provides several ways to open or create new workbooks from templates.*

TIP

Workbooks saved as templates and stored on your computer or network can be located in Windows and used to create a new workbook, which you can then open in Excel. Right-click the file and click **New**. Excel starts (if it is not already open) and displays a new workbook based on the template.

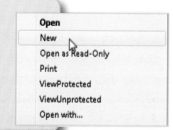

Open an Existing Workbook

Opening an existing workbook is a simple matter of navigating to the file, within or outside of Excel.

OPEN AN EXISTING WORKBOOK IN EXCEL

1. Click the **File** tab, and click **Open**. The Open dialog box appears, as shown in Figure 1-10.

TIP

The File menu (the list on the left side of the window after clicking the File tab) includes a list of your recently opened Excel files. As the list grows, the first workbooks are replaced by newer ones (by default, 22 are listed). You can "pin" a file so that it's always listed and easily available to open. Click the pushpin icon to the right of the file you want to stay on the Recent Workbooks list. To change the number of files that appear, click the **File** tab, click **Options**, click **Advanced**, and under Display, click the **Show This Number Of Recent Documents** spinner to display the number you want. Click **OK** when done.

NOTE

You can open a workbook in several ways by selecting your choice from the Open button menu at the bottom of the Open dialog box. Several of these options are discussed in later chapters.

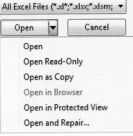

TIP

If you are unfamiliar with using the Windows 7 screen elements, such as windows and dialog boxes, or any other aspects of the operating system, consider purchasing *Windows 7 QuickSteps*, published by McGraw-Hill. Being thoroughly at home with your operating system is the basis for any work you do in Excel—or any other programs running on your Windows 7–based computer.

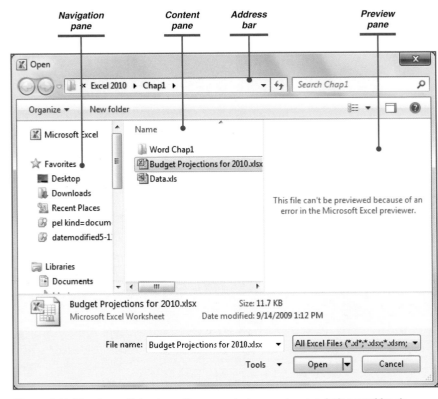

Figure 1-10: **The Open dialog box allows you to browse to an existing workbook.**

2. In the Open dialog box, use the address bar or the navigation pane containing your favorite links and folders to browse to the folder that contains the workbook you want.

3. When you have located it in the content pane and reviewed it in the preview pane, double-click the workbook.

–Or–

Click the workbook to select it, and click **Open**.

In either case, the workbook opens in Excel.

OPEN AN EXISTING WORKBOOK OUTSIDE OF EXCEL

1. In Windows, use Search tools, Windows Explorer, or the desktop (if you have template files stored on it) to locate the workbook you want to open. (The Microsoft Excel 2010 option on the Windows 7 Start menu also lists recently opened workbooks as a submenu.)

2 3 4 5 6 7 8 9 10

2. Right-click the file and click **Open**. Excel starts (if it is not already open) and displays the workbook.

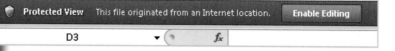

Change the Appearance of New Workbooks

You can customize how new workbooks are set up, saving you time otherwise spent manually adjusting several settings.

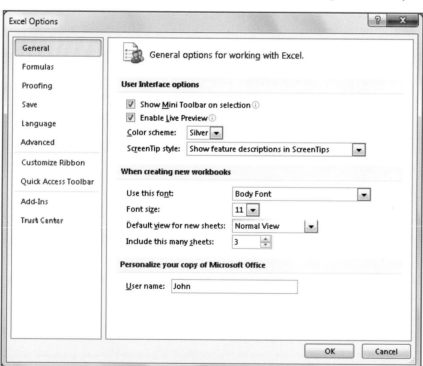

Figure 1-11: *You can create new workbooks to appear more to your liking.*

1. Click the **File** tab, and click **Options** at the bottom of the menu.

2. In the Excel Options dialog box, the General options appear, as shown in Figure 1-11. In the **When Creating New Workbooks** area, change one or more of the following settings:

- Click the **Use This Font** down arrow to display and select the font you want.

- Click the **Font Size** down arrow to display and select the text size you want (text size is listed by *points*; there are 72 points in an inch).

- Click the **Default View For New Sheets** down arrow to display and select an alternate view (see Chapter 5 for information on how you can change your layout to facilitate printing).

- Click the **Include This Many Sheets** spinner to increase or decrease the number of sheets included in the workbook. (You can easily add or remove sheets after a workbook is created—Chapter 3 describes how.)

3. Click **OK** when finished.

Save a Workbook

As you work with a workbook, it is important to periodically save it. You can have Excel do this automatically and you can also do it manually anytime you want.

UNDERSTANDING EXCEL'S XML FILE FORMATS

XML (eXtensible Markup Language) is rapidly becoming the de facto standard for a data-exchange format throughout modern computing. XML does for data what HTML (Hypertext Markup Language) did for the formatting of Web pages. By providing a consistent set of *tags* (or identifiers) for data, along with a road map of how that data is structured (a *schema*) and a file format that *transforms* the data from one use to another, documents can easily exchange information with Web services, programs, and other documents. A key feature of the file formats (identified by the "x" in the file extension, such as .xlsx) is how a file is now organized. In workbooks prior to Excel 2007, each workbook was a single binary file, such as MyBudget .xls. Office 2010 XML files are actually a collection of several files and folders that all appear as a single file, such as the workbook, MyBudget.xlsx, or the template, MyBudgetTemplate.xltx (see Figure 1-12). XML provides several key advantages over binary files in addition to data parsing. XML files are

- **Smaller**—They use ZIP compression to gain up to a 75 percent file size reduction.

- **More secure**—Executable code, such as VBA (Visual Basic for Applications), used in macros and ActiveX controls, is segregated into more secure file packages, such as macro-enabled workbooks (.xlsm) and macro-enabled templates (.xltm).

- **More easily recovered**—Individual XML files can be opened in text readers such as Notepad, so it's not an all-or-nothing proposition when opening a corrupted file.

Continued . . .

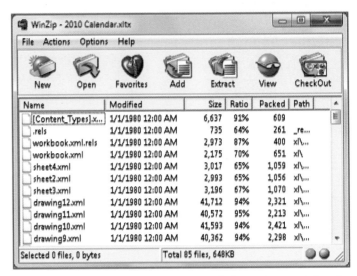

Figure 1-12: The default Excel workbook file format is a container for a myriad of XML files.

In addition, you can save changes to an existing workbook and preserve the original work.

SAVE A WORKBOOK AUTOMATICALLY

Having Excel do it automatically using AutoRecover will reduce the chance of losing data in case of a power failure or other interruption. To save your file automatically:

1. Click the **File** tab, click **Options**, and then click **Save**. The Customize How Workbooks Are Saved settings appear, as shown in Figure 1-13.

2. Select the following settings:

   - Click the **Save Files In This Format** down arrow, and select the default file format in which to save workbooks (see the "Understanding Excel File Compatibility" and "Understanding Excel's XML File Formats" QuickFacts for more information on Excel file formats).

   - Ensure the **Save AutoRecover Information Every** check box is selected, and click the **Minutes** spinner to establish how often Excel will save your work. The shorter

UNDERSTANDING EXCEL'S XML FILE FORMATS *(Continued)*

So what does all this have to do with you if you simply want to create a worksheet to track your monthly cash flow? Fortunately, very little. All this XML tagging and multiple file organizing is done behind the scenes. As far as you're concerned, you have one file per workbook or template to save, copy, delete, or perform any standard file-maintenance actions upon.

time selected will ensure you lose less work in the event of a problem, though you will find it a bit annoying if you decrease the time too much. Stay with the default and see how it works for you.

- Review the paths in the **AutoRecover File Location** and **Default File Location** text boxes. The AutoRecover file location is where you will find open files that are saved after a program or system problem. The Default file location is the initial file location that will appear in the Save As dialog box.

- If you want to remove AutoRecover protection for any open workbook, click the **AutoRecover Exceptions For** down arrow, and select the workbook. Click the **Disable AutoRecover For This Workbook Only** check box.

3. Click **OK** when finished.

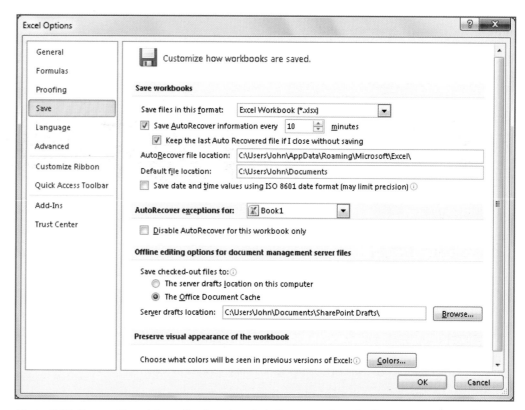

Figure 1-13: Save settings let you fine-tune how AutoRecover automatically saves your Excel files.

SAVE A WORKBOOK MANUALLY

Even if you use AutoRecover, it's a good practice to manually save your workbook after you have done any significant work. To save a workbook file:

Click the **File** tab, and click **Save**.

–Or–

Click the **Save** button 🖫 on the Quick Access toolbar (see "Customize the Quick Access Toolbar" earlier in this chapter).

–Or–

Press **CTRL+S**.

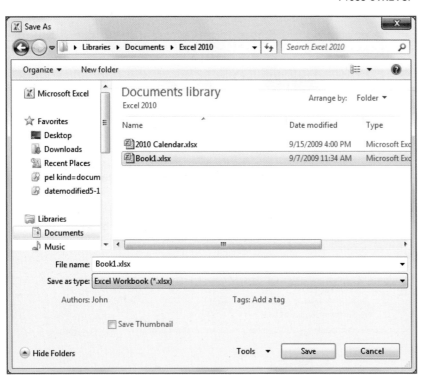

Figure 1-14: *Give a workbook a name, location, and identifying information in the Save As dialog box.*

If you haven't previously saved the workbook, the Save As dialog box will appear, as shown in Figure 1-14.

1. In the Save As dialog box, use the address bar or the navigation pane containing your favorite links and folders to browse to the folder where you want to save the workbook, if different from the default location.

2. Type a name for the workbook in the File Name text box.

3. Ensure the Save As Type box displays the correct file type. If not, click its down arrow, and select the file type you want.

4. Change or add identifying information. (More detailed document information can be added using a Document Information panel. See "Add Identifying Information" later in the chapter.)

5. Click **Save** when finished.

SAVE A COPY OF YOUR WORKBOOK

When you save a workbook under a different name, you create a copy of it. Both the original workbook and the newly named one will remain. To create a copy with a new name:

1. Click the **File** tab, and click **Save As**.

2. In the Save As dialog box, use the address bar or the navigation pane containing your favorite links and folders to browse to the folder where you want to save the copy of the workbook, if different from the default location.

NOTE

A popular way to share documents is to convert them to a graphics-based format, such as Adobe PDF (Portable Document Format) or Microsoft XPS (XML Paper Specification), that can be viewed by anyone using a free viewer program. You can save Excel workbooks in either format from the Save As Type drop-down list in the Save As dialog box or in the Share view. Chapter 9 contains more information on XPS files and sharing your data.

3. Type a name for the new workbook in the File Name text box.

4. Change any identifying information, and click **Save**.

Add Identifying Information

You can add identifying information to a workbook to make it easier to find during searches and when organizing files, especially in a shared environment (see Chapter 9 for more information on sharing Excel files).

1. Click the **File** tab. In the default Info view, several document properties appear under the preview of the workbook, as shown in Figure 1-15.

2. On the right of the window, click the text box to the right of the information you want to add or change and type identifying information, such as title, tags (words or phrases that are associated with the workbook), categories, and additional authors.

   –Or–

   Click **Properties** and then click **Show Document Panel**. You are returned to the workbook, where a Document Properties panel is added between the minimized ribbon and the worksheet. You can type identifying information in the applicable text boxes.

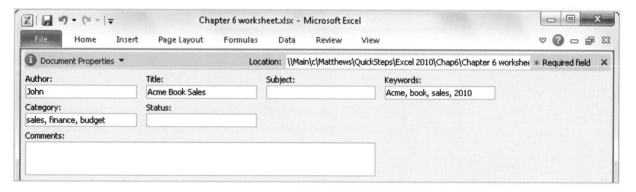

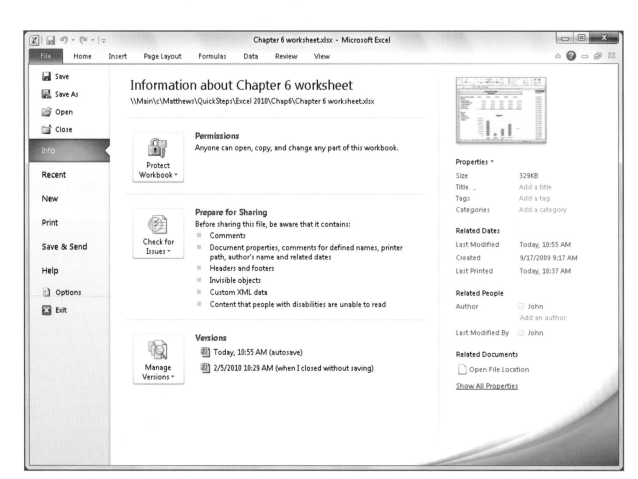

Figure 1-15: *You can more easily locate a workbook using search tools if you add identifying data.*

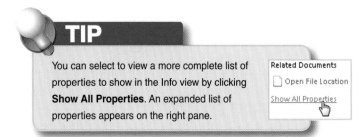

TIP

You can select to view a more complete list of properties to show in the Info view by clicking **Show All Properties**. An expanded list of properties appears on the right pane.

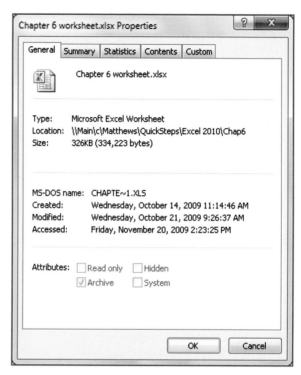

Figure 1-16: A full set of information about your workbook is available from the Advanced Properties command.

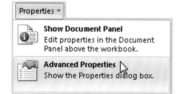

A Properties dialog box (see Figure 1-16) containing common and more advanced properties and workbook information such as the file size and location is available by clicking **Advanced Properties** from the Properties menu in either the Info view or in the Document Properties panel.

3. When finished, click the **File** tab to return to the Excel worksheet.

Exit an Excel Session

After you have saved the most recent changes to your workbook, you can close the workbook and exit Excel.

QUICKFACTS

UNDERSTANDING EXCEL FILE COMPATIBILITY

Any time a version of Office is released with a new file format, sales of the antacid Maalox spike higher for several months (from anecdotal evidence, LOL). The default XML workbook in Excel 2010 is backward-compatible all the way to Excel 5.0/95, although Excel 2010 formatting and features will not be available. If you will be opening an Excel 2010 workbook in Excel 2007, there are no issues; however, in versions of Excel that use the Excel 97-2003 file format, you have a couple of options available to you. You can save a copy of your Excel 2010 workbook (.xlsx) in the Excel 97-2003 format (.xls) using the Save As dialog box. This option is preferable if you have no control over the computers the file will be used on. If you have control over the computer environment, you can install a File Format Compatibility Pack (available from the Microsoft Office Web site) on the computers running earlier versions of Excel. This set of updates and converters will allow those computers to open, edit, and save files in the Excel 2010 .xlsx format without manually creating a separate file copy.

Legacy Excel files opened in Excel 2010 can be edited and saved in their original format. Excel lets you know you are working with a workbook in an earlier file format by adding the words "Compatibility Mode" to the end of the workbook name in the Excel window title bar. Saving the file will keep it in the legacy format, or you can convert the file to the Excel 2010 file format using the Save As Type drop-down list in the Save As dialog box.

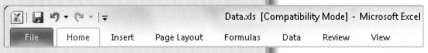

CLOSE THE WORKBOOK

1. Click the **File** tab, and click **Close**.

   –Or–

   Click the lower "X" in the upper-right corner of the Excel window.

2. If asked, click **Yes** to save any unsaved work. If you haven't previously saved the workbook, the Save As dialog box will appear so that you can locate where you want the file stored and name it (see "Save a Workbook Manually" earlier in the chapter).

EXIT EXCEL

Click the **File** tab, and click **Exit**.

–Or–

Click the upper **Close** icon (the "X" in the red box) in the upper-right corner of the Excel window.

How to...

- *Understanding Data Types*
- *Enter Text*
- *Completing an Entry*
- *Enter Numeric Data*
- *Enter Dates*
- *Formatting Numbers*
- *Use Times*
- *Understanding Excel Dates and Times*
- *Adding Data Quickly*
- *Edit Cell Data*
- *Remove Cell Contents*
- *Selecting Cells and Ranges*
- *Copy and Paste Data*
- *Using the Office Clipboard*
- *Find and Replace Data*
- *Verify Spelling*
- *Modify Automatic Corrections*

Chapter 2
Entering and Editing Data

Data is the heart and soul of Excel, yet before you can calculate data, chart it, analyze it, and otherwise *use* it, you have to place it on a worksheet. Data comes in several forms—such as numbers, text, dates, and times—and Excel handles the entry of each form uniquely. After you enter data into Excel's worksheets, you might want to make changes. Simple actions—such as removing text and numbers, copying and pasting, and moving data—are much more enhanced in Excel than the standard actions most users are familiar with.

In addition, Excel provides several tools to assist you in manipulating your data. You can have Excel intelligently continue a series without having to manually enter the sequential numbers or text. Automatic tools are available to help you verify accuracy and provide pop-ups—small toolbars related to the Excel task you're working on. These, and other ways of entering and editing data, are covered in this chapter.

UNDERSTANDING DATA TYPES

Cells in Excel are characterized by the type of data they contain. *Text* is composed of characters that cannot be used in calculations. For example, "Quarterly revenue is not meeting projection." is text, and so is "1302 Grand Ave." *Numbers* are just that: numerical characters that can be used in calculations. *Dates* and *times* occupy a special category of numbers that can be used in calculations, and are handled in a variety of ways. Excel lets you know what it thinks a cell contains by its default alignment of a cell's contents; that is, text is left-aligned and numbers (including dates and times) are right-aligned by default.

D6		f_x
	A	B	C
1	Supplies	23567	
2			

Text: left-aligned

Number: right-aligned

TIP

It is quite easy to lose track of the address of the cell you are currently working in. Excel provides several highly visible identifiers for the active cell: the Name box at the left end of the Formula bar displays the address; the column and row headings are highlighted in color; the Formula bar displays cell contents; and the cell borders are bold.

Enter Data

An Excel worksheet is a matrix, or grid, of lettered *column headings* across the top and numbered *row headings* down the side. The first row of a typical worksheet is used for column *headers*. The column headers represent categories of similar data. The rows beneath a column header contain data that is further categorized either by a row header along the leftmost column or listed below the column header. Figure 2-1 shows examples of two common worksheet arrangements. Worksheets can also be used to set up *tables* of data, where columns are sometimes referred to as *fields* and each row represents a unique *record* of data. Tables are covered in Chapter 8.

Each intersection of a row and column is called a *cell*, and is referenced first by the column location and then by the row location. The combination of a column letter and row number assigns each cell an *address*. For example, the cell at the intersection of column D and row 8 is called D8. A cell is considered *active* when it is clicked or otherwise selected as the place in which to place new data.

Enter Text

In an Excel worksheet, text is used to identify, explain, and emphasize numeric data. It comprises characters that cannot be used in calculations. You enter text by typing, just as you would in a word-processing program.

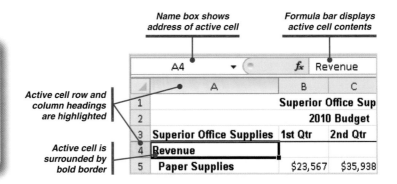

Name box shows address of active cell

Formula bar displays active cell contents

Active cell row and column headings are highlighted

Active cell is surrounded by bold border

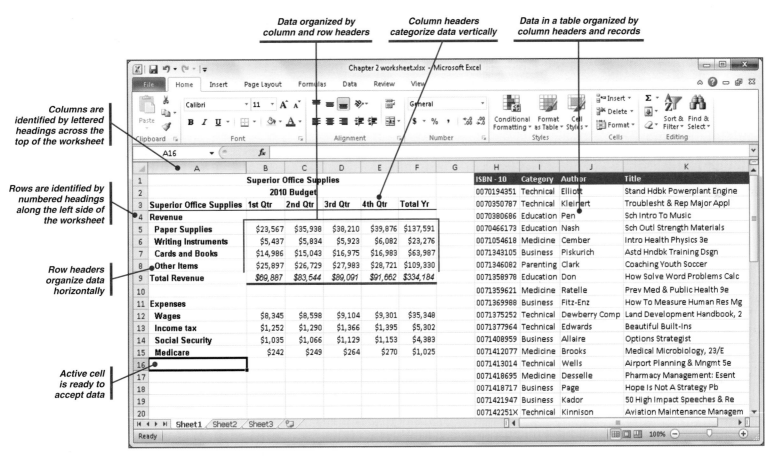

Data organized by column and row headers

Column headers categorize data vertically

Data in a table organized by column headers and records

Columns are identified by lettered headings across the top of the worksheet

Rows are identified by numbered headings along the left side of the worksheet

Row headers organize data horizontally

Active cell is ready to accept data

Figure 2-1: *The grid layout of Excel worksheets is defined by several components.*

ENTER TEXT CONTINUOUSLY

Text (and numbers) longer than one cell width will appear to cover the adjoining cells to the right of the active cell. The covered cells have not been "used"; their contents have just been hidden, as shown in Figure 2-2. To enter text on one line:

1. Click the cell where you want the text to start.

2. Type the text. The text displays in one or more cells (see rows 2 and 4 in Figure 2-2).

3. Complete the entry. (See the "Completing an Entry" QuickSteps later in the chapter for several ways to do that.)

NOTE

See Chapter 3 for ways to increase column width to accommodate the length of text in a cell.

QUICKSTEPS

COMPLETING AN ENTRY

You can complete an entry using the mouse or the keyboard and control where the active cell goes next.

STAY IN THE ACTIVE CELL

To complete an entry and keep the current cell active, click **ENTER** on the Formula bar.

MOVE THE ACTIVE CELL TO THE RIGHT

To complete the entry and move to the next cell in the same row, press **TAB**.

MOVE THE ACTIVE CELL TO THE NEXT ROW

To complete the entry and move the active cell to the next row, press **ENTER**. The active cell moves to the *beginning cell* in the next row (see Note on the next page).

CHANGE THE DIRECTION OF THE ACTIVE CELL

1. Click the **File** tab, click **Options**, and then click the **Advanced** option.

2. Under Editing Options, click **After Pressing Enter, Move Selection** to select it if it is not already selected.

3. Click the **Direction** down arrow, and click a direction. Down is the default.

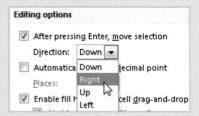

4. Click **OK** when finished.

MOVE THE ACTIVE CELL TO ANY CELL

To complete the entry and move the active cell to any cell in the worksheet, click the cell you want to become active.

Figure 2-2: *Text in a cell can cover several cells or be placed on multiple lines.*

WRAP TEXT ON MULTIPLE LINES

You can select a cell and wrap text at the end of its column width, much like how a word-processing program wraps text to the next line when entered text reaches its right margin.

1. Click the cell where you want to enter text.

2. Type all the text you want to appear in a cell. The text will continue to the right, overlapping as many cells as its length dictates (see row 4 in Figure 2-2).

3. Press **ENTER** to complete the entry. (See the "Completing an Entry" QuickSteps.) Click the cell a second time to select it.

4. Click the **Home** tab at the left end of the ribbon. In the Alignment group, click the **Wrap Text** button. The text wraps within the confines of the column width, increasing the row height as necessary (see row 6 in Figure 2-2).

NOTE

The *beginning cell* is in the same column where you first started entering data. For example, if you started entering data in cell A5 and continued through E5, pressing TAB between entries A5 through D5 and pressing ENTER in E5, the active cell would move to A6 (the first cell in the next row). If you had started entering data in cell C5, after pressing ENTER at the end of that row of entries, the active cell would move to C6, the cell below it.

TIP

You can cause a number to be interpreted by Excel as text by typing an apostrophe (') in front of it and completing the entry. The "number" is left-aligned as text and a green triangle is displayed in the upper-left corner of the cell. When selected, an error icon displays next to the cell, indicating a number is stored as text.

G	H
	ISBN - 10
◇	0070194350
	0070194351

TIP

You can convert a number to scientific notation from the Home tab Number group on the ribbon. Click the **Number Format** down arrow, and click **Scientific** near the bottom of the list. To set the number of decimal places, click the **Increase Decimal** or **Decrease Decimal** button at the bottom of the Number group. Also, note that the Number Format box displays the type of number format in the selected cell.

CONSTRAIN TEXT ON MULTIPLE LINES

When you want to constrain the length of text in a cell:

1. Click the cell where you want to enter text.
2. Type the text you want to appear on the first line.
3. Press **ALT+ENTER**. The insertion point moves to the beginning of a new line.
4. Repeat steps 2 and 3 for any additional lines of text. (See row 8 in Figure 2-2.)
5. Complete the entry. (See the "Completing an Entry" QuickSteps.)

Enter Numeric Data

Numbers are numerical data, from the simplest to the most complex. Excel provides several features to help you more easily work with numbers used to represent values in various categories, such as currency, accounting, and mathematics.

ENTER NUMBERS

Enter numbers by simply selecting a cell and typing the numbers.

1. Click the cell where you want the numbers entered.
2. Type the numbers. Use decimal places, thousands separators, and other formatting as you type, or have Excel format these things for you. (See the "Formatting Numbers" QuickSteps later in this chapter.)
3. Complete the entry. (See the "Completing an Entry" QuickSteps.)

ENTER NUMBERS USING SCIENTIFIC NOTATION

Exponents are used in scientific notation to shorten (or round off) very large or small numbers. The shorthand scientific notation display does not affect how the number is used in calculations.

1. Click the cell where you want the data entered.
2. Type the number using three components:
   - **Base:** For example, 4, 7.56, –2.5.
   - **Scientific notation identifier:** Type the letter "e."

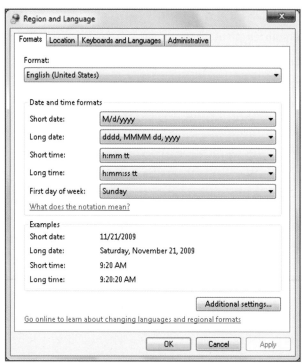

Figure 2-3: *You can change how Excel and other Windows programs display dates.*

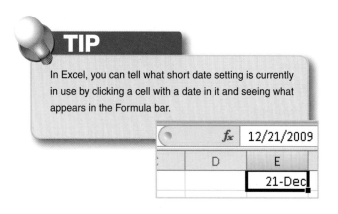

- **Exponent:** The number of times 10 is multiplied by itself. Positive exponent numbers increment the base number to the right of the decimal point, negative numbers to the left. For example, scientific notation for the number 123,456,789.0 is written to two decimal places as 1.23×10^8. In Excel, you would type 1.23e8.

3. After completing the entry (see the "Completing an Entry" QuickSteps), it will display as:

$$1.23E+08$$

Enter Dates

If you can think of a way to enter a date, Excel can probably recognize it as such. For example, Table 2-1 shows how Excel handles different ways to make the date entry use the date of March 1, 2010 (assuming it is sometime in 2010) in a worksheet.

In cases when a year is omitted, Excel assumes the current year.

TYPING THIS...	DISPLAYS THIS AFTER COMPLETING THE ENTRY
3/1, 3-1, 1-mar, or 1-Mar	1-Mar
3/1/10, 3-1-10, 3/1/2010, 3-1-2010, 3-1/10, or 3-1/2010	3/1/2010
Mar 1, 10, March 1, 2010, 1-mar-10, or 1-Mar-2010	1-Mar-10

Table 2-1: *Examples of Excel Date Formats*

CHANGE THE DEFAULT DISPLAY OF DATES

Two common date formats (long and short) are displayed by default in Excel based on settings in the Windows Region And Language item in Control Panel, shown in Figure 2-3.

1. In Windows 7, click **Start** and click **Control Panel**.

2. In Control Panel Category view, click the **Clock, Language, And Region** category, and then click **Region And Language**.

   –Or–

   In Icons view, click **Regional And Language Options**.

3. On the Formats tab, click **Additional Settings**.

4. Click the **Date** tab, click the **Short Date Format** down arrow, and select a format. Similarly, change the long date format, as necessary.

5. Click **OK** twice and close Control Panel.

QUICKSTEPS

FORMATTING NUMBERS

Numbers in a cell can be formatted in any one of several numeric categories by first selecting the cell containing the number. You can then use the tools available in the Home tab Number group or have the full range of options available to you from the Format Cells dialog box.

DISPLAY THE NUMBER TAB

Click the **Dialog Box Launcher** in the lower-right corner of the Number group. The Format Cells dialog box appears with the Number tab displayed (shown in Figure 2-5).

ADD OR DECREASE DECIMAL PLACES

1. On the Number tab of the Format Cells dialog box, choose the appropriate numeric category (Number, Currency, Accounting, Percentage, or Scientific) from the Category list box.

2. In the Decimal Places text box, enter a number or use the spinner to set the number of decimal places you want. Click **OK**.

   –Or–

   In the ribbon's Home tab Number group, click the **Increase Decimal** or **Decrease Decimal** button.

   Continued . . .

FORMAT DATES

You can change how a date is displayed in Excel by choosing a new format.

1. Right-click the cell that contains the date you want to change. (See the "Selecting Cells and Ranges" QuickSteps later in the chapter to see how to apply formats to more than one cell at a time.)

2. Click **Format Cells** on the context menu. The Format Cells dialog box appears. If needed, click the **Number** tab and then the **Date** category, as shown in Figure 2-4.

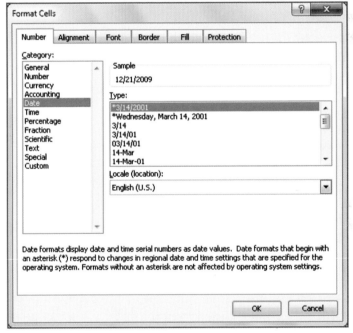

*Figure 2-4: **You can choose from among several ways to display dates in Excel.***

3. Select a format from the Type list.

   –Or–

   Use custom number codes to create a new format. To learn about number format codes, search Excel Help for the topic "Create or delete a custom number format."

4. You can see how the new date format affects your date in the Sample area. Click **OK** when finished.

QUICKSTEPS

FORMATTING NUMBERS *(Continued)*

ADD A THOUSANDS SEPARATOR

On the Number tab of the Format Cells dialog box, click the **Number** category, and click **Use 1000 Separator (,)**. Click **OK**.

–Or–

In the ribbon's Home tab Number group, click the **Comma Style** button in the Number group.

ADD A CURRENCY SYMBOL

1. On the Number tab, choose the appropriate numeric category (Currency or Accounting) from the Category list box.

2. Click **OK** to accept the default dollar sign ($), or choose another currency symbol from the Symbol drop-down list, and click **OK**.

   –Or–

   Click the **Accounting Number Format** button **$ ▾** in the Number group. (You can change the currency symbol by clicking the down arrow next to the current symbol and choosing another one.)

CONVERT A DECIMAL TO A FRACTION

1. On the Number tab, click the **Fraction** category.

2. Click the type of fraction you want. View it in the Sample area, and change the type if needed. Click **OK**.

CONVERT A NUMBER TO A PERCENTAGE

1. On the Number tab, click the **Percentage** category.

2. In the Decimal Places text box, enter a number or use the spinner to set the number of decimal places you want. Click **OK**.

   –Or–

Continued . . .

Figure 2-5: The Format Cells Number tab provides a complete set of numeric formatting categories and options.

Use Times

Excel's conventions for time are as follows:

- Colons (:) are used as separators between hours, minutes, and seconds.
- AM is assumed unless you specify PM or when you enter a time from 12:00 to 12:59.
- AM and PM do not display in the cell if they are not entered.
- You specify PM by entering a space followed by "p," "P," "pm," or "PM."
- Seconds are not displayed in the cell if not entered.
- AM, PM, and seconds are displayed in the Formula bar of a cell that contains a time.

ENTER TIMES

1. Select the cell in which you want to enter a time.
2. Type the hour followed by a colon.
3. Type the minutes followed by a colon.
4. Type the seconds, if needed.

QUICKSTEPS

FORMATTING NUMBERS *(Continued)*

Click the **Percent Style** button  in the Number group.

FORMAT ZIP CODES, PHONE NUMBERS, AND SOCIAL SECURITY NUMBERS

1. On the Number tab, click the **Special** category.

2. Select the type of formatting you want. Click **OK**.

QUICKFACTS

UNDERSTANDING EXCEL DATES AND TIMES

If you select a cell with a date and open the Number Format list in the Number group, you'll notice several of the formats show examples with a number around 40,000. Is this just an arbitrary number Excel has cooked up to demonstrate the example formats? Hardly. Dates and times in Excel are assigned values so that they can be used in calculations (Chapter 4 describes how to use formulas and functions). Dates are assigned a serial value starting with January 1, 1900 (serial value 1). The number you see on the Number Format list is the value of the date in the active cell (you can convert a date to its serial value by changing the format from Date to Number). For example, January 1, 2010, has a serial value of 40,179. Times are converted to the decimal equivalent of a day. For example, 4:15 P.M. is converted to .68. Since Excel considers dates and times as numerics, they are right-aligned in a cell. If you see what you think is a date but it is left-aligned, Excel is treating it as text, not a date, and you would receive an error message if you tried to use it in a formula.

NOTE

Formatting also can be applied to cells in advance of entering numbers (or text) so that the attributes are displayed as you complete the entry. Simply select the cells and apply the formatting. See the "Selecting Cells and Ranges" QuickSteps later in the chapter for ways to select cells.

5. Type a space and <u>PM</u>, if needed.

6. Complete the entry.

CHANGE THE DEFAULT DISPLAY OF TIMES

Times are displayed by default in Excel based on settings configured in the Windows Region And Language feature of Control Panel. To change the default settings:

1. In Windows 7, click **Start** and click **Control Panel**.

2. In Category view, click the **Clock**, **Language, And Region** category, and then click **Region And Language**.

   –Or–

   In Icons view, click **Region And Language**.

3. On the Formats tab, click the **Short Time** and/or **Long Time** down arrow, and select the formats you want.

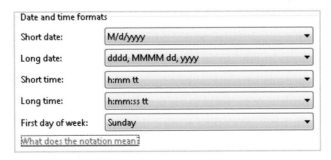

4. Click **What Does The Notation Mean?** to view an explanation of the time symbology.

5. Click **OK** and close Control Panel.

TIP

To enter the current time in a cell, click the cell and press **CTRL+SHIFT+:**. The current time in the form h:mm AM/PM is displayed.

CAUTION

Changing the *system* date/time formats in Region And Language changes the date and time formats used by all Windows programs. Dates and times previously entered in Excel may change to the new setting unless they were formatted using the features in Excel's Format Cells dialog box.

QUICKSTEPS

ADDING DATA QUICKLY

Excel provides several features that help you quickly add more data to existing data with a minimum of keystrokes.

USE AUTOCOMPLETE

Excel will complete an entry for you after you type the first few characters of data that appear in a previous entry in the same column. Simply press **ENTER** to accept the completed entry. To turn off this feature if you find it bothersome:

1. Click the **File** tab, click **Options**, and click the **Advanced** option.

2. Under Editing Options, click **Enable AutoComplete For Cell Values** to remove the check mark.

FILL DATA INTO ADJOINING CELLS

1. Select the cell that contains the data you want to copy into adjoining cells.

Continued . . .

FORMAT TIMES

You can change how a time is displayed in Excel by choosing a new format.

1. Select the cell that contains the time you want to change. (See the "Selecting Cells and Ranges" QuickSteps later in the chapter for how to apply formats to more than one cell at a time.)

2. Click the **Dialog Box Launcher** arrow in the Home tab Number group. The Format Cells dialog box appears with the Number tab displaying the Custom category.

3. Under Type, select a format.

   –Or–

   Use custom number codes to create a new format. To learn about number format codes, search Excel Help for the topic "Create or delete a custom number format."

4. You can see how the new time format will affect your time in the Sample area. Click **OK** when finished.

Edit Data

The data-intensive nature of Excel necessitates easy ways to change, copy, or remove data already entered on a worksheet. In addition, Excel has facilities to help you find and replace data and check the spelling.

Edit Cell Data

You have several choices on how to edit data, depending on whether you want to replace all the contents of a cell or just part of the contents, and whether you want to do it in the cell or in the Formula bar.

EDIT CELL CONTENTS

To edit data entered in a cell:

- Double-click the text in the cell where you want to begin editing. An insertion point is placed in the cell. Type the new data, use the mouse to select characters to be overwritten or deleted, or use keyboard shortcuts. Complete the entry when finished editing. (See the "Completing an Entry" QuickSteps earlier in the chapter.)

  –Or–

	C	D
1	January	Feberary
2		

QUICKSTEPS

ADDING DATA QUICKLY *(Continued)*

2. Point to the fill handle in the lower-right corner of the cell. The pointer turns into a cross.

3. Drag the handle in the direction you want to extend the data until you've reached the last cell in the range you want to fill.

4. Open the Smart tag ▦+ by clicking it, and select fill options.

–Or–

Select the contiguous cells you want to fill in with the data in a cell (see the "Selecting Cells and Ranges" QuickSteps later in the chapter). In the Home tab Editing group, click the **Fill** button, ▦▾ and click the direction of the fill.

CONTINUE A SERIES OF DATA

Data can be *logically* extended into one or more adjoining cells. For example, 1 and 2 extend to 3, 4...; Tuesday extends to Wednesday, Thursday...; January extends to February, March...; and 2004 and 2005 extend to 2006, 2007....

1. Select the cell or cells that contain a partial series. (See the "Selecting Cells and Ranges" QuickSteps later in the chapter for more information on selecting more than one cell.)

Continued ...

• Select the cell to edit, and then click the cell's contents in the Formula bar where you want to make changes. Type the new data, use the mouse to select characters to overwrite or delete, or use keyboard shortcuts. Click **Enter** on the Formula bar or press **ENTER** to complete the entry.

–Or–

• Select the cell to edit, and press **F2**. Edit in the cell using the mouse or keyboard shortcuts. Complete the entry.

REPLACE ALL CELL CONTENTS

Click the cell and type new data. The original data is deleted and replaced by your new characters.

CANCEL CELL EDITING

Before you complete a cell entry, you can revert back to your original data by pressing **ESC** or clicking **Cancel** on the Formula bar.

Remove Cell Contents

You can easily delete cell contents, move them to other cells, or clear selective attributes of a cell.

TIP

To undo a data-removal action, even if you have performed several actions since removing the data, click **Undo** on the Quick Access toolbar next to the File tab (or press **CTRL+Z**) for the most recent action. For earlier actions, continue clicking **Undo** to work your way back; or click the down arrow next to the button, and choose the action from the drop-down list.

1   3   4   5   6   7   8   9   10

QUICKSTEPS

ADDING DATA QUICKLY *(Continued)*

2. Point to the fill handle in the lower-right corner of the last cell. The pointer turns into a cross.

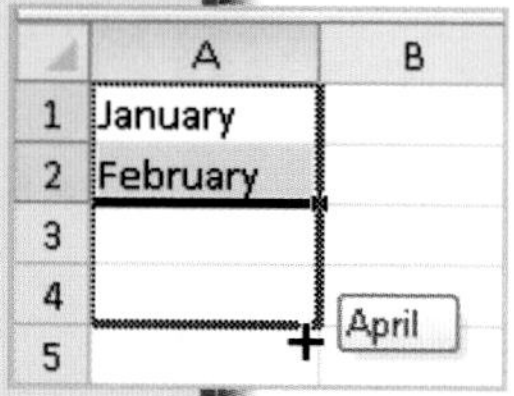

3. Drag the handle in the direction you want until you've reached the last cell in the range to complete the series.

4. To copy the partial series into the adjoining cells instead of extending the series, drag the fill handle to cover as many occurrences of the copy you want, click the Smart tag, and click Copy Cells (see Figure 2-6).

REMOVE THE FILL HANDLE

To hide the fill handle and disable AutoFill:

1. Click the **File tab**, under Excel click **Options**, and click the **Advanced** option.

2. Under Editing Options, click **Enable Fill Handle And Cell Drag And Drop** to remove the check mark.

ENTER DATA FROM A LIST

Previously entered data in a column can be selected from a list and entered with a click.

1. Right-click the cell at the bottom of a column of data.

2. Select **Pick From Drop-Down List** from the context menu, and then click the data you want to enter in the cell.

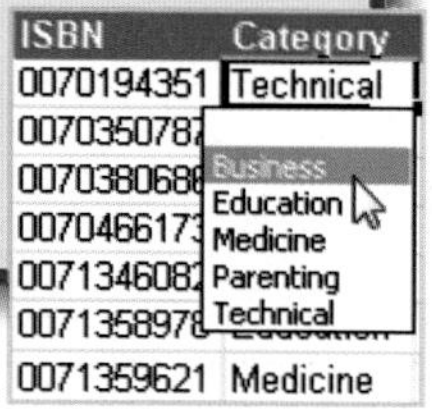

TIP

You can fill data into the active cell from the cell above it or to its left by clicking **CTRL+D** or **CTRL+R**, respectively.

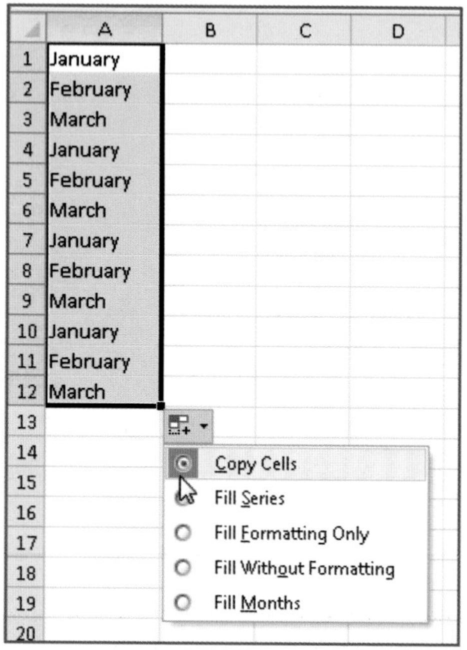

Figure 2-6: *You can copy a series (January, February, and March, in this case) by using the Smart tag that appears after dragging the fill handle.*

DELETE DATA

Remove all contents (but not formatting) from a cell by selecting the cell and pressing DELETE. You can delete the contents of more than one cell by selecting the cells or the cell range and pressing DELETE. (See the "Selecting Cells and Ranges" QuickSteps for more information on selecting various configurations.)

MOVE DATA

Cell contents can be removed from one location and placed in another location of equal size. Select the cell or range you want to move. Then:

● Place the pointer on any edge of the selection, except the lower-right corner where the Fill handle resides, until it turns into a cross with arrowhead tips. Drag the cell or range to the new location.

10					
11	**Expenses**				
12	**Wages**	$8,345	$9,104	$9,301	$35,348
13	**Income tax**	$1,252	$1,366	$1,395	$5,302
14	**Social Security**	$1,035	$1,129	$1,153	$4,383
15	**Medicare**	$242	$264	$270	$1,025
16					
17					

QUICKSTEPS

SELECTING CELLS AND RANGES

The key to many actions in Excel is the ability to select cells in various configurations and use them to perform calculations. You can select a single cell, nonadjacent cells, and adjacent cells (or *ranges*).

SELECT A SINGLE CELL

Select a cell by clicking it, or move to a cell using the arrow keys or by completing an entry in a cell above or to the left.

SELECT NONADJACENT CELLS

Select a cell and then press **CTRL** while clicking the other cells you want to select. The selected cells remain highlighted.

$8,345	$9,104
$1,252	$1,366
$1,035	$1,129
$242	$264

SELECT A RANGE OF ADJACENT CELLS

Select a cell and drag over the additional cells you want to include in the range.

–Or–

Select the first cell in the range, press and hold **SHIFT**, and click the last cell in the range.

Continued . . .

–Or–

- On the Home tab Clipboard group, click **Cut**. Select the new location, and click **Paste** in the Clipboard group. (See "Copy and Paste Data" later in this chapter for more information on pasting options.)

REMOVE SELECTED CELL CONTENTS

A cell can contain several components, including:

- **Formats**—Consisting of number formats, conditional formats (formats that display if certain conditions apply), and borders

- **Contents**—Consisting of formulas and data

- **Comments**—Consisting of notes you attach to a cell

- **Hyperlinks**—Consisting of links to other ranges on the current worksheet, to other worksheets in the current workbook, other workbooks or other files, and Web pages in Web sites (see Chapter 10 for information on using hyperlinks)

1. Choose which cell components you want to clear by selecting the cell or cells.

2. On the Home tab Editing group, click the **Clear** button, and click the applicable item from the menu. (Clicking **Clear Contents** performs the same action as pressing **DELETE**.)

Copy and Paste Data

Data you've already entered on a worksheet (or in other programs) can be copied to the same or other worksheets, or even to other Windows programs (see Chapter 10 for information on using data with other programs). You first *copy* the data to the Windows Clipboard, where it is temporarily stored.

QUICKSTEPS

SELECTING CELLS AND RANGES
(Continued)

SELECT ALL CELLS ON A WORKSHEET

Click the **Select All** button in the upper-left corner of the worksheet, or press **CTRL+A**.

E6	▼

	A	B
1		Superior
2		20
3	Superior Office Supplies	1st Qtr
4	Revenue	

Select All points to upper-left corner.

SELECT A ROW OR COLUMN

Click a row (number) heading or column (letter) heading.

	H ↓	I
	ISBN	Category
	0070194351	Technical
	0070350787	Technical
	0070380686	Education

SELECT ADJACENT ROWS OR COLUMNS

Drag down the row headings or across the column headings.

SELECT NONADJACENT ROWS OR COLUMNS

Select a row or column heading, and then press **CTRL** while clicking other row or column headings you want selected.

RESIZE AN ADJACENT SELECTION

Press **SHIFT** and click the cell you want to be at the end of the selection.

SELECT A COMBINATION OF CELLS

By dragging, combined with clicking while pressing **CTRL** or **SHIFT**, you can include single cells, rows, columns, and ranges all in one selection. Figure 2-7 shows one example.

After selecting a destination for the data, you *paste* it into the cell or cells. You can copy all the data in a cell or only part of it. You can paste it on your worksheet one time, in one location, or at different locations several times. (The copied data remains on the Clipboard until you replace it with another copy action.) While many computer users are familiar with a basic copy, Excel's paste feature lets you selectively paste attributes of the data and even shows you a preview of how the pasted information will look in its new location.

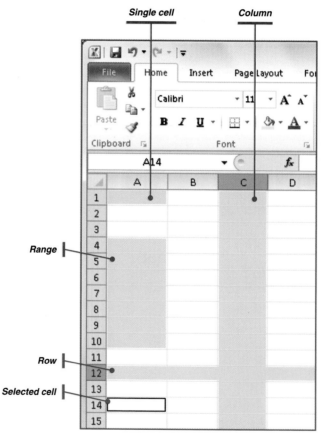

Figure 2-7: You can include a single cell, a row, a column, and a range all in one selection.

TIP

To select larger numbers of adjacent cells, rows, or columns, click the first item in the group, and then press **SHIFT** while clicking the last item in the group.

TIP

Another way to send information to the Clipboard is to *cut* the data. When you cut data ✄ Cut , like a copy action, information is placed on the Clipboard and removes any existing data already there. However, when you cut data, it is removed from its original location (it's essentially moved), unlike copying, where the data is retained at its original location.

COPY DATA

1. Select the cells that contain the data you want to copy; or double-click a cell, and select the characters you want to copy.

2. In the Home tab Clipboard group, click the **Copy** down arrow, and click **Copy** (to copy data as letters and characters), or click **Copy As Picture** to choose a picture format of the material (see Chapter 7 for more information on working with pictures and graphics).

–Or–

Press **CTRL+C**.

In either case, the selected data is copied to the Clipboard and the border around the cells displays a flashing dotted line.

| Social Security | | $1,035 | $1,129 | $1,153 | $4,383 |

PASTE DATA

Once data is placed on the Windows Clipboard through a *copy* action, you can selectively include or omit formulas, values, formatting, comments, arithmetic operations, and other cell properties *before* you copy or move data. (See Chapter 4 for information on formulas, values, and arithmetic operations.) You can preview several variations of a paste by choosing from several tools, either on the ribbon or from a dialog box. Even after you perform a paste, you can easily change your mind by selecting and previewing paste options from a Smart tag.

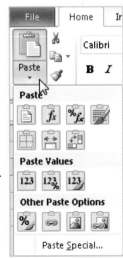

1. Select the location (a cell or range) for the cut or copied data.

2. On the Home tab Clipboard group, click the **Paste** down arrow. A menu of several pasting tools appears, each as an icon.

–Or–

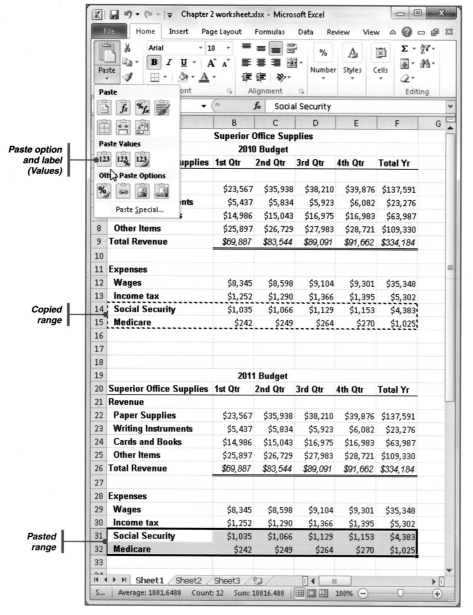

Right-click the selected cell or range, and on the context menu, view a few tools under Paste Options, or even more tools by pointing to Paste Special.

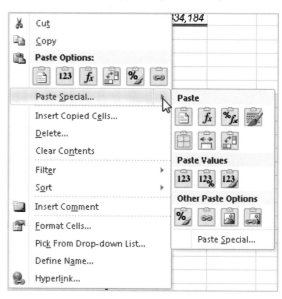

3. Point to each tool to see a short description of the pasting characteristic(s) it supports. As you point to an icon, the cell or range you had selected will show how the pasting characteristic affects the data, as shown in Figure 2-8.

4. Click the tool you want to use to perform the paste. If you want a different pasting tool, click the Smart tag 📋 (Ctrl) ▾ that appears next to the pasted cell or range and select another option.

5. Repeat steps 1 through 4 to paste the copied data to other locations. Press **ESC** when finished to remove the flashing border around the source cells.

Figure 2-8: You can preview how each tool will show your pasted data.

6. Alternatively, you can choose options from a list in a dialog box without previewing the effects. After selecting the destination cell or cells to where you want the data copied or moved, in the Clipboard group, click the **Paste** down arrow, and click **Paste Special**; or right-click the destination cells, and click **Paste Special**. The Paste Special dialog box appears, as shown in Figure 2-9.

7. Select the paste options you want in the copied or moved cells, and click **OK**.

Figure 2-9: *Pasting options are listed in the Paste Special dialog box.*

Find and Replace Data

In worksheets that might span thousands of rows and columns (over one million rows and over 16,000 columns are possible), you need the ability to locate data quickly, as well as to find instances of the same data so that consistent replacements can be made.

FIND DATA

1. In the Home tab Editing group, click **Find & Select**, and click **Find**; or press **CTRL+F** to open the Find And Replace dialog box with the Find tab displayed.

2. Type the text or number you want to find in the Find What text box.

3. Click **Options** to view the following options to refine the search (see Figure 2-10):

- **Format**—Opens the Find Format dialog box, where you select from several categories of number, alignment, font, border, pattern, and protection formats.

- **Choose Format From Cell**—(From the Format drop-down list) lets you click a cell that contains the format you want to find.

UICKSTEPS

USING THE OFFICE CLIPBOARD

(Continued)

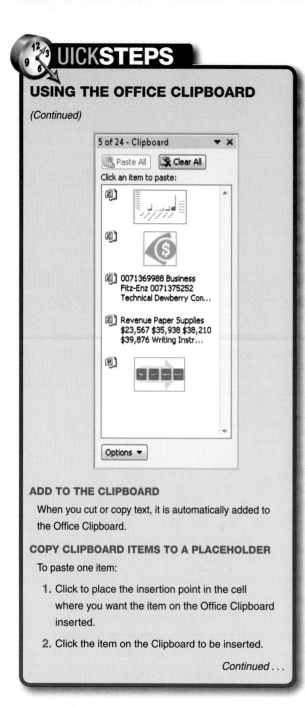

ADD TO THE CLIPBOARD

When you cut or copy text, it is automatically added to the Office Clipboard.

COPY CLIPBOARD ITEMS TO A PLACEHOLDER

To paste one item:

1. Click to place the insertion point in the cell where you want the item on the Office Clipboard inserted.

2. Click the item on the Clipboard to be inserted.

Continued . . .

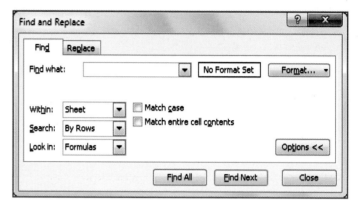

Figure 2-10: **The Find tab lets you refine your search based on several criteria.**

- **Within**—Limits your search to the current worksheet or expands it to all worksheets in the workbook.

- **Search**—Lets you search to the right by rows or down by columns. You can search to the left and up by pressing **SHIFT** and clicking **Find Next**.

- **Look In**—Focuses the search to just formulas, values, or comments.

- **Match Case**—Lets you choose between uppercase or lowercase text.

- **Match Entire Cell Contents**—Searches for an exact match of the characters in the Find What text box.

4. Click **Find All** to display a table of all occurrences (shown here), or click **Find Next** to find the next singular occurrence.

USING THE OFFICE CLIPBOARD

(Continued)

To paste all items:

1. Click to place the insertion point in the cell where you want the items on the Office Clipboard inserted.

2. Click **Paste All** on the Clipboard.

DELETE ITEMS ON THE CLIPBOARD

1. To delete all items, click **Clear All** on the Clipboard task pane.

2. To delete a single item, point to an item, click the arrow next to it, and click **Delete**.

SET CLIPBOARD OPTIONS

1. On the Clipboard task pane, click the **Options** down arrow at the bottom. A context menu is displayed.

2. Click an option to select or deselect it:

   • **Show Office Clipboard Automatically** always shows the Office Clipboard when copying.

   • **Show Office Clipboard When CTRL+C Pressed Twice** shows the Office Clipboard when you press **CTRL+C** twice to make two copies (in other words, copying two items to the Clipboard will cause the Clipboard to be displayed).

   • **Collect Without Showing Office Clipboard** copies items to the Clipboard without displaying it.

   • **Show Office Clipboard Icon On Taskbar** displays the icon ▣ on the notification area of the taskbar when the Clipboard is being used.

   • **Show Status Near Taskbar When Copying** displays a message about the items being added to the Clipboard as copies are made.

REPLACE DATA

The Replace tab of the Find And Replace dialog box looks and behaves similar to the Find tab covered earlier.

1. In the Home tab Editing group, click **Find And Select**, and click **Replace**; or press **CTRL+H** to open the Find And Replace dialog box with the Replace tab displayed.

2. Enter the text or number to find in the Find What text box; enter the replacement characters in the Replace With text box. If formatting or search criteria are required, click **Options**. See "Find Data" for the options' descriptions.

3. Click **Replace All** to replace all occurrences in the worksheet, or click **Replace** to replace occurrences one at a time.

FIND SPECIFIC EXCEL OBJECTS

You can quickly locate key Excel objects, such as formulas and comments, without having to type any keywords. The objects you can directly search for are listed on the Find & Select drop-down menu.

1. In the Home tab Editing group, click **Find & Select**. The drop-down menu lists several categories of objects from which you can choose.

2. Click the item whose instances you want selected. The first instance is surrounded by a light border, and all other instances in the worksheet are selected/highlighted (see Figure 2-11).

   –Or–

   Click **Go To Special** to open a dialog box of the same name, and select from several additional objects. Click **OK** after making your selection.

3. To remove the selection/highlight from found objects, click **Find & Select** again, and click **Select Objects** to turn off that feature.

B7			▼	f_x	14986	
▲	A	B	C	D	E	F
1	Superior Office Supplies					
2	2010 Budget					
3	Superior Office Supplies	1st Qtr	2nd Qtr	3rd Qtr	4th Qtr	Total Yr
4	Revenue					
5	Paper Supplies	$23,567	$35,938	$38,210	$39,876	$137,591
6	Writing Instruments	$5,437	$5,834	$5,923	$6,082	$23,276
7	Cards and Books	$14,986	$15,043	$16,975	$16,983	$63,987
8	Other Items	$25,897	$26,729	$27,983	$28,721	$109,330
9	Total Revenue	$69,887	$83,544	$89,091	$91,662	$334,184

Figure 2-11: Certain Excel objects, such as comments, can be located and identified with just a few clicks.

NOTE

The Go To option on the Find And Select drop-down menu lets you find cells and ranges by name or address. Using the Go To dialog box in this manner is covered in Chapter 4.

TIP

If the correct spelling of a misspelled word is not shown in the Suggestions list box, edit the word in the Not In Dictionary text box, and click **Add To Dictionary** to include it in a custom dictionary that is checked in addition to the main dictionary.

Verify Spelling

You can check the spelling of selected cells—or the entire worksheet—using Excel's main dictionary and a custom dictionary you add words to (both dictionaries are shared with other Office programs).

1. Select the cells to check; to check the entire worksheet, select any cell.

2. In the Review tab Proofing group, click **Spelling** or press **F7**. When the spelling checker doesn't find anything to report, you are told the spelling check is complete. Otherwise, the Spelling dialog box appears, as shown in Figure 2-12.

3. Choose to ignore one or more occurrences of the characters shown in the Not In Dictionary text box, or change the characters by picking from the Suggestions list and clicking one of the Change options.

4. Click **AutoCorrect** if you want to automatically replace words in the future. (See "Modify Automatic Corrections," next, for more information on using AutoCorrect.)

5. Click **Options** to change language or custom dictionaries and set other spelling criteria.

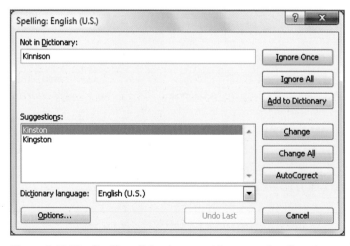

Figure 2-12: The Spelling dialog box provides several options to handle misspelled or uncommon words.

Figure 2-13: *AutoCorrect provides several automatic settings and lets you add words and characters that are replaced with alternatives.*

Modify Automatic Corrections

Excel automatically corrects common data entry mistakes as you type, replacing characters and words you choose with other choices. You can control how this is done.

1. Click the **File** tab, click **Options**, click the **Proofing** option, and click **AutoCorrect Options**. The AutoCorrect dialog box appears, as shown in Figure 2-13. As appropriate, do one or more of the following:

   - Choose the type of automatic corrections you do or do not want from the options at the top of the dialog box.

   - Click **Exceptions** to set capitalization exceptions.

   - Click **Replace Text As You Type** to turn off automatic text replacement (turned on by default).

   - Add new words or characters to the Replace and With lists, and click **Add**; or select a current item in the list, edit it, and click **Replace**.

   - Delete replacement text by selecting the item in the Replace and With lists and clicking **Delete**.

2. Click **OK** when you are done.

How to...

Chapter 3
Formatting a Worksheet

Arguably, the primary purpose of a worksheet is to provide a grid to calculate numbers, generally regarded as a rather boring display of numeric data. Excel provides you with the tools to adjust and rearrange the row-and-column grid to meet your needs, but it goes much further to bring emphasis, coordinated colors, and other features that let you add *presentation* to your data.

In this chapter you will learn how to add and delete cells, rows, and columns, and how to change their appearance, both manually and by having Excel do it for you. You will see how to change the appearance of text, how to use themes and styles for a more consistent look, and how to add comments to a cell to better explain important points. Techniques to better display workbooks and change worksheets are also covered.

Don't ever worry about running out of rows or columns in a worksheet. You can have up to 1,048,576 rows and 16,384 columns in each Excel worksheet. As a bit of tourist information, the last cell address in a worksheet is XFD1048576.

QUICKSTEPS

ADDING AND REMOVING ROWS, COLUMNS, AND CELLS

You can insert or delete rows one at a time or select adjacent and nonadjacent rows to perform these actions on them together. (See Chapter 2 for information on selecting rows, columns, and cells.)

ADD A SINGLE ROW

1. Select the row below where you want the new row.

2. In the Home tab Cells group, click the **Insert** down arrow, and click **Insert Sheet Rows**; or right-click a cell in the selected row, and click **Insert**.

ADD MULTIPLE ADJACENT ROWS

1. Select the number of rows you want immediately below the row where you want the new rows.

2. In the Home tab Cells group, click the **Insert** down arrow, and click **Insert Sheet Rows**; or right-click a cell in the selected rows, and click **Insert**.

ADD ROWS TO MULTIPLE NONADJACENT ROWS

1. Select the number of rows you want immediately below the first row where you want the new rows.

2. Hold down the **CTRL** key while selecting the number of rows you want immediately below any other rows.

Continued . . .

Work with Cells, Rows, and Columns

Getting a worksheet to look the way you want will probably involve adding and removing cells, rows, and/or columns to appropriately separate your data and remove unwanted space. You might also want to adjust the size and type of cell border and add comments to provide ancillary information about the contents of a cell. This section covers these features and more.

Adjust Row Height

You can change the height of a row manually or by changing cell contents.

CHANGE THE HEIGHT USING A MOUSE

1. Select one or more rows (they can be adjacent or nonadjacent).

2. Point at the bottom border of a selected row heading until the pointer changes to a cross with up and down arrowheads.

3. Drag the border up or down to the row height you want (as you are dragging, the row height is shown in *points*—there are 72 points to an inch—and in pixels).

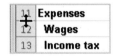

CHANGE THE HEIGHT BY ENTERING A VALUE

1. Select the rows you want to adjust.

2. In the Home tab Cells group, click **Format**, and under Cell Size, click **Row Height**; or right-click a cell in the selected rows, and click **Row Height**. The Row Height dialog box appears.

3. Type a new height in points, and click **OK**. The cell height changes, but the size of the cell contents stays the same.

QUICKSTEPS

ADDING AND REMOVING ROWS, COLUMNS, AND CELLS *(Continued)*

3. In the Home tab Cells group, click the **Insert** down arrow, and click **Insert Sheet Rows**; or right-click any selection, and click **Insert**.

ADD A SINGLE COLUMN

1. Select the column to the right of where you want the new column.

2. In the Home tab Cells group, click the **Insert** down arrow, and click **Insert Sheet Columns**; or right-click a cell in the selected column, and click **Insert**.

ADD MULTIPLE ADJACENT COLUMNS

1. Select the number of columns you want immediately to the right of the column where you want the new columns.

2. In the Home tab Cells group, click the **Insert** down arrow, and click **Insert Sheet Columns**; or right-click a cell in the selected columns, and click **Insert**.

ADD COLUMNS TO MULTIPLE NONADJACENT COLUMNS

1. Select the number of columns you want immediately to the right of the first column where you want the new columns.

2. Hold down the **CTRL** key while selecting the number of columns you want immediately to the right of any other columns.

3. In the Home tab Cells group, click the **Insert** down arrow, and click **Insert Sheet Columns**; or right-click any selection, and click **Insert**.

ADD CELLS

1. Select the cells adjacent to where you want to insert the new cells.

Continued . . .

CHANGE ROW HEIGHT BY CHANGING CELL CONTENTS

1. Select one or more cells, rows, or characters that you want to change in height.

2. Change the cell contents. Examples of the various ways to do this include:

- **Changing font size:** In the Home tab Font group, click the **Font Size** down arrow, and click a size from the drop-down list. (You can drag up and down the list of font sizes and see the impact of each on the worksheet before selecting one, as shown in Figure 3-1.)

- **Placing characters on two or more lines within a cell:** Place the insertion point at the end of a line or where you want the line to break, and press **ALT+ENTER**.

- **Inserting graphics or drawing objects:** See Chapter 7 for information on working with graphics.

When a selected object changes size or a new object is inserted, if its height becomes larger than the original row height, the height of all cells in the row(s) will be increased. The size of the other cell's contents, however, stays the same.

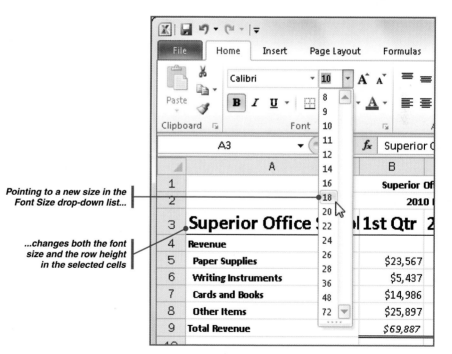

Pointing to a new size in the Font Size drop-down list...

...changes both the font size and the row height in the selected cells

Figure 3-1: *You can preview the effects of changing row heights by increasing or decreasing the font size in selected cells.*

QUICKSTEPS

ADDING AND REMOVING ROWS, COLUMNS, AND CELLS (Continued)

2. In the Home tab Cells group, click the **Insert** down arrow, and click **Insert Cells**; or right-click the cell, and click **Insert**.

3. In the Insert dialog box, choose the direction to shift the existing cells to make room for the new cells. Click **OK**.

REMOVE CELLS, ROWS, AND COLUMNS

1. Select the single or adjacent items (cells, rows, or columns) you wish to remove. If you want to remove nonadjacent items, hold down the **CTRL** key while clicking them.

2. In the Home tab Cells group, click the **Delete** down arrow, and click the command applicable to what you want to remove; or right-click the selection, and click **Delete**.

3. When deleting selected cells, the Delete dialog box appears. Choose from which direction to fill in the removed cells, and click **OK**.

MERGE CELLS

Select the cells you want to combine into one cell.

1. In the Home tab Alignment group, click the **Merge & Center** down arrow. (If all you want to do is merge and center, click the button.)

2. Click the applicable tool from the drop-down list.

CHANGE ROW HEIGHT TO FIT THE SIZE OF CELL CONTENTS

Excel automatically adjusts row height to accommodate the largest object or text size added to a row. If you subsequently removed larger objects or text and you need to resize to fit the remaining objects, you can do so using AutoFit.

- Double-click the bottom border of the row heading for a row or selected rows.

  –Or–

- Select the cell or rows you want to size. In the Home tab Cells group, click **Format** and click **AutoFit Row Height**.

The row heights(s) will adjust to fit the highest content.

Adjust Column Width

As with changing row height, you can change the width of a column manually or by changing cell contents.

CHANGE THE WIDTH USING A MOUSE

1. Select one or more columns (columns can be adjacent or nonadjacent).

2. Point at the right border of a selected column heading until the pointer changes to a cross with left and right arrowheads.

3. Drag the border to the left or right to the width you want.

CHANGE THE WIDTH BY ENTERING A VALUE

1. Select the columns you want to adjust.

2. In the Home tab Cells group, click **Format** and click **Column Width**; or right-click the cell, and click **Column Width**. The Column Width dialog box appears.

3. Type a new width, and click **OK**. The cell width changes, but the size of the cell contents stays the same.

NOTE

You cannot change the width of a single cell without changing the width of all cells in the column.

TIP

The default column width for a worksheet is determined by the average number of characters in the default font that will fit in the column (not in points, as with row height). For example, the default Calibri 11 pt. font provides a standard column width of 8.43 characters. If you want to change the default column width, in the Home tab Cells group, click **Format** and click **Default Width**. Type a width and click **OK**. Columns at the original standard width will change to reflect the new value.

TIP

If you hide one or more rows or columns beginning with column A or row 1, it does not look like you can drag across the rows or columns on both sides of the hidden rows or columns to unhide them. However, you can by selecting the row or column to the right or below the hidden row or column and dragging the selection into the heading. Then when you click **Unhide** from the context menu or **Unhide Rows** or **Unhide Columns** from the Format menu, the hidden object will appear. If you don't do this, you won't be able to recover the hidden row or column.

CHANGE COLUMN WIDTH TO FIT THE SIZE OF CELL CONTENTS

- Double-click the right border of the column header for the column or selected columns.

 –Or–

- Select the cell or columns you want to size. In the Home tab Cells group, click **Format** and click **AutoFit Column Width**.

The column width(s) will adjust to fit the longest entry.

Hide and Unhide Rows and Columns

Hidden rows and columns provide a means to temporarily remove rows or columns from view without deleting them or their contents.

HIDE ROWS AND COLUMNS

1. Select the rows or columns to be hidden (see Chapter 2).
2. In the Home tab Cells group, click **Format**, click **Hide & Unhide**, and click **Hide Rows** or **Hide Columns**; or right-click the selection, and click **Hide**.

 –Or–

 Drag the bottom border of the rows to be hidden *up*, or drag the right border of the columns to be hidden to the *left*.

The row numbers or column letters of the hidden cells are omitted, as shown in Figure 3-2. (You can also tell cells are hidden by the slightly darker border in the row or column headers between the hidden rows or columns.)

UNHIDE ROWS OR COLUMNS

1. Drag across the row or column headings on both sides of the hidden rows or columns.
2. In the Home tab Cells group, click **Format**, click **Hide & Unhide**, and click **Unhide Rows** or **Unhide Columns**.

 –Or–

 Right-click the selection and click **Unhide**.

Change Cell Borders

Borders provide a quick and effective way to emphasize and segregate data on a worksheet. You can create borders by choosing from samples or by setting them up in a dialog box. Use the method that suits you best.

Darker heading border identifies hidden rows and columns

	A	B	C	F
1	Superior Office Supplies			
2	2010 Budget			
3	Superior Office Supplies	1st Qtr.	2nd Qtr	Total Yr
4	Revenue			
5	Paper Supplies	$23,567	$35,938	$137,59
9	Total Revenue	$69,887	$83,544	$334,18
10				
11	Expenses			
12	Wages	$8,345	$8,598	$35,34
13	Income tax	$1,252	$1,290	$5,30
14	Social Security	$1,035	$1,066	$4,38
15	Medicare	$242	$249	$1,02

Figure 3-2: Rows 6, 7, and 8 and columns D and E are hidden in this worksheet.

PICK A BORDER

1. Select the cell, range, row, or column whose border you want to modify.

2. In the Home tab Font group, click the **Border** down arrow, and select the border style you want. (The style you choose remains as the available border style on the button.)

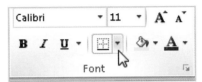

3. To remove a border, select the cell(s), click the **Border** down arrow, and click **No Border**.

PREVIEW BORDERS BEFORE YOU CHANGE THEM

1. Select the cell, range, row, or column that you want to modify with a border.

2. In the Home tab Font group, click the **Border** down arrow, and click **More Borders**.

–Or–

In the Home tab Font group, click the **Dialog Box Launcher**, or right-click the selection, and click **Format Cells**. Click the **Border** tab in the Format Cells dialog box.

In either case, the Format Cells dialog box appears with the Border tab displayed, as shown in Figure 3-3.

3. In the Border area in the center of the dialog box, you will see a preview of the selected cells. Use the other tools in the dialog box to set up your borders.

- **Presets buttons**—Set broad border parameters by selecting to have no border, an outline border, or an inside "grid" border (can also be changed manually in the Border area).

- **Line area**—Select a border style and color (see "Change Themed Colors" later in the chapter for information on color options).

- **Border buttons**—Choose where you want a border (click once to add the border; click twice to remove it).

4. Click **OK** to apply the borders.

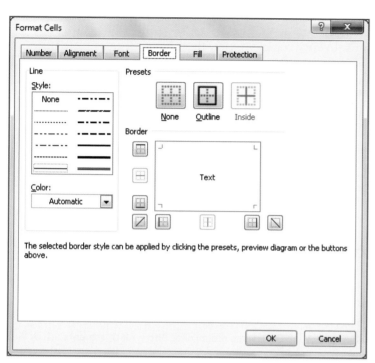

Figure 3-3: *You can build and preview borders for selected cells in the Border tab.*

TIP

To change the user name that appears in a comment, click the **File** tab, click **Options**, and click the **General** option. Under Personalize Your Copy Of Microsoft Office, edit the name in the User Name text box, and click **OK**.

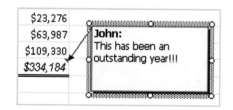

DRAW BORDERS

1. In the Home tab Font group, click the **Border** down arrow, and under Draw Borders, select the color and style of border you want.

2. From the Border menu, click **Draw Border** to draw an outer border.

   –Or–

   Click **Draw Border Grid** to include interior borders.

3. Use the pencil mouse pointer to drag over the cells you want to have a border.

$8,345	$8,593	$9,104
$1,252	$1,290	$1,366
$1,035	$1,066	$1,129

4. If you want to change a drawn border, click **Erase Border** and drag over a border to remove it.

5. When you are finished, press **ESC** to turn off the border drawing feature.

Add a Comment

A comment acts as a "notepad" for cells, providing a place on the worksheet for explanatory text that can be hidden until needed.

1. Select the cell where you want the comment.

2. In the Review tab Comments group, click **New Comment**; or right-click the cell, and click **Insert Comment**. In either case, a text box labeled with your user name is attached to the cell.

3. Type your comment and click anywhere on the worksheet to close the comment. An indicator icon (red triangle) in the upper-right corner of the cell shows that a comment is attached.

NOTE

If you have a TabletPC, you will have an additional contextual tab available to you that provides drawing and highlighting tools. To open the Pens tab (Ink Tools), in the Review tab Ink group, click **Start Inking**. (On all computers, you can view/hide ink annotations by clicking **Show Ink** in the Comments group.)

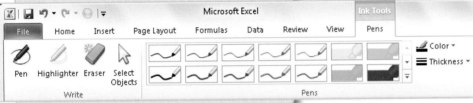

TIP

The default behavior for comments is to show the indicator icon (red triangle) and display the comment text when the mouse pointer is hovered over a cell containing a comment. You can also choose to always show the comment text and indicators or to not show the indicators and text. Click the **File** tab, click **Options**, and click the **Advanced** option. In the Display area, under For Cells With Comments, Show, select the behavior you want, and click **OK**.

For cells with comments, show:
- ○ No comments or indicators
- ● Indicators only, and comments on hover
- ○ Comments and indicators

TIP

You can also delete comments by selectively clearing them from a cell. In the Home tab Editing group, click **Clear** and then click **Clear Comments** from the drop-down menu.

VIEW COMMENTS

You can view an individual comment, view them in sequence, or view all comments on a worksheet.

● To view any comment, point to or select a cell that displays an indicator icon (red triangle) in its upper-right corner. The comment stays displayed as long as your mouse pointer remains in the cell.

● To view comments in sequence, in the Review tab Comments group, click **Next**. The next comment in the worksheet, moving left to right and down the rows, displays until you click another cell or press **ESC**. Click **Previous** in the Comments group to reverse the search direction.

● To keep the comment displayed while doing other work, select the cell that contains the comment. In the Review tab Comments group, click **Show/Hide Comment**; or right-click the cell, and click **Show/Hide Comments**. (Click either command to hide the comment.)

● To view all comments in a worksheet and keep the comment displayed while doing other work, in the Review tab Comments group, click **Show All Comments**. (Click the command a second time to hide all comments.)

EDIT A COMMENT

1. Select a cell that displays an indicator icon (red triangle) in its upper-right corner.

2. In the Review tab Comments group, click **Edit Comment**; or right-click the cell, and click **Edit Comment**.

3. Edit the text, including the user name if appropriate. Click anywhere in the worksheet when finished.

DELETE A COMMENT

1. Select the cell or cells that contain the comments you want to delete.

2. In the Review tab Comments group, click **Delete**; or right-click the cell, and click **Delete Comment**.

NOTE

Moving a comment only moves the editing text box's position in relationship to its parent cell—it does not move the comment to other cells. The new location of moved comments only appears when editing the comment or when you display all comments in the worksheet; otherwise, when either the cell is selected or the mouse hovers over the cell, it appears in its default position.

FORMATTING COMMENTS

You can apply several formatting techniques to comments, including changing text, borders, and color. These and other attributes are changed using the Format Comment dialog box, available after a comment is opened for editing (see "Edit a Comment").

CHANGE THE APPEARANCE OF COMMENT TEXT

1. To change the formatting of existing text, select the text first. If you do not select existing text, only new text you type will show the changes after you make them.

2. Right-click the interior of the comment, and click **Format Comment**. Make and preview the changes you want in the Font tab, and click **OK**. Alternatively, in the Home tab Font group, click the applicable control to change the font, size, and styling (see "Change Fonts" later in this chapter).

Continued . . .

MOVE AND RESIZE A COMMENT

Open the comment (see "Edit a Comment").

- To **resize**, point to one of the corner or mid-border sizing handles. When the pointer becomes a double arrow-headed line, drag the handle in the direction you want to increase or decrease the comment's size.

- To **move**, point at the wide border surrounding the comment. When the pointer becomes a cross with arrowhead tips, drag the comment to where you want it.

COPY A COMMENT

1. Select the cell that contains the comment you want to copy (only the comment will be added to a new cell, not any other cell contents).

2. In the Home tab Clipboard group, click **Copy**; or right-click the cell, and click **Copy**; or press **CTRL+C**. The cell is surrounded by a flashing border.

3. Select the cells to which you want the comment copied. Then, in the Clipboard group, click the **Paste** down arrow, and click **Paste Special**. In the Paste Special dialog box, under Paste, click **Comments**, and then click **OK**.

4. Repeat step 3 to paste the comment into other cells. When finished, press **ESC** to remove the flashing border.

Apply Formatting

Formatting gives life to a worksheet, transforming a rather dull collection of text and numbers into pleasing colors, shades, and variations in size and effects that bring attention to points you are trying to emphasize. You can apply or create *themes* (consistent use of color, fonts, and graphics effects) to give your worksheets a coordinated appearance. If you want more control, you can apply *styles* (consistent formatting parameters applicable to specific worksheet objects) and *direct formatting* (use of ribbon buttons and dialog boxes) to cells and text.

FORMATTING COMMENTS *(Continued)*

CHANGE A COMMENT'S COLOR AND BORDER

1. Right-click the border of the comment, and click **Format Comment**.

2. In the Format Comment dialog box, click the **Colors And Lines** tab.

3. Click the **Fill Color** down arrow to open the gallery. Click the new color you want (see "Change Themed Colors" later in the chapter for information on color options).

4. In the Linc area, change the attributes that control the comment's border. Click **OK** when finished.

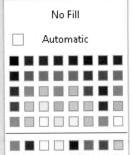

No Fill

☐ Automatic

More Colors...
Fill Effects...

TIP

To quickly determine the theme currently in effect, click the **Page Layout** tab, and point to the **Themes** button in the Themes group. The tooltip displays the current theme (similarly, point to the **Fonts** button to see the current theme fonts in use).

Themes

Current: Office Theme

Change the overall design of the entire document, including colors, fonts, and effects.

_____

❷ **Press F1 for more help.**

(See the "Understanding Excel Formatting" QuickFacts for more information on these formatting types.) In addition, you can transfer formatting attributes from one cell to others.

Apply Themes

Themes are the most hands-off way to add a coordinated look and feel to a worksheet. Built-in themes control the formatting of themed elements, such as the color of table headers and rows and the font used in chart text. In addition, you can change themes and modify themed elements (colors, fonts, and graphic effects).

CHANGE THE CURRENT THEME

By default, Excel applies the Office theme to new workbooks. You can easily view the effects from the other built-in themes and change to the one you prefer.

1. In the Page Layout tab Themes group, click **Themes**. A gallery of the available themes (built-in, custom, and a selection from those available from Office Online) is displayed, as shown in Figure 3-4.

2. Point to each theme and see how colors, fonts, and graphics change in themed elements. The best way to view changes is to create a table and associated chart, and with it displayed, point to each theme in the gallery and see how the table and chart look (see Figure 3-4). Chapters 6 and 8 provide more information on charts and tables, respectively.

3. Click the theme you want, and save your workbook.

CHANGE THEMED COLORS

Each theme comes with 12 primary colors (see the "Understanding Excel Formatting" QuickFacts) affecting text, accents, and hyperlinks. You can choose a theme with different colors or modify each constituent color.

1. In the Page Layout tab Themes group, click **Colors**. The drop-down list displays the built-in and online themes and 8 of the 12 colors associated with each theme.

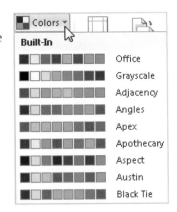

Colors

Built-In

Office
Grayscale
Adjacency
Angles
Apex
Apothecary
Aspect
Austin
Black Tie

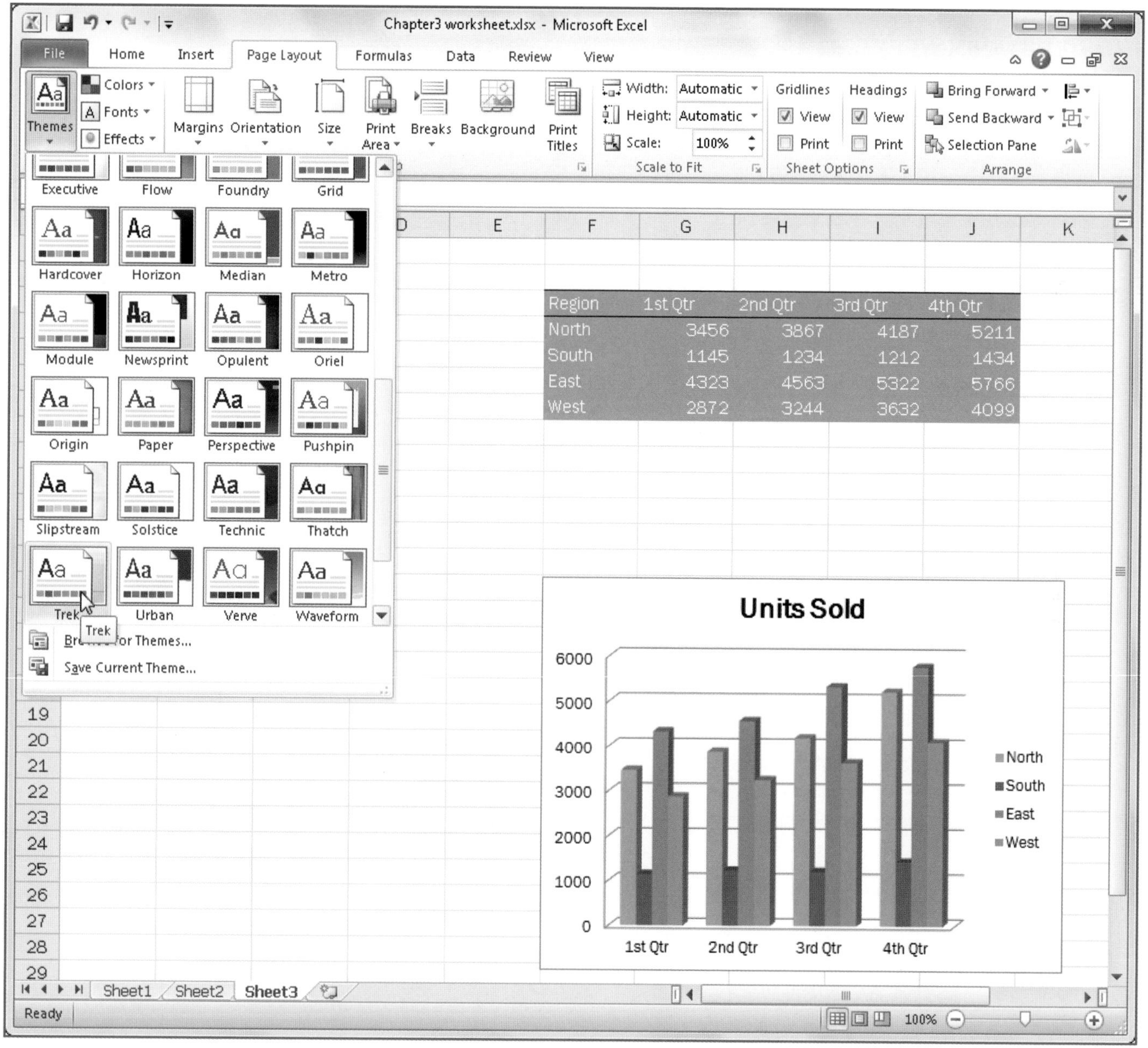

Figure 3-4: *Excel provides 40 built-in professionally designed themes.*

QUICKFACTS

UNDERSTANDING EXCEL FORMATTING

There are a plethora of ways you can change the appearance of text and worksheet elements. Without having a sense of the "method behind the madness," it's easy to become confused and frustrated when attempting to enhance your work. Excel (as well as Microsoft Word and Microsoft PowerPoint, and to a lesser degree, Microsoft Access) operates on a hierarchy of formatting assistance (see Figure 3-5). The higher a formatting feature is on the stack, the broader and more automatic are its effects; the lower on the stack, the more user intervention is required, although you will have more control over the granularity of any given feature.

- **Themes** are at the top of the formatting heap. Themes provide an efficiently lazy way to apply professionally designed color, font, and graphic elements to a workbook. Each theme (with names like Office, Currency, and Solstice) includes 12 colors (4 text colors, 6 accent colors, and 2 hyperlink colors), along with 6 shades of each primary theme color. Separate collections of theme fonts are available for headings and body text (the default workbook theme is Office, which is where the Calibri font comes from that you see in new workbooks). When you switch themes, all theme-affected elements are changed. You can modify existing themes and save them, creating your own theme.

- **Styles** occupy the middle tier of Excel formatting. Styles apply consistent formatting to directed Excel components, such as cells, tables, charts, and PivotTables. Styles, similar to themes, can be modified and saved for your own design needs.

Continued . . .

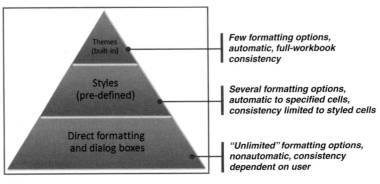

Figure 3-5: Excel provides three levels of formatting assistance.

2. At the bottom of the list, click **Create New Theme Colors**. The Create New Theme Colors dialog box displays each constituent theme color and a sample displaying the current selections (see Figure 3-6).

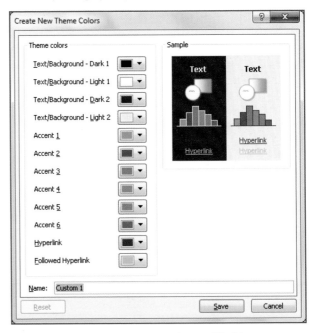

Figure 3-6: Each theme color can be modified from an essentially infinite number of choices.

UNDERSTANDING EXCEL FORMATTING *(Continued)*

Both themes and styles are supported by several galleries of their respective formatting options, and provide a live preview by hovering your mouse pointer over each choice. Certain attributes of a style are *themed*, meaning they are consistent with the current theme and change accordingly.

- **Direct formatting** is the feature most of us have used to get the look we want, found in buttons on the ribbon and formatting dialog boxes divided into several tabs of options. Direct formatting provides the greatest control and access to formatting features, but even though Excel now provides live previews for many options, most still require you to accept the change, view the result in the workbook, and then repeat the process several times to get the result you want (and then start all over when moving, for example, from formatting a table to a chart).

So how do you best put this hierarchy to work? Start at the top by applying a theme. If its formatting works for you, you're done! If you need more customization, try simply changing to a different theme. Need more options? Try applying a style to one of the style-affected components. Finally, if you need total control, use a component's formatting dialog box and ribbon buttons to make detailed changes. When you're all done, save all your changes as a new theme that you can apply to new workbooks, and also to your Word documents and PowerPoint presentations.

3. Click the theme color you want to change. A gallery of colors displays and provides the following three options from which you select a new color:

- **Theme Colors** displays a matrix of the 12 primary colors in the current theme and 6 shades associated with each. Click a color and see the change in the Sample area of the Create New Theme Colors dialog box.

- **Standard Colors** displays the 10 standard colors in the color spectrum (red through violet). Click the color you want.

- **More Colors** opens the Colors dialog box, shown in Figure 3-7, from where you can select a custom color by clicking a color and using a slider to change its shading, or by selecting a color model and entering specific color values. In addition, you can click the **Standard** tab and select from a hexagonal array of Web-friendly colors.

4. Repeat step 3 for any other theme color you want to change. If you get a bit far afield in your color changes, don't panic. Click **Reset** at the bottom of the Create New Theme Colors dialog box to return to the default theme colors.

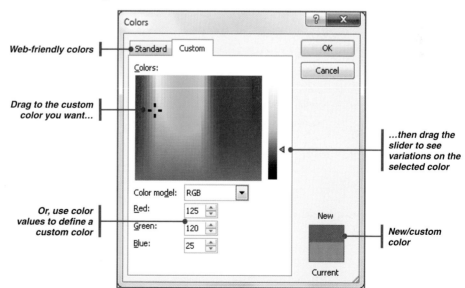

Figure 3-7: The Colors dialog box offers the greatest control of custom color selection, as well as a collection of standard Web-friendly colors.

5. Type a new name for the color combination you've selected, and click **Save**. Custom colors are available for selection at the top of the theme Colors drop-down list.

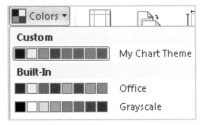

CHANGE THEMED FONTS

Each theme includes two fonts. The *body* font is used for general text entry (the Calibri font in the default Office theme is the body font). A *heading* font is also included and used in a few cell styles (see "Use Cell Styles" later in this chapter).

1. In the Page Layout tab Themes group, click **Fonts**. The drop-down list, shown in Figure 3-8, displays a list of theme font combinations (heading and body). The current theme font combination is highlighted.

2. Point to each combination to see how the fonts will appear on your worksheet.

3. Click the combination you want, or click **Create New Theme Fonts** at the bottom of the drop-down list (see Figure 3-8).

4. In the Create New Theme Fonts dialog box, click either or both the **Heading Font** and **Body Font** down arrows to select new fonts. View the new combination in the Sample area.

5. Type a new name for the font combination you've selected, and click **Save**. Custom fonts are available for selection at the top of the theme Fonts drop-down list.

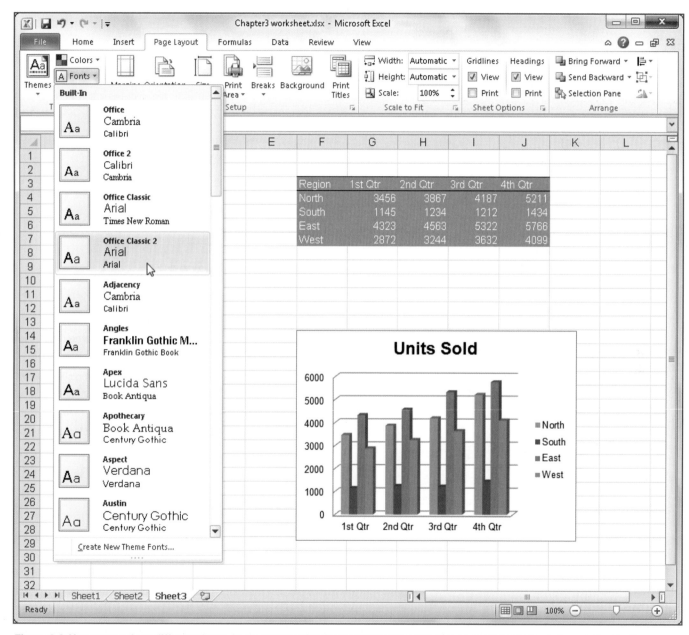

Figure 3-8: You can see how different theme body and heading font combinations affect your worksheet simply by pointing to them.

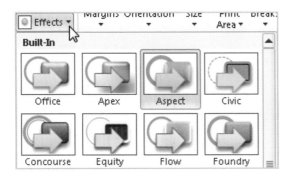

CHANGE THEMED GRAPHIC EFFECTS

Shapes, illustrations, pictures, and charts include graphic effects that are controlled by themes. Themed graphics are modulated in terms of their lines (borders), fills, and effects (such as shadowed, raised, and shaded). For example, some themes simply change an inserted rectangle's fill color, while other themes affect the color, the weight of its border, and whether it has a 3-D appearance.

1. In the Page Layout tab Themes group, click **Effects**. The drop-down list displays a gallery of effects. The current effect is highlighted.

2. Point to each effect to see how it changes your worksheet, assuming you have a theme-based graphic or other element inserted on the worksheet (see Chapters 6 and 7 for information on inserting charts and graphics).

3. Click the effect you want.

Create Custom Themes

Changes you make to a built-in theme (or to a previously created custom theme) can be saved as a custom theme and reused in other Office 2010 documents.

1. Make color, font, and effects changes to the current theme (see "Apply Themes" earlier in this chapter).

2. In the Page Layout tab Themes group, click **Themes** and click **Save Current Theme**. The Save Current Theme dialog box appears with the custom Office themes folder displayed, as shown in Figure 3-9.

3. Name the file and click **Save** to store the theme in the Document Themes folder.

   –Or–

   Name the file and browse to the folder where you want to store it. Click **Save** when finished.

Use Cell Styles

Cell styles allow you to apply consistent formatting to specific cells, and let you make changes to styled cells with a few mouse clicks instead of changing each cell individually. Excel provides dozens of predefined styles, categorized by use. One category, themed cell styles, has the additional advantage of being fully integrated with the current theme. Colors associated with a theme change will automatically

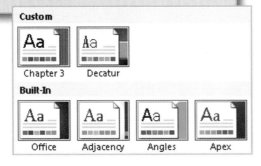

CAUTION

Saved custom themes that are not stored in the default Document Themes folder will not be displayed in the Custom area of the Themes drop-down list. You will need to locate them to apply them (see the "Searching for Themes" QuickSteps).

NOTE

Styles also can be applied to charts, tables, and PivotTables. Using styles with these Excel components is covered in their respective chapters later in this book.

TIP

The easiest way to ensure a common look and feel to your Excel 2010 workbooks is to create or apply the theme you want and save the workbook as a template. In addition to the theme-controlled aspects of a workbook, the template allows you to consistently re-create formulas, tables, charts, and all else that Excel has to offer. Chapter 1 describes saving workbooks as templates.

QUICKSTEPS

SEARCHING FOR THEMES

You can quickly find individual theme files and themed documents, and apply them to your workbook. In addition, you can use prebuilt themes that are available from Office.com.

LOCATE AND APPLY THEMES

You can apply themes from other files to your workbooks, either as individual theme files or from other Office 2010 files that have themes applied to them.

1. In the Page Layout tab Themes group, click **Themes** and click **Browse For Themes** at the bottom of the gallery.

2. In the Choose Theme Or Themed Document dialog box, browse to the folder where the themes or themed documents are located. Only those documents will display. (*Themed documents* are Office 2010 files that contain a theme, such as Word files, Excel workbooks, PowerPoint presentations, Access databases, and their respective templates.)

3. If you are only looking for theme files (.thmx), click **Office Themes And Themed Documents**, and click **Office Themes (.thmx)**.

Continued . . .

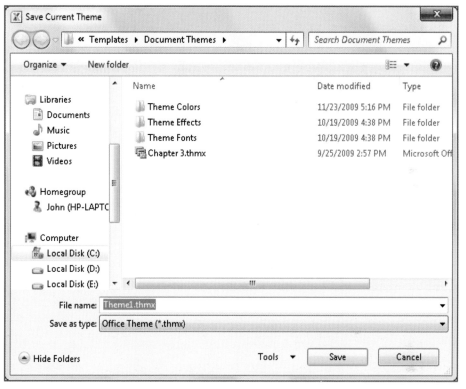

Figure 3-9: *Custom themes are saved as individual files, along with custom theme colors, effects, and fonts.*

carry over to themed cell styles, preserving the coordinated appearance of your worksheet. Of course, you can modify any applied style and save the changes to create your own custom style.

APPLY A STYLE

1. Select the cells you want to format with a style.

2. In the Home tab Styles group, click **Cell Styles**. A gallery of cell styles is displayed, as shown in Figure 3-10.

3. Point to several styles in the gallery to see how each style affects your selected cells.

4. Click the style that best suits your needs. The style formatting is applied to your selected cells.

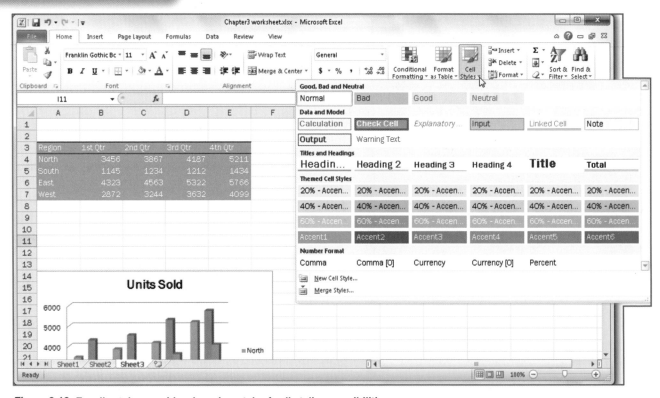

QUICKSTEPS

SEARCHING FOR THEMES (Continued)

4. Select the Office document whose theme you want to apply or the theme file you want to apply, and click **Open**.

ACQUIRE THEMES FROM OFFICE.COM

In the Page Layout tab Themes group, click **Themes** and below the gallery of Built-In themes, click one of the themes you acquired from Office.com, often from a template you downloaded. Since these are Office themes and are shared across products, you may acquire them from the work you do in other Office products such as Word or PowerPoint.

CREATE A CUSTOM STYLE

You can create your own style by starting with a predefined style and making changes, or you can start from scratch and apply all formatting directly, using the formatting tools on the ribbon or in a formatting dialog box. In either case, you can save your changes as a custom style and apply it from the Cell Styles gallery.

1. Use one or more, or a combination, of the following techniques to format at least one cell as you want:

- Apply a predefined style to the cell(s) you want to customize.

- Use the formatting tools in the ribbon (Home tab Font, Alignment, and Number groups).

- Right-click a cell to be styled, click **Format Cells**, and use the six tabs in the Format Cells dialog box to create the styling format you want. Click **OK** when finished.

Figure 3-10: Excel's styles provide a broad swatch of cell styling possibilities.

NOTE

The default font used in each style is derived from the current theme. When you change themes, the font used in styled cells will change according to the font used in the new theme. Themed cell styles, unlike other cell styles, will additionally change color as applicable to the new theme.

TIP

You can avoid going back and forth between the Page Layout and Home tabs to apply themes and styles by placing the respective galleries on the Quick Access toolbar. Right-click a gallery icon, and click **Add To Quick Access Toolbar**; or right-click anywhere in the open gallery, and click **Add Gallery To Quick Access Toolbar**.

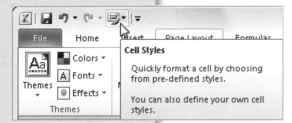

NOTE

Direct formatting using the ribbon and the Format Cells dialog box is discussed in other sections of this chapter.

TIP

To quickly create a style based on an existing style, right-click the existing style in the Cells Styles gallery, and click **Duplicate**. In the Style dialog box, type a name for the new style, make any formatting changes by clicking **Format**, and click **OK** twice.

2. In the Home tab Styles group, click **Cell Styles** and click **New Cell Style** at the bottom of the gallery.

3. In the Style dialog box, type a name for your style, and review the six areas of affected style formatting. If necessary, click **Format** and make formatting adjustments in the Format Cells dialog box. Click **OK** to apply formatting changes.

4. Click **OK** in the Style dialog box to create the style. The new custom style will be displayed in the Custom area at the top of the Cell Styles gallery.

CHANGE A CELL STYLE

1. In the Home tab Styles group, click **Cell Styles**.

2. Right-click a style (custom or predefined) in the gallery, and click **Modify**.

3. In the Style dialog box, click **Format** and make any formatting adjustments in the Format Cells dialog box. Click **OK** to apply the formatting changes.

4. Click **OK** in the Style dialog box to save changes to the style.

REMOVE A CELL STYLE

You can remove a style's formatting applied to selected cells, or you can completely remove the cell style from Excel (and concurrently remove all style formatting from affected cells).

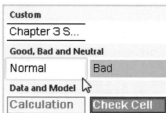

- To remove style formatting from cells, select the cells, click **Cell Styles** in the Styles group, and click the **Normal** style.

- To permanently remove a style, click **Cell Styles** in the Styles group, right-click the cell style you want removed, and click **Delete**.

ADD CELL STYLES FROM OTHER WORKBOOKS

1. Open both the workbook whose styles you want to add and the workbook where you want the styles to be added in the same Excel window.

2. In the View tab Window group, click **Switch Windows** and click the workbook to which you want the styles added, making it the active workbook.

3. In the Home tab Styles group, click **Cell Styles** and below the gallery, click **Merge Styles**.

4. In the Merge Styles dialog box, click the workbook from which you want to add styles. Click **OK**.

Change Fonts

Each *font* is composed of a *typeface*, such as Calibri; a *style*, such as italic; and a size. Other characteristics, such as color and super/subscripting, further distinguish text. Excel also provides several underlining options that are useful in accounting applications.

1. On a worksheet, select:
   - Cells to apply font changes to all characters
   - Characters to apply font changes to just the selected text and numbers

2. Use one of the following techniques to access font tools and options:
   - On the ribbon, click the **Home** tab, and click the appropriate Font group tools (see Figure 3-11).

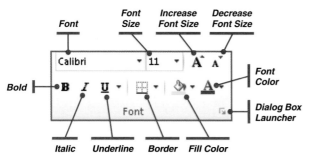

Figure 3-11: Font group tools apply formatting to text.

TIP

When selected, the Normal Font check box on the Font tab of the Format Cells dialog box (see Figure 3-12) resets font attributes to the defaults defined in the Normal template. The Normal template is an ever-present component of Excel (if you delete it, Excel will re-create another) that defines startup values in the absence of any other template.

- Double-click or right-click a cell or selection, and use the font tools available on the mini-toolbar (you might need to move the cursor over the faded toolbar to see it more clearly).

- Click the Font group **Dialog Box Launcher** arrow (located in the lower-right corner of group).

- Right-click a cell or selection, click **Format Cells**, and then click the **Font** tab.

3. In the latter two cases, the Format Cells dialog box appears with the Font tab displayed, as shown in Figure 3-12. Make and preview changes, and click **OK** when finished.

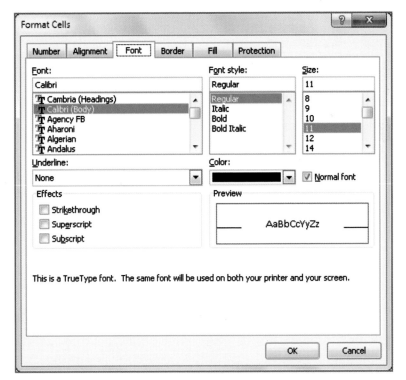

*Figure 3-12: **Change the appearance of text by changing its font and other characteristics.***

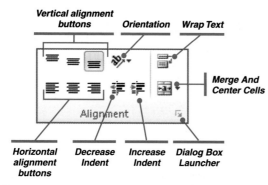

Vertical alignment buttons | Orientation | Wrap Text

Merge And Center Cells

Alignment

Horizontal alignment buttons | Decrease Indent | Increase Indent | Dialog Box Launcher

Figure 3-13: Alignment group tools allow you to reposition text.

Change Alignment and Orientation

You can modify how characters appear within a cell by changing their alignment, orientation, and "compactness."

1. Select the cells whose contents you want to change.

2. Use one of the following techniques to access font tools and options:

   • On the ribbon, click the **Home** tab, and click the appropriate Alignment group tools (see Figure 3-13).

   • Click the Alignment group **Dialog Box Launcher**.

   • Right-click a cell or selection, click **Format Cells**, and then click the **Alignment** tab.

3. In the latter two cases, the Format Cells dialog box appears with the Alignment tab displayed, as shown in Figure 3-14. The specific features of the Alignment tab are described in Table 3-1.

4. Click **OK** when you are finished.

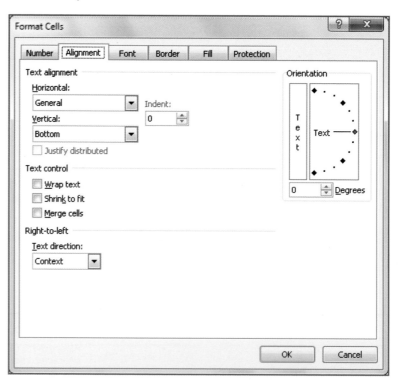

Figure 3-14: The Alignment tab provides detailed text-alignment options.

FEATURE	OPTION	DESCRIPTION
Text Alignment, Horizontal	General	Right-aligns numbers, left-aligns text, and centers error values; Excel default setting
	Left (Indent)	Left-aligns characters with optional indentation spinner
	Center	Centers characters in the cell
	Right (Indent)	Right-aligns characters with optional indentation spinner
	Fill	Fills cell with recurrences of content
	Justify	Justifies the text in a cell so that, to the degree possible, both the left and right ends are vertically aligned
	Center Across Selection	Centers text across one or more cells; used to center titles across several columns
	Distributed (Indent)	Stretches cell contents across cell width by adding space between words, with optional indentation spinner
Text Alignment, Vertical	Top	Places the text at the top of the cell
	Center	Places the text in the center of the cell
	Bottom	Places the text at the bottom of the cell; Excel's default setting
	Justify	Evenly distributes text between the top and bottom of a cell to fill it by adding space between lines
	Distributed	Vertically arranges characters equally within the cell (behaves the same as Justify)
Orientation		Angles text in a cell by dragging the red diamond up or down or by using the Degrees spinner
Text Control	Wrap Text	Moves text that extends beyond the cell's width to the line below
	Shrink To Fit	Reduces character size so that cell contents fit within cell width (cannot be used with Wrap Text)
	Merge Cells	Creates one cell from contiguous cells, "increasing" the width of a cell without changing the width of the column(s)
Right To Left, Text Direction	Context	Text entry flows according to keyboard language in use
	Left To Right	Text entry flows from the left as in Western countries
	Right To Left	Text entry flows from the right as in many Middle Eastern and East Asian countries

Table 3-1: Text-Alignment Options in Excel

Add a Background

You can add color and shading to selected cells to provide a solid background. You can also add preset patterns, either alone or in conjunction with a solid background for even more effect.

1. Select the cell, range, row, or column that you want to modify with a background.

2. In the Home tab Alignment group, click its **Dialog Box Launcher**.

   –Or–

   Right-click the selection and click **Format Cells**.

   In either case, the Format Cells dialog box appears.

3. Click the **Fill** tab (see Figure 3-15), and choose colored and/or patterned fills.

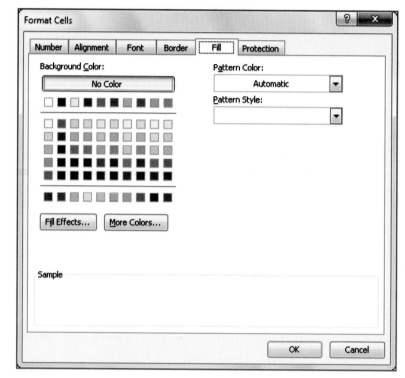

Figure 3-15: Use the Fill tab to apply colored or patterned backgrounds to cells.

USE SOLID COLORED BACKGROUNDS

1. In the Fill tab, click one of the color options in the Background Color area (see "Change Themed Colors" earlier in this chapter for information on the various color options).

   –Or–

   Click **Fill Effects** to apply blended fills, as shown in Figure 3-16. Preview your selections in the Sample area, and click **OK**.

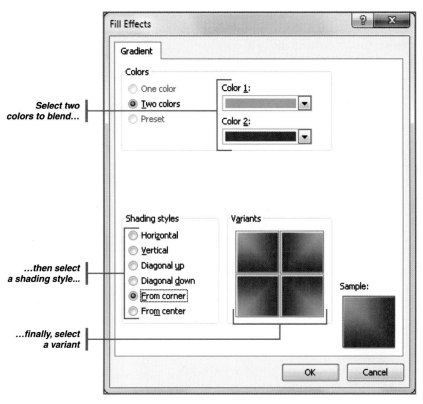

Select two colors to blend...

...then select a shading style...

...finally, select a variant

Figure 3-16: You can add pizzazz to cell fills using gradient effects.

2. Preview your selections in the larger Sample area at the bottom of the Fill tab, and click **OK** when finished.

USE PATTERNED BACKGROUNDS

1. In the Fill tab, click the **Pattern Style** down arrow to display a gallery of patterns. Click the design you want, and see it enlarged in the Sample area at the bottom of the Fill tab.

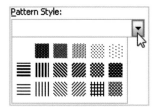

NOTE

If you choose Automatic for the Pattern Color in the Format Cells Fill tab, the pattern is applied to the background color, but if you pick both a background color and a pattern color, the colors are merged.

CAUTION

When the Format Painter is turned on by double-clicking it, every time you select an object on the worksheet, formatting will be applied to it. For this reason, be sure to turn off the Format Painter immediately after you are done copying formats.

TIP

You can also copy formatting by using Paste Preview, Paste Special, and the Paste Options Smart tag (see Chapter 2).

2. If you want to colorize the pattern, click the **Pattern Color** down arrow to display the color gallery (see "Change Themed Colors" earlier in this chapter for information on the various color options), and select one of the color options.

3. Click **OK** when finished to close the Format Cells dialog box.

Copy Formatting

You can manually copy formatting from one cell to other cells using the Format Painter, as well when you are inserting cells.

USE THE FORMAT PAINTER

1. Select the cell whose formatting you want to copy.

2. In the Home tab Clipboard group, click the **Format Painter** button once if you only want to apply the formatting one time.

   –Or–

   Double-click the **Format Painter** button to keep it turned on for repeated use.

3. Select the cells where you want the formatting applied.

4. If you single-clicked the Format Painter before applying it to your selection, it will turn off after you apply it to your first selection; if you double-clicked the button, you may select other cells to continue copying the formatting.

5. Double-click the **Format Painter** to turn it off, or press ESC.

ATTACH FORMATTING TO INSERTED CELLS, ROWS, AND COLUMNS

Click the **Insert Options** Smart tag (the paintbrush icon that appears after an insert), and choose from which direction you want the formatting applied, or choose to clear the formatting.

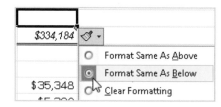

Arrange and Organize Worksheets

Excel provides several features to help you work with and view worksheets. You can retain headers at the top of the worksheet window as you scroll through hundreds of rows, split a worksheet, and view worksheets from several workbooks. In addition, there are several techniques you can use to add, remove, copy, and organize worksheets (see Chapter 5 for features that allow you to adjust worksheet layout parameters that support pagination and printing).

Lock Rows and Columns

You can lock (or *freeze*) rows and columns in place so that they remain visible as you scroll. Typically, row and column headers are locked in larger worksheets, where you are scrolling through large numbers of rows or columns. You can quickly lock the first row and/or first column in a worksheet, or you can select the rows or columns to freeze.

LOCK ROWS

- In the View tab Window group, click **Freeze Panes** and click **Freeze Top Row**. The top row (typically, your header row) remains in place as you scroll down.

  –Or–

- Select the row below the rows you want to lock, click **Freeze Panes** and click **Freeze Panes**. A thin border displays on the bottom of the locked row, as shown in Figure 3-17. All rows above the locked row remain in place as you scroll down.

LOCK COLUMNS

- In the View tab Window group, click **Freeze Panes** and click **Freeze First Column**. The leftmost column (typically, your header column) remains in place as you scroll to the right.

  –Or–

- Select the column to the right of the columns you want to lock, click **Freeze Panes** and click **Freeze Panes**. A thin border displays on the right side of the locked column. All columns to the left of the locked column remain in place as you scroll to the right.

NOTE

Freezing panes is not the same as freezing data. In an external data range, you can prevent the data from being refreshed, thereby freezing it. See Chapter 8 for more information on external data ranges.

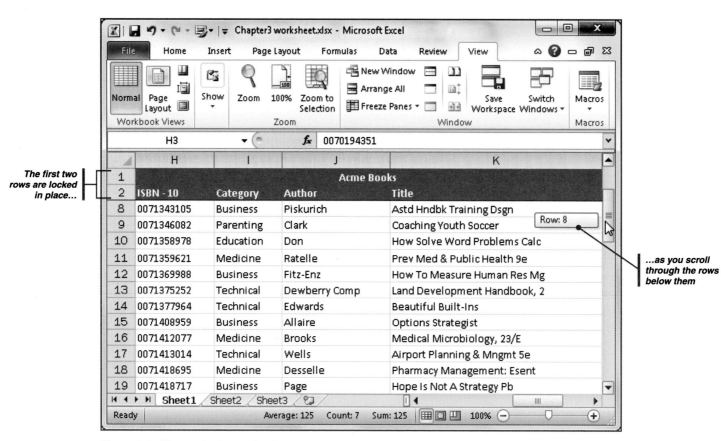

The first two rows are locked in place...

...as you scroll through the rows below them

Figure 3-17: You can lock rows in place and scroll through only those rows below the frozen rows.

LOCK ROWS AND COLUMNS TOGETHER

1. Select the cell that is below and to the right of the range you want to lock.

2. In the View tab Window group, click **Freeze Panes** and click **Freeze Panes**. A thin border displays below the locked rows and to the right of the locked columns. The range will remain in place as you scroll down or to the right.

Two locked columns

	H	I	J	K
1			Acme Books	
2	ISBN - 10	Category	Author	Title
3	0070194351	Technical	Elliott	Stand Hdbk Powerplant Engine
4	0070350787	Technical	Kleinert	Troublesht & Rep Major Appl
5	0070380686	Education	Pen	Sch Intro To Music
6	0070466173	Education	Nash	Sch Outl Strength Materials
7	0071054618	Medicine	Cember	Intro Health Physics 3e
8	0071343105	Business	Piskurich	Astd Hndbk Training Dsgn
9	0071346082	Parenting	Clark	Coaching Youth Soccer
10	0071358978	Education	Don	How Solve Word Problems Calc
11	0071359621	Medicine	Ratelle	Prev Med & Public Health 9e
12	0071369988	Business	Fitz-Enz	How To Measure Human Res Mg
13	0071375252	Technical	Dewberry Comp	Land Development Handbook, 2

Locked rows

UNLOCK ROWS AND COLUMNS

In the View tab Window group, click **Freeze Panes** and click **Unfreeze Panes**.

Split a Worksheet

You can divide a worksheet into two independent panes of the same data, as shown in Figure 3-18.

1. To split the worksheet horizontally, drag the row split icon down the worksheet to where you want the split.

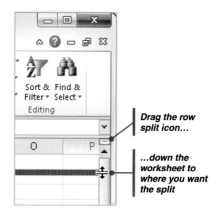

Drag the row split icon...

...down the worksheet to where you want the split

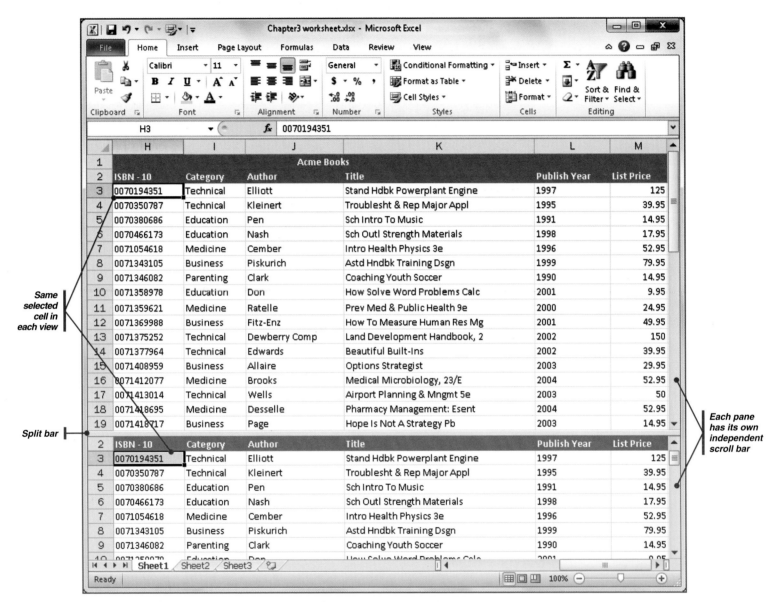

Figure 3-18: *A split worksheet provides two independent views of the same worksheet.*

Same selected cell in each view

Split bar

Each pane has its own independent scroll bar

WORKING WITH WORKSHEETS

Excel provides several tools you can use to modify the number and identification of worksheets in a workbook.

ADD A WORKSHEET

Right-click the worksheet tab to the right of where you want the new worksheet, click **Insert**, and click **OK**.

–Or–

On the worksheet bar, click **Insert Worksheet**. A new worksheet is added to the right of any current tabs.

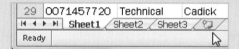

DELETE A WORKSHEET

Right-click the worksheet tab of the worksheet you want to delete, and click **Delete**.

MOVE OR COPY A WORKSHEET

You can move or copy worksheets within a workbook or between open workbooks by dragging a worksheet's tab. (See "View Worksheets from Multiple Workbooks" for steps to arrange multiple open workbooks to facilitate dragging objects between them.)

- To move a worksheet, drag the worksheet tab to the position on the worksheet bar where you want it to appear.

- To copy a worksheet, press and hold **CTRL**, and drag the worksheet tab to the position on the worksheet bar where you want it to appear.

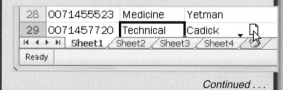

Continued . . .

–Or–

To split the worksheet vertically, drag the column split icon (at the right end of the horizontal scroll bar) to the left to where you want the split.

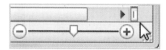

In either case, a split bar is displayed either across or down the worksheet.

2. Use the scroll bars to view other data within each pane.

3. Remove the split bar by double-clicking it.

View Worksheets from Multiple Workbooks

You can divide the Excel worksheet area so that you can view worksheets from multiple workbooks. This arrangement makes it easy to copy data, formulas, and formatting among several worksheets. (See Chapter 9 for information on sharing data.)

1. Open the workbooks that contain the worksheets you want to view. (See Chapter 1 for information on opening existing workbooks.)

2. In the View tab Window group, click **Arrange All**. The Arrange Windows dialog box appears.

3. Select an arrangement and click **OK**. (Figure 3-19 shows an example of tiling four workbooks.)

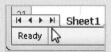
4. To change the arrangement, simply close the worksheets you do not want to view by selecting a worksheet to close and clicking the ⌧ in its upper-right corner. Return a worksheet to full view in the Excel window by double-clicking its title bar.

Compare Workbooks

Excel provides a few tools that allow easy comparison of two workbooks.

1. Open the workbooks you want to compare.

2. In the View tab Window group, click **View Side By Side** 🔲. If you have only two workbooks open, they will appear next to one another. If you have more than two workbooks open, you can select the workbook to view along with the currently active workbook from the Compare Side By Side dialog box.

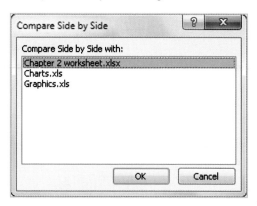

By default, both workbook windows will scroll at the same rate. To turn off this feature, click **Synchronous Scrolling** ▤ in the Window group.

TIP

To change how two workbooks are displayed for side-by-side comparison (horizontally or vertically), use the Arrange Windows dialog box described in the section, "View Worksheets from Multiple Workbooks."

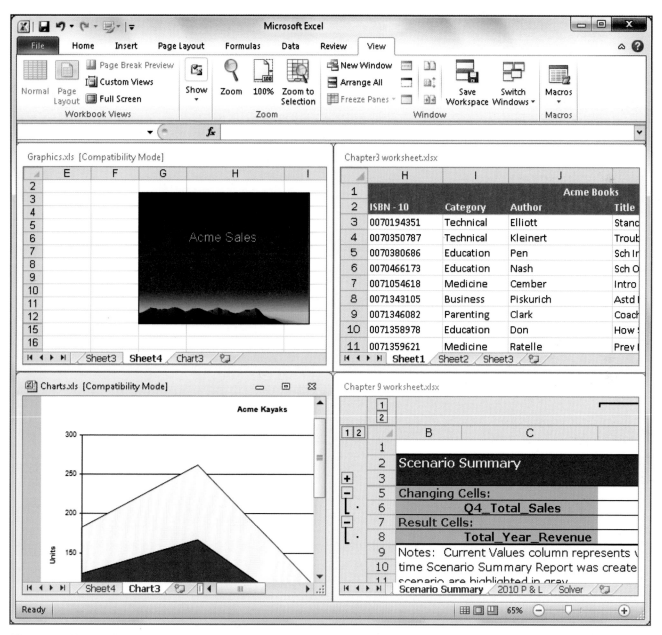

Figure 3-19: *You can look at several workbooks at the same time to compare them or to transfer information among them.*

Chapter 4

Using Formulas and Functions

Excel lets you easily perform powerful calculations using formulas and functions. Formulas are mathematical statements that follow a set of rules and use a specific syntax. In this chapter you will learn how to reference cells used in formulas, how to give cells names so that they are easily input, how to use conditional formatting to identify cells that satisfy criteria you specify, and how to build formulas. Functions—ready-made formulas that you can use to get quick results for specific applications, such as figuring out loan payments—are also covered. Finally, you will learn about several tools Excel provides to find and correct errors in formulas and functions.

UNDERSTANDING CELL REFERENCING TYPES

There are three basic methods and one extended method for referencing cells used in formulas that adhere to the Excel default "A1" cell reference scheme used in this book.

- **Relative references** in formulas move with cells as cells are copied or moved around a worksheet. This is the most flexible and common way to use cell references, and is the Excel default, displayed as A1 in the worksheet and Formula bar. For example, if you sum a list of revenue items for the first quarter, =SUM(B5:B8), and then copy and paste that summary cell to the summary cells for the other three quarters, Excel will deduce that you want the totals for the other quarters to be =SUM(C5:C8), =SUM(D5:D8), and =SUM(E5:E8). Figure 4-1 shows how this appears on the worksheet.

- **Absolute references** do not change cell addresses when you copy or move formulas. Absolute references are displayed in the worksheet and Formula bar with the dollar sign preceding the reference, for example, $A$1.

- **Mixed references** include one relative and one absolute cell reference. Such references are displayed in the worksheet and Formula bar with a dollar sign preceding the absolute reference but no dollar sign before the relative reference. For example, $A1 indicates absolute column, relative row; A$1 indicates relative column, absolute row.

- **External (or 3-D) references** are an extended form of relative, absolute, and mixed cell references. They are used when referencing cells from other worksheets or workbooks. Such a reference might look like this in the worksheet and Formula bar: [*workbook name*]*worksheet name*!A1.

Reference Cells

Formulas typically make use of data already entered in worksheets and need a scheme to locate, or *reference,* that data. Shortcuts are used to help you recall addresses as well as a *syntax,* or set of rules, to communicate to Excel how you want cells used.

Change Cell References

To change cell referencing:

1. Select the cell that contains the formula reference you want to change.

2. In the Formula bar, select the cell address, and press **F4** to switch the cell referencing, starting from a relative reference to the following in this order:

   - Absolute ($A$1)
   - Mixed (relative column, absolute row) (A$1)
   - Mixed (absolute column, relative row) ($A1)
   - Relative (A1)

   –Or–

   Edit the cell address by entering or removing the dollar symbol ($) in front of row and/or column identifiers.

Change to R1C1 References

You can change the A1 cell referencing scheme used by Excel to an older style that identifies both rows and columns numerically, starting in the upper-left corner of the worksheet, rows first, and adds a leading *R* and *C* for clarification. For example, cell B4 in R1C1 reference style is R4C2.

1. Click the **File** tab, click **Options**, and click the **Formulas** option.

2. Under Working With Formulas, click the **R1C1 Reference Style** check box.

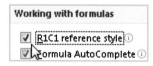

3. Click **OK** when finished.

Name Cells

TIP

To view formulas instead of cell values (see Figure 4-1), in the Formulas tab Formula Auditing group, click **Show Formulas**. Click the button a second time to return to a value display.

You can name a cell (MonthTotal, for example) or a range to refer to physical cell addresses, and then use the names when referencing the cell in formulas and functions. Names are more descriptive, easier to remember, and often quicker to enter than A1-style cell references. You can name a cell directly on the worksheet, use a dialog box and provide amplifying information, or use column or row names.

NAME A CELL OR RANGE DIRECTLY

1. Select the cells you want to reference.
2. Click the **Name** box at the left end of the Formula bar.

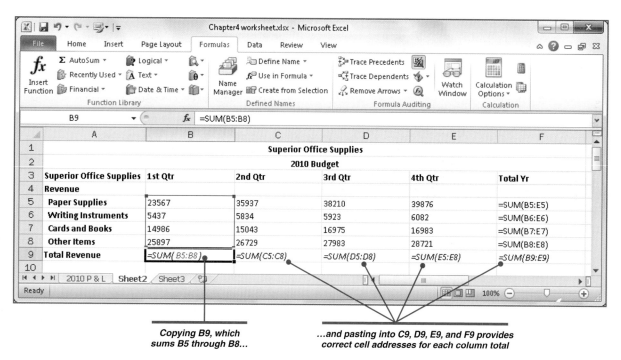

Copying B9, which sums B5 through B8...

...and pasting into C9, D9, E9, and F9 provides correct cell addresses for each column total

Figure 4-1: Using relative references, Excel logically assumes cell addresses in copied formulas.

3. Type a name (see the accompanying Caution for naming rules), and press **ENTER**. (See "Use the Name Manager" for ways to modify cell names.)

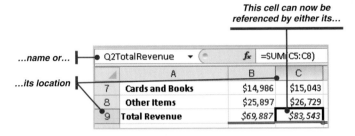

NAME A CELL OR RANGE IN A DIALOG BOX

1. Select the cells you want to reference.

2. In the Formulas tab Defined Names group, click **Define Name**.

   –Or–

   Right-click the selection and click **Define Name**.

   In the either case, the New Name dialog box appears, shown in Figure 4-2.

3. Type a name for the cell or range (see the accompanying Caution for naming rules).

4. Click the **Scope** down arrow, and select whether the name applies to the entire workbook or to one of its worksheets.

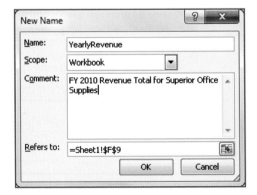

Figure 4-2: You can easily name cells and add descriptive information.

QUICKSTEPS

USING CELL REFERENCE OPERATORS

Cell reference operators (colons, commas, and spaces used in an address, such as E5:E10 E16:E17,E12) provide the syntax for referencing cell ranges, unions, and intersections.

REFERENCE A RANGE

A *range* defines a block of cells.

Type a colon (:) between the upper-leftmost cell and the lower-rightmost cell (for example, B5:C8).

● × ✓ ƒx	=SUM(B5:C8)
B	C
$23,567	$35,938
$5,437	$5,834
$14,986	$15,043
$25,897	$26,729

REFERENCE A UNION

A *union* joins multiple cell references.

Type a comma (,) between separate cell references (for example, B5,B7,C6).

● × ✓ ƒx	=SUM(B5,B7,C6)
B	C
$23,567	$35,938
$5,437	$5,834
$14,986	$15,043

REFERENCE AN INTERSECTION

An *intersection* is the overlapping, or common, cells in two ranges.

Type a space (press the SPACEBAR) between two range-cell references (for example, B5:B8 B7:C8). B7 and B8 are the common cells (and are summed in this example).

● × ✓ ƒx	=SUM(B5:B8 B7:C8)
B	C	D
$23,567	$35,938	$38
$5,437	$5,834	$5
$14,986	$15,043	$16
$25,897	$26,729	$27

5. If desired, type a comment that more fully explains the meaning of the named cells. Comments can be upwards of 1,000 characters and will appear as a tooltip when the name is used in formulas and functions.

=SUM(B9+y	
ƒx YEAR	
ƒx YEARFRAC	
▣ YearlyRevenue	FY 2010 Revenue Total for Superior Office Supplies
ƒx YIELD	
ƒx YIELDDISC	
ƒx YIELDMAT	

6. If you want to modify the cell or cells to be named, click the **Refers To** text box, and type the reference (starting with the equal [=] sign), or reselect the cells from the worksheet.

7. Click **OK** when finished.

Go to a Named Cell

Named cells are quickly found and selected for you.

C18	▼	●	ƒx
Cards_and_Books			B
Other_Items			
Paper_Supplies			$23,567
Q2TotalRevenue		nt:	$5,437
Writing_Instruments			$14,986
YearlyRevenue			$25,897
8 Other Items			

Click the **Name** box down arrow to open the drop-down list, and click the named cell or range you want to go to.

–Or–

In the Home tab Editing group, click **Find & Select** and click **Go To**. In the Go To dialog box, double-click the named cell or range you want to go to.

Use the Name Manager

Excel provides several related tools and a Name Manager to help you manage and organize your named cells. To open the Name Manager:

In the Formulas tab Defined Names group, click **Name Manager**. The Name Manager window opens, as shown in Figure 4-3, listing all named cells in the workbook.

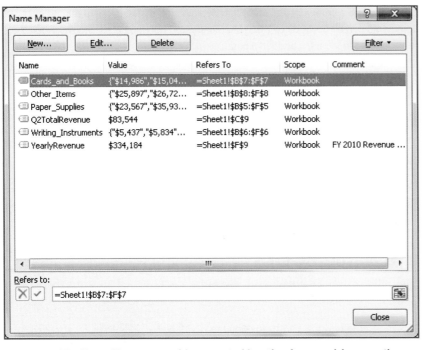

Figure 4-3: The Name Manager provides a central location for organizing, creating, and modifying named cells.

CHANGE CELL NAMES

1. Select the name of the cell reference whose parameters you want to change, and click **Edit**.

2. In the Edit Name dialog box, type a new name, add or change the comment, and/or modify the cell reference (you cannot change the scope). Click **OK** when finished.

DELETE NAMED CELLS

1. Select the name of the cell reference that you want to delete (to select more than one cell name to delete, hold down the **CTRL** key while clicking noncontiguous names in the list; or select the first name in a contiguous range, and hold down **SHIFT** while clicking the last name in the range).

2. Click **Delete** and click **OK** to confirm the deletion.

SORT AND FILTER NAMED CELLS

If you have several named cells in a workbook, you can easily view only the ones you are interested in.

1. To sort named cells, click a column heading to change the sort order from ascending (numerals first 0–9, then A–Z) to descending (Z–A, numerals last 9–0). Click the heading a second time to return to the original order.

–Or–

To see only specific categories of named cells, click **Filter** and click the category of named cells you want to see. Only named cells that belong in the category you select will appear in the list of cell names.

2. To return a filtered list to a complete list of named cells, click **Filter** and click **Clear Filter**.

VIEW MORE DATA

The default width of the Name Manager and its columns might not readily display longer cell names, references, or comments.

- To increase a column width, drag the right border of the column heading to the right as far as you need.
- To increase the width of the window, drag either the window's right or left border to the left or right, respectively.

Build Formulas

Formulas are mathematical equations that combine *values* and *cell references* with *operators* to calculate a result. Values are actual numbers or logical values, such as True and False, or the contents of cells that contain numbers or logical values. Cell references point to cells whose values are to be used, for example, E5:E10, E12, and MonthlyTot. Operators, such as + (add), > (greater than), and ^ (use an exponent), tell Excel what type of calculation to perform or logical comparison to apply. Prebuilt formulas, or *functions*, that return a value also can be used in formulas. (Functions are described later in this chapter.)

Create a Formula

You create formulas by either entering or referencing values. The character that tells Excel to perform a calculation is the equal sign (=), and it must precede any combination of values, cell references, and operators.

Excel formulas are calculated from left to right according to an ordered hierarchy of operators. For example, exponents precede multiplication and division, which precede addition and subtraction. You can alter the calculation order (and results) by using parentheses; Excel performs the calculation within the innermost parentheses first. For example, =12+48/24 returns 14 (48 is divided by 24, resulting in 2; then 12 is added to 2). Using parentheses, =(12+48)/24 returns 2.5 (12 is added to 48, resulting in 60; then 60 is divided by 24).

ENTER A SIMPLE FORMULA

1. Select a blank cell, and type an equal sign (=).

   –Or–

   Select a blank cell and click in the Formula bar in the blank area directly to the right of the Insert Function f_x icon. The function area expands with the addition of the Cancel ✗ and Enter ✓ icons.

   The equal sign displays both in the cell and in the Formula bar, as will the additional characters you type. The insertion point (where Excel expects you to type the next character) is placed to the right of the equal sign in either the cell or Formula bar, depending on where you typed it.

2. Type a value, such as 64.

3. Type an operator, such as +.

4. Type a second value, such as 96.

5. Complete the entry by pressing **ENTER** or clicking **Enter** on the Formula bar; or add additional values and operators, and then complete the entry. The result of your equation displays in the cell. (See Chapter 2 for other methods to complete an entry.)

USE CELL REFERENCES

The majority of formulas use the values in other cells to produce a result, that is, the cell that contains the formula may have no value of its own—it's derived from other cells whose values are manipulated by arithmetic operators. For example, the cell at the bottom of several values contains a formula that sums the values to produce a total.

1. Select a blank cell, and type an equal sign (=). The equal sign displays in the cell and in the Formula bar.

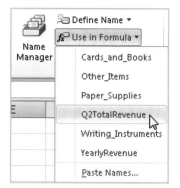

2. Enter a cell reference in one of the following ways:

- Type a cell reference (for example, B4) that contains the value you want.
- Click the cell whose value you want. A blinking border surrounds the cell.
- Select a named cell. In the Formulas tab Defined Names group, click **Use In Formula**, and click the named cell you want.

3. Type an operator.

4. Enter another cell reference or a value.

5. Complete the entry by pressing **ENTER**; or add additional cell references, values, and operators, and then complete the entry. The result of your formula is displayed in the cell, as shown in Figure 4-4.

Figure 4-4: A formula in Excel comprises cell references, values, and named cells.

QUICKSTEPS

ADDING A SYMBOLIC FORMULA

Another way to add a formula, though it won't work as one, is to use the Equation Editor, an Office-wide tool. This will allow you to display the characters of a complex formula without actually performing the calculation. To install the Equation Editor (it is not part of an Express Office installation):

1. Click **Start**, click **Control Panel**, and then under **Programs**, click **Uninstall A Program**. Select your version of Office, and click **Change**.

2. In the Change Your Installation Of Microsoft Office dialog box, click **Add Or Remove Features**, and click **Continue**. Click the **plus sign** (+) next to Office Tools, and click the **Equation Editor** down arrow.

3. Click **Run From My Computer**, and click **Continue**.

4. To use the Equation Editor, restart Excel, select where you want the equation placed, and then in the Insert tab Symbols group, click **Equation**.

TIP

If you do not see the Cancel, Enter, and Insert Function buttons in the Formula bar when editing or creating a formula, click anywhere in the Formula bar and they will be displayed.

Edit a Formula

You can easily change a formula after you have entered one.

1. Double-click the cell that contains the formula you want to change. The formula is displayed in the cell and in the Formula bar. Cell references for each cell or range are color-coded.

	=SUM(F5+F6+63987+Other_Items)	
E	**F**	**G**
4th Qtr	**Total Yr**	
$39,876	$137,591	
$6,082	$23,276	
$16,983	$63,987	
$28,721	$109,330	
$91,662	=SUM(F5 + F6 +63987+ Other_Items)	
	SUM(**number1**, [number2], ...)	

2. Edit the formula by:
   - Making changes directly in the cell or on the Formula bar
   - Dragging the border of a colored cell or range reference to move it to a new location
   - Dragging a corner sizing-box of a colored cell or range reference to expand the reference

3. Complete the entry by pressing ENTER.

Move Formulas

You move formulas by cutting and pasting. When you move formulas, Excel uses absolute referencing—the formula remains exactly the same as it was originally with the same cell references. (See "Change Cell References" earlier in the chapter for more information on cell referencing.)

1. Select the cell whose formula you want to move.

2. In the Home tab Clipboard group, click **Cut** or press CTRL+X.

   –Or–

   Right-click the cell whose formula you want to move, and click **Cut**.

3. Select the cell where you want to move the formula.

4. In the Home tab Clipboard group, click **Paste** or press **CTRL+V**.

   –Or–

   Right-click the cell where you want to move the formula, and under Paste Options, click **Paste**.

Copy Formulas

When you copy formulas, relative referencing is applied. Therefore, cell referencing in a formula will change when you copy the formula, unless you have made a reference absolute. If you do not get the results you expect, click **Undo** on the Quick Access toolbar, and change the cell references before you copy again.

COPY FORMULAS INTO ADJACENT CELLS

1. Select the cell whose formula you want to copy.

2. Point at the fill handle in the lower-right corner of the cell, and drag over the cells where you want the formula copied.

	A	B	C
4	**Revenue**		
5	**Paper Supplies**	$23,567	$35,937
6	**Writing Instruments**	$5,437	$5,834
7	**Cards and Books**	$14,986	$15,043
8	**Other Items**	$25,897	$26,729
9	**Total Revenue**	$69,887	

COPY FORMULAS INTO NONADJACENT CELLS

1. Select the cell whose formula you want to copy.

2. In the Home tab Clipboard group, click **Copy** or press **CTRL+C**.

   –Or–

   Right-click the cell you want to copy, and click **Copy**.

3. Copy formatting along with the formula by selecting the destination cell. Then, in the Home tab Clipboard group, click **Paste** and then click the **Paste** icon.

   –Or–

   Copy just the formula by selecting the destination cell. Then, in the Home tab Clipboard group, click the **Paste** down arrow, and click the **Formulas** icon.

Recalculate Formulas

By default, Excel automatically recalculates formulas affected by changes to a value, to the formula itself, or to a changed named cell. You also can recalculate more frequently using the tips presented in Table 4-1.

TO CALCULATE...	IN...	PRESS...
Formulas, and formulas dependent on them, that have changed since the last calculation	All open workbooks	F9
Formulas, and formulas dependent on them, that have changed since the last calculation	The active worksheet	SHIFT+F9
All formulas, regardless of any changes since the last calculation	All open workbooks	CTRL+ALT+F9
All formulas, regardless of any changes since the last calculation, after rechecking dependent formulas	All open workbooks	CTRL+SHIFT+ALT+F9

Table 4-1: Formula Recalculations in Excel

To turn off automatic calculation and select other calculation options:

Calculate Now

Calculate Sheet

Calculation

1. In the Formulas tab Calculation group, click **Calculation Options**.

2. In the drop-down menu, click **Manual**. You can also force an immediate calculation by clicking **Calc Now** to recalculate the workbook or clicking **Calc Sheet** to recalculate the active worksheet.

Use External References in Formulas

You can *link* data using cell references to worksheets and workbooks other than the one you are currently working in. For example, if you are building a departmental budget, you could link to each division's budget workbook and have any changes made to formulas in those workbooks be applied automatically to your total budget workbook. Changes made to the *external* references in the *source* workbooks are automatically updated in the *destination* workbook when the destination workbook is opened or when the source workbooks are changed and the destination workbook is open.

TIP

It is a good practice to save and close the source workbook before saving the destination workbook.

CREATE EXTERNAL REFERENCE LINKS

1. Open both the source and destination workbooks in your computer.

2. Arrange the workbooks so that they are all displayed. For example, in the View tab Window group, click **Arrange**, click **Tiled**, and click **OK**. (See Chapter 2 for more information on arranging workbooks in the Excel window.)

3. In the destination worksheet, create the formula or open an existing formula.

4. Place the insertion point in the formula where you want the external reference.

5. In the source workbook, click the cell whose cell reference you want. The external reference is added to the formula, as shown in Figure 4-5.

6. Press **ENTER** to complete the entry.

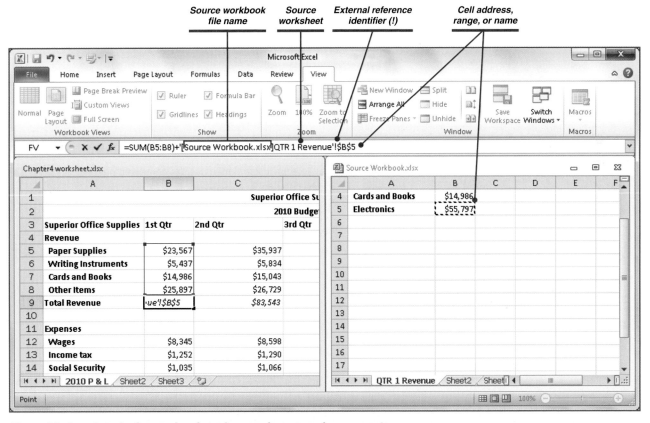

Figure 4-5: *An external reference in a formula comprises several components.*

UPDATE AND MANAGE EXTERNAL REFERENCES

You can control how external references are updated, check on their status, and break or change the link.

1. Open the destination workbook.

2. In the Data tab Connections group, click **Edit Links**. The Edit Links dialog box appears, as shown in Figure 4-6.

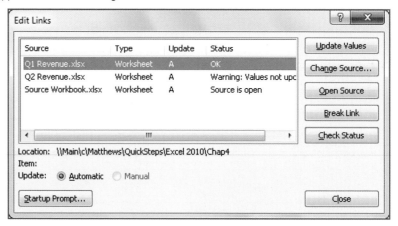

Figure 4-6: You can update and manage links in the Edit Links dialog box.

3. Select a link and then use the command buttons on the right side of the dialog box to perform the action you want.

4. Click **Close** when finished.

UPDATE LINKS

When you open a destination workbook with external links to source workbooks, you are potentially introducing a security risk to your computer by allowing data from other sources into your system. By default, automatic updating is disabled and the user opening a destination workbook needs to provide permission to enable the links (unless the source workbooks are open on the same computer as the destination workbook).

1. Open the destination workbook. A message box, as shown in Figure 4-8, opens to tell you that updating links will use new data from the source files and warns you about the possibility of sharing confidential information. Click **Update**, assuming you trust the source file; click **Don't Update** if you do not.

CAUTION

If you break an external reference link in the Edit Links dialog box, all formulas using external references are converted to values. Broken links cannot be undone except by reestablishing the links.

TIP

If you are unsure of the origination of the source workbooks when updating links in a destination workbook, open the Edit Links dialog box to view the files involved in the links. See how in the section "Update and Manage External References."

NOTE

As there can be a myriad of combinations of links and referencing in your workbooks from source files on your own computer to lose on networks, there are also several permutations of security warnings you may see, depending on your specific circumstance. To try and describe each situation and show its result would take an entire chapter and not really provide much value. Suffice it to say that when you see security warnings, read them carefully, and just be cognizant of what you are accepting.

Figure 4-7: The Trust Center provides a focal point for accessing privacy and security information and settings for Office 2010 programs.

Figure 4-8: To protect you from erroneous or malicious data, Office asks if you want to update external links.

2. When you open the source file, which also has a link to an external workbook, unless default settings have been changed, a Security Warning message displays below the ribbon notifying you that automatic link updating is disabled. Click **Enable Content** to allow updates to occur.

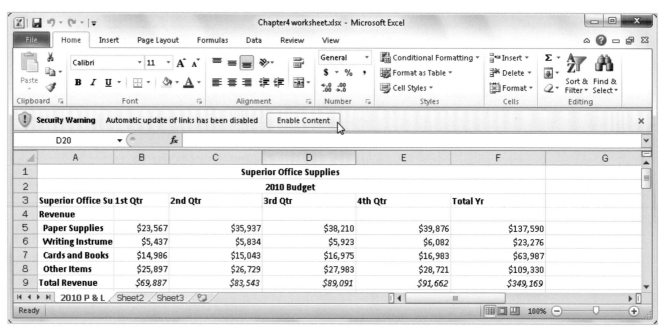

3. For additional protection, if your source workbook is located in a network location (that is, not on the same computer as your destination workbook), a second warning is displayed. Assuming you trust the source data, click **Yes**. The links will be updated.

Figure 4-9: The Trust Center allows you to set the degree to which you trust the links among your workbooks.

CHANGE AUTOMATIC LINK UPDATING FOR ALL WORKBOOKS

You can change how links are updated in the Trust Center security settings window.

1. Click the **File** tab, click **Options**, and click the **Trust Center** option. In the Trust Center window, click **Trust Center Settings**.

2. In the Trust Center security settings window, click the **External Content** category, shown in Figure 4-9.

3. In the Security Settings For Workbook Links area, select the automatic link updating behavior you want, and click **OK** twice.

CHANGE AUTOMATIC LINK UPDATING FOR INDIVIDUAL WORKBOOKS

You can choose to not display the security alert in a destination workbook prompting users to update links. You can also choose to update links, or not, without user intervention.

Before you can allow automatic link updating in an individual workbook, you must enable it in the Trust Center for all workbooks. See how in "Change Automatic Link Updating for All Workbooks."

1. Open the destination workbook whose security alert behavior you want to change.

2. In the Data tab Connections group, click **Edit Links**, and click **Startup Prompt**.

3. In the Startup Prompt dialog box, select the behavior you want, click **OK**, and click **Close**. The next time the workbook is opened, the new behavior will be enabled.

TIP

The number of conditional format scenarios that can be applied to a cell is only limited by your system's memory.

NOTE

If your selected cells don't change as you point to different style options, Live Preview has been turned off. To turn on Live Preview, click the **File** tab, click **Options**, and click the **General** option. Under User Interface Options, select **Enable Live Preview**, and click **OK**.

4	Revenue	
5	Paper Supplies	$23,567
6	Writing Instruments	$5,437
7	Cards and Books	$14,986
8	Other Items	$25,897
9	Total Revenue	$69,887

Data bars

Format Conditionally

Excel 2010 continues to improve the ease and capabilities with which data can be identified in a worksheet based on rules you select. Rules are organized into several types that allow you to easily format cells that compare values against each other; meet specific values, dates, or other criteria; match top and bottom percentile values you choose; match values above or below an average; or identify unique or duplicate values. If no preexisting rule accommodates your needs, you can use a formula to set up criteria that cells must match.

COMPARE CELLS

You can highlight the comparative values of selected cells by using one of three formatting styles:

- **Data bars** display in each cell colored bars whose length is proportional to their value as compared to the other values in the selection.

- **Color scales** blend two or three colors (such as a green-yellow-red traffic light metaphor) to differentiate among high to low values.

4	Revenue	
5	Paper Supplies	$23,567
6	Writing Instruments	$5,437
7	Cards and Books	$14,986
8	Other Items	$25,897
9	Total Revenue	$69,887

Color scales

- **Icon sets** use from three to five similar icons (such as the red and black circles used in *Consumer Reports*) to differentiate among high to low values.

4	Revenue			
5	Paper Supplies	●	$23,567	$35,938
6	Writing Instruments	○	$5,437	$5,834
7	Cards and Books	◐	$14,986	$15,043
8	Other Items	●	$25,897	$26,729
9	Total Revenue		$69,887	$83,544

Icon sets

1. Select the cells that will be compared.

2. In the Home tab Styles group, click **Conditional Formatting** and click the style you want to see a submenu of options.

3. Point to each option to see a live preview of its effect on your selected data, as shown in Figure 4-10. Click the option you want to use.

Point to a conditional formatting style and see the effect on selected cells

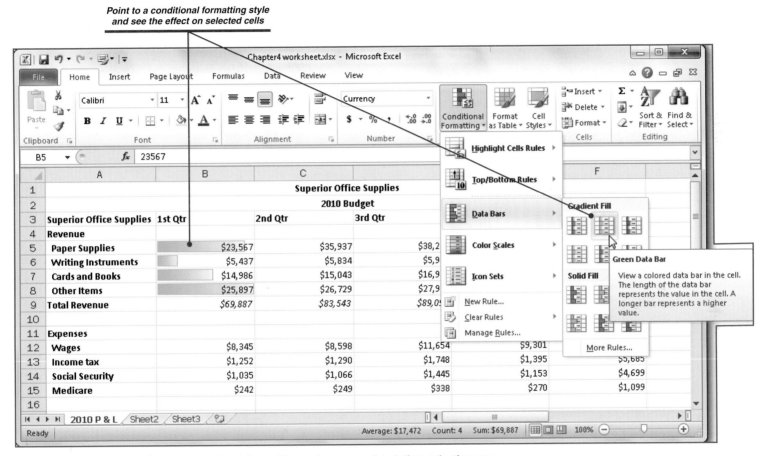

Figure 4-10: You can see a live preview of each formatting style on your data before selecting one.

4. For more choices of each style, click **More Rules** at the bottom of each of their respective submenus.

5. In the New Formatting Rule dialog box, under Edit The Rule Description, you can change from one style to another and, depending on the style, change colors, change the values attributed to an icon or color, and make other customizations (see Figure 4-11). Click **OK** when finished.

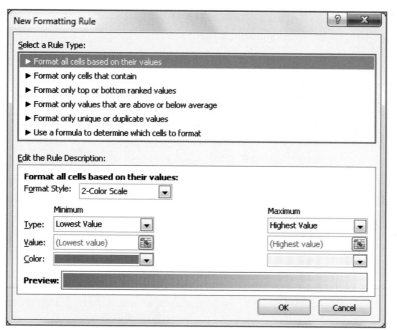

Figure 4-11: Each style has a set of customizations (or rules) that apply to how data is visually identified.

FORMAT CELLS THAT MATCH VALUES OR CONDITIONS

Excel provides several preexisting rules that let you easily format cells that meet established criteria.

1. Select the cells that will be formatted if they meet conditions you select.

2. In the Home tab Styles group, click **Conditional Formatting** and click **Highlight Cells Rules** to view a submenu of rules that compare values to conditions.

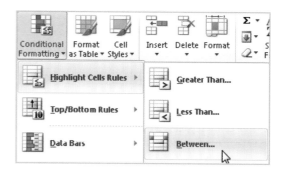

–Or–

Click **Top/Bottom Rules** to view a submenu that lets you select cells based on top/bottom ranking or whether they're above or below the average of the selected cells.

3. For more choices, click **More Rules** at the bottom of each of the respective submenus.

4. In the New Formatting Rule dialog box, under Edit The Rule Description, you can change criteria and the formatting you want applied (see Chapter 3 for more information on using the Format Cells dialog box). Click **OK** when finished.

TIP

When changing values in dialog boxes for conditional formatting, as in the New Formatting Rule dialog box (and when setting up functions, described later in this chapter), you can type a value or formula in the associated text box, or you can select a cell that contains the value or formula you want and have it entered for you. When selecting a cell, click the **Collapse Dialog** button to shrink the dialog box so that you can see more of the worksheet. Click **Expand Dialog** to return to the full-size dialog box.

MANAGE CONDITIONAL FORMATTING RULES

Using the Conditional Formatting Rules Manager, you can view any conditional formatting rules in a workbook as well as edit, delete, reorder, and create new rules.

1. In the Home tab Styles group, click **Conditional Formatting** and click **Manage Rules**. The Conditional Formatting Rules Manager appears, as shown in Figure 4-12.

2. Click the **Show Formatting Rules For** down arrow to select the scope of where you want to look for rules.

3. Select a rule and perform one or more of the following actions:

   - Click **Edit Rule** to open the Edit Formatting Rule dialog box and change criteria or conditions. Click **OK** to close the Edit Formatting Rule dialog box.

   - Click **Delete Rule** to remove it (alternatively, you can click **Clear Rules** on the Conditional Formatting drop-down menu to remove all rules in the selected cells or worksheet).

   - Click the up and down arrows to change the order in which rules are applied (rules are applied in order from top to bottom).

   - Click the **Stop If True** check box to discontinue further rules from being applied if the selected rule is satisfied as being True.

4. Click **New Rule** to open the New Formatting Rule dialog box and create a new rule. Click **OK** to close the New Formatting Rule dialog box.

5. Click **OK** when finished.

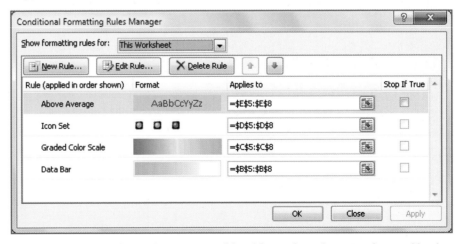

Figure 4-12: You can view and manage conditional formatting rules set up in a workbook.

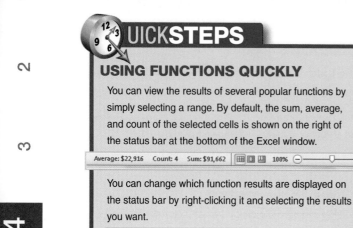

USING FUNCTIONS QUICKLY

You can view the results of several popular functions by simply selecting a range. By default, the sum, average, and count of the selected cells is shown on the right of the status bar at the bottom of the Excel window.

Average: $22,916   Count: 4   Sum: $91,662   100%

You can change which function results are displayed on the status bar by right-clicking it and selecting the results you want.

✓	Average	$22,916
✓	Count	4
	Numerical Count	
	Minimum	
	Maximum	
✓	Sum	$91,662

TIP

You do not need to type the closing parenthesis; Excel will add it for you when you complete the entry. However, it is good practice to include a closing parenthesis for each opening parenthesis. This is especially true if you use complex, nested functions that include other functions as arguments. (You may nest up to 64 levels!)

Use Functions

Functions are prewritten formulas that you can use to perform specific tasks. They can be as simple as =PI(), which returns 3.14159265358979, the value of the constant pi; or they can be as complex as =PPMT(rate,per,nper,pv,fv,type), which returns a payment on an investment principal.

A function comprises three components:

- **Formula identifier**, the equal sign (=), is required when a function is at the beginning of the formula.
- **Function name** identifies the function, and typically is a two- to five-character uppercase abbreviation.
- **Arguments** are the values acted upon by functions to derive a result. They can be numbers, cell references, constants, logical (True or False) values, or a formula. Arguments are separated by commas and enclosed in parentheses. A function can have upto 255 arguments.

Enter a Function

You can enter functions on a worksheet by typing or by a combination of typing and selecting cell references, as described earlier in this chapter for formulas. In addition, you can search for and choose functions from Excel's library of built-in functions.

TYPE A FUNCTION

To type a function in a cell on the worksheet:

1. Select a blank cell, and type an equal sign (=). The equal sign displays in the cell and the Formula bar.

2. Start typing the function name, such as <u>AVERAGE</u>, <u>MAX</u>, or <u>PMT</u>. As you start typing, functions with related spellings are displayed. Click any to see a description of the function.

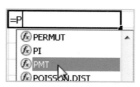

=P

- ƒx PERMUT
- ƒx PI
- ƒx PMT
- ƒx POISSON.DIST

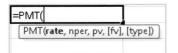

NOTE

You can create your own functions using Excel's built-in programming language, VBA (Visual Basic for Applications). Using VBA to programmatically customize Excel is beyond the scope of this book.

3. Double-click the function you want. The function name and open parenthesis are entered for you. Excel displays a tooltip showing arguments and proper syntax for the function.

4. Depending on the function, for each argument you need to do none, one, or both of the following:

- Type the argument.
- Select a cell reference.

5. Type a comma to separate arguments, and repeat steps 4 and 5 as necessary.

6. Type a closing parenthesis, and press **ENTER** or click **Enter** on the Formula bar to complete the entry. A value will be returned. (If a *#code* is displayed in the cell or a message box displays indicating you made an error, see "Find and Correct Errors" later in this chapter.)

INSERT A FUNCTION

You can find the function you want using the Function Wizard or using the function category buttons on the ribbon.

In either case, the wizard helps you enter arguments for the function you chose.

1. Select a blank cell. In the Formulas tab Function Library group, click the relevant function category button, and scroll to the function you want. Point to a function and wait a second to see a tooltip that describes it. When ready, click the function and skip to step 5 to view its arguments.

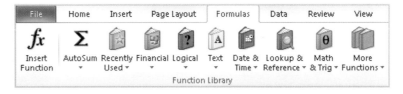

–Or–

Click **Insert Function** in the Function Library group or its button on the Formula bar, f_x or press **SHIFT+F3**. The Insert Function dialog box appears, as shown in Figure 4-13.

2. Type a brief description of what you want to do in the Search For A Function text box, and click **Go**. A list of recommended functions is displayed in the Select A Function list box.

–Or–

Open the **Select A Category** drop-down list, and select a category.

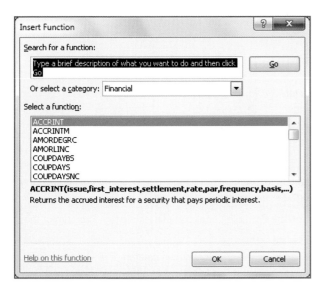

Figure 4-13: You can search for and select functions from Excel's extensive library in the Insert Function dialog box.

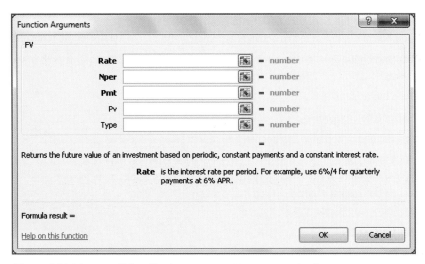

Figure 4-14: Type or click cell references to enter argument values.

3. Click the function you want from the Select A Function list box. Its arguments and syntax are shown, as well as a description of what the function returns.

4. If you need more assistance with the function, click **Help On This Function**. A Help topic provides details on the function and an example of how it's used.

5. Click **OK** to open the Function Arguments dialog box, shown in Figure 4-14. The function's arguments are listed in order at the top of the dialog box, and the beginning of the function displays in the cell and in the Formula bar.

6. Enter values for the arguments by typing or clicking cell references. Click the **Collapse Dialog** button to shrink the dialog box so that you can see more of the worksheet. The formula on the worksheet is built as you enter each argument.

7. Click **OK** to complete the entry.

Enter a Sum in Columns or Rows Quickly

AutoSum uses the SUM function to add contiguous numbers quickly.

1. Select a blank cell below a column or to the right of a row of numbers.

2. In the Formulas tab Function Library group, click **AutoSum**. The cells Excel "thinks" you want to sum above or to the left of the blank cell are enclosed in a border, and the formula is displayed in the cell and in the Formula bar.

	A	B	C
11	Expenses		
12	Wages	$8,345	
13	Income tax	$1,252	
14	Social Security	$1,035	
15	Medicare	$242	
16		=SUM(B12:B15)	
17		SUM(**number1**, [number2], ...)	

3. Modify the cells to be included in the sum by dragging a corner sizing-box, editing the formula in the cell or the Formula bar, or by selecting cells.

4. Press **ENTER** or click **Enter** on the Formula bar to complete the entry. The sum of the selected cells is returned.

5. Alternatively, for an even faster sum, select a contiguous column or row of cells, and click **AutoSum**. The sum is entered in the first blank cell at either the bottom of a column of cells or to the right of a row of cells.

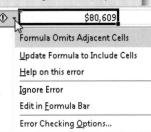

$80,609
Formula Omits Adjacent Cells
Update Formula to Include Cells
Help on this error
Ignore Error
Edit in Formula Bar
Error Checking Options...

Find and Correct Errors

Excel provides several tools that help you see how your formulas and functions are constructed, recognize errors in formulas, and better locate problems.

Check for Errors

Excel can find errors and provide possible solutions.

1. In the Formulas tab Formula Auditing group, click **Error Checking**. If you have an error on the worksheet, the Error Checking dialog box appears, as shown in Figure 4-15.

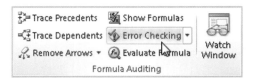

2. Use the command buttons on the right side of the dialog box to perform the indicated action. Click **Next** or **Previous** to check on other errors.

3. Click **Options** to view the Excel Options Formulas window (see Figure 4-16), where you can customize error checking.

- **Error Checking**, **Enable Background Error Checking** lets you turn on or off error checking as you enter formulas and determines the color of flagged cells that contain errors. Errors are flagged in green by default.

- **Error Checking Rules** provide several criteria that cells are checked against for possible errors.

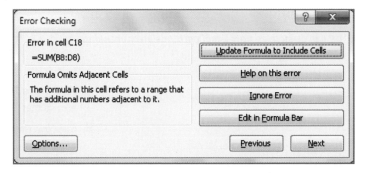

*Figure 4-15: **You can manage how errors are checked and locate cells that contain errors.***

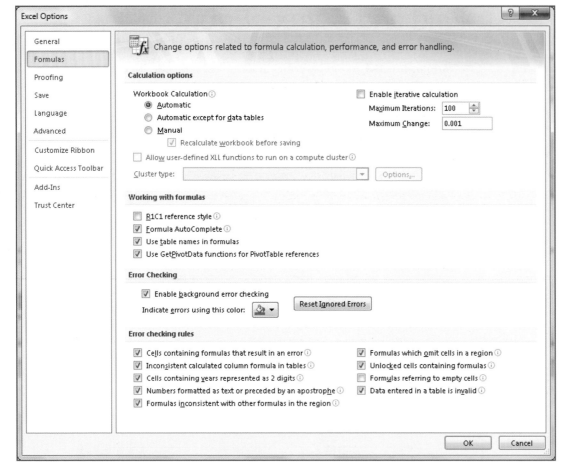

Figure 4-16: You can customize how Excel performs error checking.

Trace Precedent and Dependent Cells

Precedent cells are referenced in a formula or function in another cell; that is, they provide a value to a formula or function. *Dependent* cells contain a formula or function that uses the value from another cell; that is, they depend on the value in another cell for their own value.

This interwoven relationship of cells can compound one error into many, making a visual representation of the cell dependencies a vital error-correction tool.

1. Click a cell that uses cell references and/or is itself used as a reference by another cell in its formula or function.

2. In the Formulas tab Formula Auditing group, click **Trace Precedents** to display blue arrows that point to the cell from other cells.

3	Superior Office Supplies	1st Qtr
4	Revenue	
5	Paper Supplies	$23,567
6	Writing Instruments	$5,437
7	Cards and Books	$14,986
8	Other Items	$25,897
9	Total Revenue	$69,887

–Or–

Click **Trace Dependents** to display blue arrows that point to other cells.

3. Click the **Remove Arrows** down arrow, and select whether to remove precedent, dependent, or all arrows.

Watch a Cell

You can follow what changes are made to a cell's value as its precedent cells' values are changed, even if the cells are not currently visible.

1. In the Formulas tab Formula Auditing group, click **Watch Window**. The Watch Window window opens.

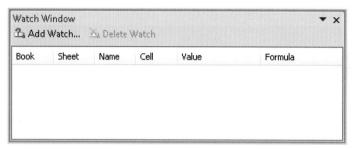

2. Click **Add Watch** to open the Add Watch dialog box.

3. Select the cell or cells you want to watch, and click **Add**. Each selected cell will be listed individually in the Watch Window. As changes are made to a precedent cell, the value of the cells "being watched" will be updated according to the recalculation options you have set. (See "Recalculate Formulas" earlier in the chapter.)

4. Close the Watch Window window when you are done.

Evaluate a Formula in Pieces

You can see what value will be returned by individual cell references or expressions in the order they are placed in the formula.

1. Select the cell that contains the formula you want to evaluate.

2. In the Formulas tab Formula Auditing group, click **Evaluate Formula**. The Evaluate Formula dialog box, shown in Figure 4-17, appears.

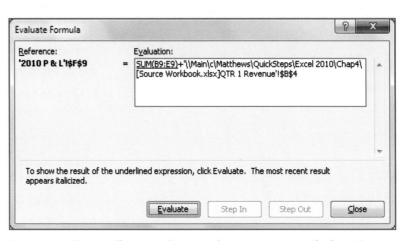

Figure 4-17: You can dissect each expression or component of a formula to see its cell reference, its formula, and its value.

3. Do one or more of the following:

- Click **Evaluate** to return the value of the first cell reference or expression. The cell reference or expression is underlined.

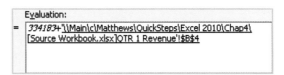

- Continue clicking **Evaluate** to return values for each of the cell references or expressions (again, underlined) to the right in the formula. Eventually, this will return the value for the cell.

- Click **Restart** to start the evaluation from the leftmost expression. (The Evaluate button changes to Restart after you have stepped through the formula.)

- Click **Step In** to view more data on the underlined cell reference.

- Click **Step Out** to return to the formula evaluation.

4. Click **Close** when finished.

How to...

Chapter 5
Viewing and Printing Data

In this chapter you will learn how to organize a worksheet to better view the information it contains and print just the information you want. Excel provides several tools and options, such as headers, footers, and titles, that enhance a worksheet for viewing, distribution, or printing. Other features let you change the layout of your worksheet to better accommodate how you want to present the data, from changing the zoom level to dividing the worksheet into pages. Printing to page-sized dimensions is a prime consideration when modifying the layout of a worksheet, regardless if the pages are printed on paper or converted to digital formats, such as Microsoft XML Paper Specification (XPS) or Portable Document Format (PDF) documents, or Web pages. Excel also provides a robust previewing feature so you can review your settings before actually distributing or printing your work.

UNDERSTANDING EXCEL VIEWS

Excel provides several ways to view a worksheet, each one suited to display your information in a specific format and purpose. Excel views are available from the View tab Workbook Views group. The three most popular views (Normal, Page Layout, and Page Break Preview) also have buttons available on the right end of the status bar, as shown in Figure 5-1. Switching between views is easily accomplished with these tools. To return to the previous view after switching to Full Screen view, press **ESC**.

- **Normal** view is the row-and-column view that spreadsheet users have been using since VisiCalc first appeared on IBM PCs in 1981, and is how Excel displays its worksheets by default. Data is shown screen by scrolling screen, without regard to how the data would appear on individual pages.

- **Page Layout** view displays the data as it will appear on a printed or digital page and lets you make adjustments prior to printing, such as providing rulers for precise measurement of objects, changing page orientation and margins, and adding headers and footers. You can work in Page Layout view as you do in Normal view to enter data, create formulas, and perform other standard Excel actions throughout the worksheet.

- **Page Break Preview** view shows only the area of the worksheet that contains data, and is parsed into page-sized representations. You can interactively adjust the page boundaries to determine where the worksheet breaks into pages. You can work in Page Break Preview view as you do in Normal view to enter data, create formulas, and perform other standard Excel actions in any page that is represented in the view.

Continued . . .

Lay Out a Worksheet

You can transform an otherwise nondescript worksheet full of text and numbers into an easy-to-follow, organized report by adding or modifying features that assist viewing or printing. The following sections will show you how to add headers and footers, use headings as page titles, define pages, and change other organizational and visual enhancements to your worksheets.

Add Headers and Footers

Custom *headers* and *footers* that print on each page can greatly enhance the appearance of your printed data. Headers and footers (see Figure 5-2) are dedicated areas of the page—headers at the top and footers at the bottom—where you can place titles, page numbers, dates, and even add pictures.

CREATE A SIMPLE HEADER AND/OR FOOTER

Excel provides several prebuilt header and footer formats you can select. The formats contain ordinary text and formatting codes that automatically add information such as page numbers.

1. Display the worksheet where you want to add a header and/or footer.

2. In the Insert tab Text group, click **Header & Footer**. A contextual Header & Footer Tools Design tab displays on the ribbon, the worksheet appears in Print Layout view, and the insertion point is placed in the center header text box at the top of the page, as shown in Figure 5-3.

3. In the Header & Footer group, click either **Header** or **Footer**, and select one of the built-in formats from the drop-down list. Each format contains one, two, or three elements, separated by commas. Single-element formats are placed in the center header/footer text box on the worksheet; two-element formats are placed in the left and center or right and center text boxes; and three-element formats are placed in the left, center, and right text boxes.

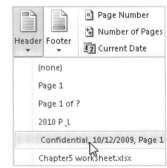

4. To make changes to the default format, see "Customize a Header and Footer," next.

TIP

To see more of a worksheet, click **Minimize The Ribbon** ⌃ to the left of the Help icon on the tab name row, or press **CTRL+F1** to collapse the ribbon groups and display only the tabs bar. Click **Minimize The Ribbon** or press the key combination a second time to return the ribbon to its full height. To see even more, in the View tab, Workbook Views group, click **Full Screen** to see only the worksheet and row/columns headings (press **ESC** to return to the previous view).

TIP

To remove content codes inserted by the Auto Header and Auto Footer formats, simply select the ampersand (&) preceding the code and the code itself—for example, &[File]—and press **DELETE**.

CUSTOMIZE A HEADER AND FOOTER

1. Display the worksheet where you want to add a header and/or footer.

2. In the Insert tab Text group, click **Header & Footer**. A contextual Header & Footer Tools Design tab displays on the ribbon, the worksheet appears in Print Layout view, and the insertion point is placed in the center header text box at the top of the page (see Figure 5-3).

3. If you want to start from a built-in format, select one from the Header or Footer drop-down lists (see "Create a Simple Header and/or Footer").

4. Click one of the three text boxes (left, center, or right) where you want to add text or objects to the header (top of the page) or footer (bottom of the page). The alignment in a text box is the same as the location of its section; for example, the left section is left-aligned.

5. If desired, place the insertion point where you want it, for example, within any existing characters. Then do one or more of the following:

   - Type characters.

   - Click a button from the Header & Footer Elements group to add an element. (See the "Adding Content to Headers and Footers" QuickSteps for information on what the tools do.)

   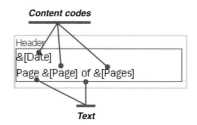

   - Use a combination of typing and features provided by the buttons.

   Content codes

   Header &[Date] Page &[Page] of &[Pages]

   Text

   - Press **ENTER** at the end of a line to place text or objects on multiple lines.

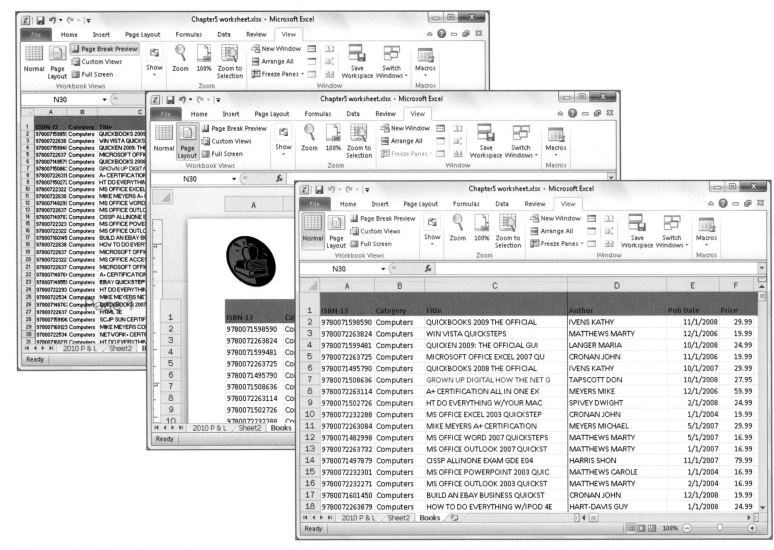

Figure 5-1: Excel views allow you to see and use your data in the row-and-column matrix, with or without consideration for how it will look formatted to fit a page.

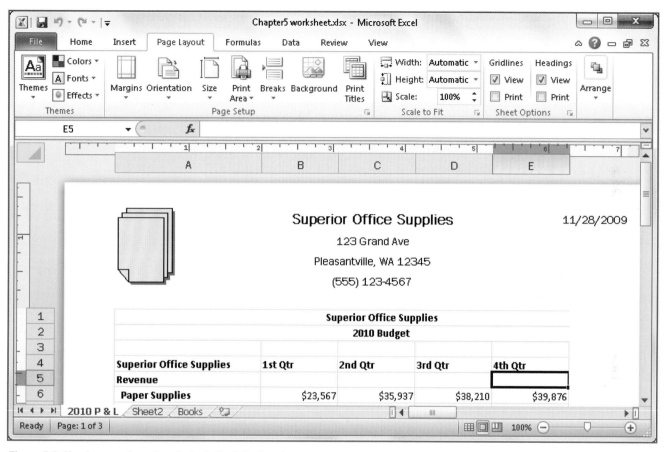

Figure 5-2: *Headers can be set up to look like letterhead.*

When finished, click outside the text boxes or press **ESC** to see how the codes and text are displayed.

6. To change to Normal view, click **Normal** ⊞ on the status bar.

    –Or–

    In the View tab Workbook Views group, click **Normal**.

10/12/2009
Page 1 of 6

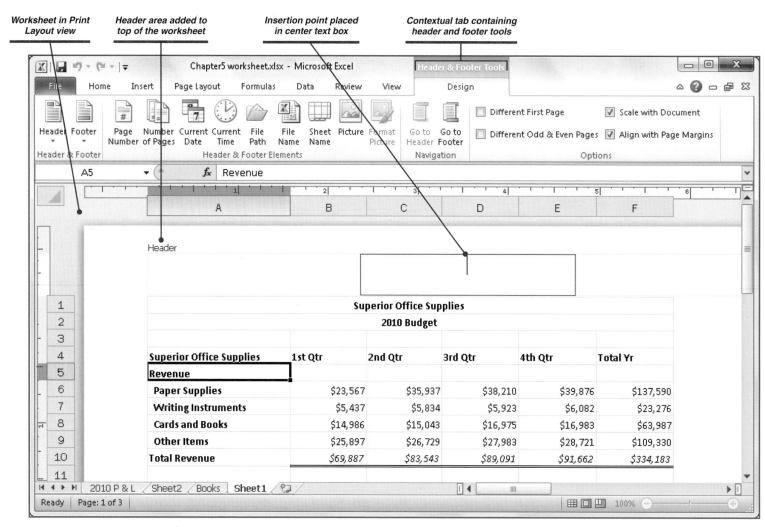

Worksheet in Print Layout view — **Header area added to top of the worksheet** — **Insertion point placed in center text box** — **Contextual tab containing header and footer tools**

Figure 5-3: Choosing to add a header or footer switches Excel into Print Layout view with the tools you need create or change them.

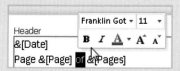

QUICKSTEPS

ADDING CONTENT TO HEADERS AND FOOTERS

Create or edit existing headers and footers by clicking **Header & Footer** in the Insert tab Text group (or double-click an existing header/footer). Use the tools on the Header & Footer Tools Design tab to add content and select other options.

CHANGE CHARACTER FONT, STYLE, AND SIZE

1. Select the text you want to format. Move the mouse off the selection to see a mini-toolbar of formatting tools.

2. Select the font, font style, size, and other effects you want characters to display.

INSERT PAGE NUMBERS

To add a page number on every printed page:

1. Click the left, center, or right text box you want, positioning the insertion point where you want the page number to appear with other text and spacing.

2. Click the **Page Number** button.

INSERT THE TOTAL NUMBER OF PAGES

To add the total number of pages, typically combined with the page number of the page, for example, Page 1 of 2:

1. Click the text box you want, positioning the insertion point where you want the total number of pages to appear.

2. Click the **Number Of Pages** button.

Continued . . .

Add Pictures to Headers and Footers

To insert pictures, such as photos, clip art, and other digital graphic files, in the header or footer:

1. Display the worksheet where you want to add a header and/or footer.

2. In the Insert tab Text group, click **Header & Footer**. Click the text box you want, positioning the insertion point where you want the picture to appear.

3. In the Header & Footer Elements group, click **Picture**. In the Insert Picture dialog box, locate the picture you want, and click **Open**. A picture code is entered into the header or footer. Click outside the text box or press **ESC** to display the picture.

4. To change the picture's size, orientation, or other formatting, click the area where the picture code was placed, and click **Format Picture** in the Header & Footer Elements group. Make your changes in the Format Picture dialog box (see Figure 5-4), and click **OK** (see Chapter 7 for more information on formatting pictures).

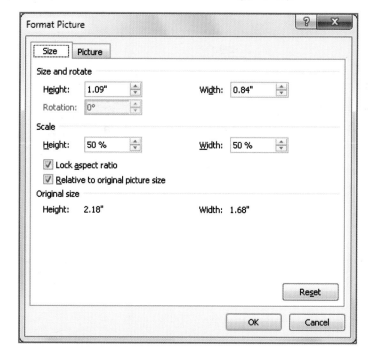

Figure 5-4: You can size, trim, and control other aspects of pictures placed in headers or footers.

ADDING CONTENT TO HEADERS AND FOOTERS *(Continued)*

INSERT THE DATE AND/OR TIME

To add the current date or time in the form mm/dd/yyyy or hh:mm (in this format, Excel omits A.M. and P.M. is added—see Chapter 2 for more information on date and time formats):

1. Click the text box where you want the date and/or time to appear.

2. Click the respective **Current Date** or **Current Time** button.

INSERT THE WORKBOOK'S PATH AND FILE NAME

To insert the path and file name of the workbook:

1. Click the text box you want, positioning the insertion point where you want the path and/or file name to appear.

2. Click the respective **File Path** or **File Name** button (File Path includes the file name).

INSERT THE WORKSHEET NAME

To insert the name of the worksheet:

1. Click the text box where you want the worksheet name to appear.

2. Click the **Sheet Name** button.

USE MORE THAN ONE HEADER AND/OR FOOTER

By default, the header and/or footer you create is displayed on each page of the worksheet. You can change this behavior from the Header & Footer Tools Design tab Options group. Select one or both of the following check boxes:

- **Different First Page** provides a unique header and/or footer on the first page of a worksheet.

- **Different Odd & Even Pages** lets you alternate a header and/or footer on every other page.

Change Margins

You can change the distance between the edges of the page and where worksheet text and pictures start printing, as well as where headers and footers start printing.

1. In the Page Layout tab Page Setup group, click **Margins**. A drop-down menu lists standard settings for normal, wide, and narrow margins, as well as the last set of custom margins used.

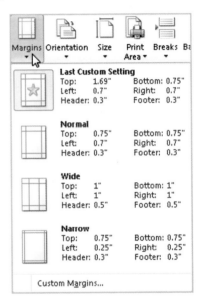

2. Select one of the margin combinations or click **Custom Margins** for more options. The Margins tab of the Page Setup dialog box appears, as shown in Figure 5-5. (You can access this dialog box directly by clicking the **Dialog Box Launcher** in the lower-right corner of the Page Setup group.)

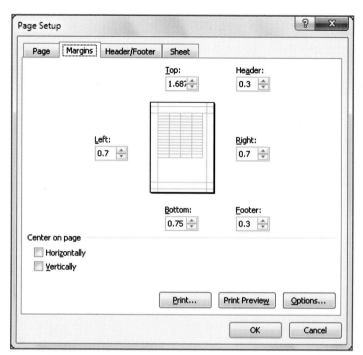

Figure 5-5: *Page and header margins are set in the Margins tab of the Page Setup dialog box.*

ADJUST PAGE MARGINS

1. Adjust the **Top**, **Bottom**, **Left**, and/or **Right** spinners to change the distance that text and pictures start printing from the page edges. As you click a spinner, the preview area shows the location of the margin you are working on.

2. Click **OK** when finished making changes in the Page Setup dialog box.

CENTER PRINTED DATA BETWEEN MARGINS

Under Center On Page, select one or both of the following check boxes:

- Click **Horizontally** to realign data centered between the left and right margins.
- Click **Vertically** to realign data centered between the top and bottom margins.

ADJUST HEADER AND FOOTER MARGINS

You can change the distance a header starts printing from the top edge of a page or the distance a footer starts printing from the bottom edge of the page.

1. Adjust the **Header** and/or **Footer** spinners to change the distance that header or footer text and pictures appear from the top or bottom page edge, respectively.

2. Click **OK** when finished making changes in the Page Setup dialog box.

Select Page Orientation

Pages can be laid out in *portrait* orientation, where a standard 8½ × 11-inch piece of paper is printed, with the sides being the longer dimension, or in *landscape* orientation, where the top and bottom edges are longer. You can also shrink or enlarge the data displayed in a worksheet, or *scale* it, to get more data to display and print on a page or focus in on a specific region.

In the Page Layout tab Page Setup group, click **Orientation** and click the layout (**Portrait** (tall) or **Landscape** (wide)) that works best for how your data is arranged in the worksheet.

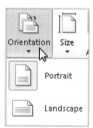

Use Headings as Page Titles

You can retain text in the top rows or left columns of a worksheet for long lists of horizontal or vertical data so that the headings appear on every page in Page Layout view and, when printed, keep you from having to return to the start of the worksheet to see what category of data is being displayed (see Figure 5-6).

Figure 5-6: *Repeating headings on every page makes it easier to keep track of data in long worksheets.*

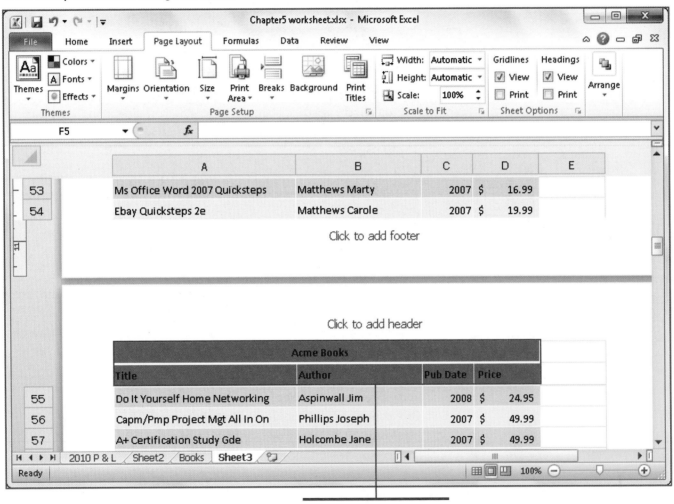

Repeated headings on every page

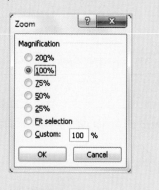

WORKING WITH ZOOM

You can change the magnification (or *zoom*) of a worksheet to see text and objects larger or smaller than the default size, as well as to see less or more of the worksheet on the screen. The worksheet will retain the new appearance until you change the zoom again.

SELECT A ZOOM PERCENTAGE

1. In the View tab Zoom group, click **Zoom**.

   –Or–

   Click the current zoom percentage on the right side of the status bar.

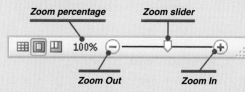

2. In either case, the Zoom dialog box appears. Click a preset magnification percentage (100% being the default).

3. Click **OK** when finished.

Continued . . .

---

1. In the Page Layout tab Page Setup group, click **Print Titles**. The Page Setup dialog box appears with the Sheet tab displayed.

2. Under Print Titles, click the **Collapse Dialog** button to the right of:

   - **Rows To Repeat At Top** to create horizontal titles at the top of every page

     –Or–

   - **Columns To Repeat At Left** to create vertical titles along the leftmost column of every page

3. Select the rows or columns you want to appear on each page. The rows or columns are outlined in a dotted rectangle, and the row/column numbers appear in the collapsed dialog box.

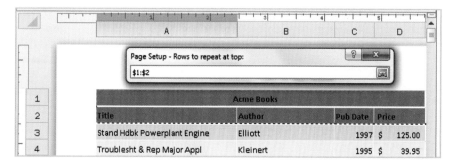

4. Click **Close** in the collapsed dialog box. The row or column reference appears in the respective text box on the Sheet tab.

5. Click **OK** when finished.

Print the Data

In this section you will see how to print different segments of a workbook or worksheet, how to preview your settings and make adjustments, and how to change aspects related to the physical device(s) you use to print.

Change the Order in Which Pages Print

Excel assumes a portrait (tall) page orientation and logically prints down the worksheet as far as there is data. It then moves to the right one page width and

QUICKSTEPS

WORKING WITH ZOOM *(Continued)*

SELECT A CUSTOM MAGNIFICATION

In the View tab Zoom group, click **Zoom**, click **Custom**, and type a custom percentage.

–Or–

Drag the **Zoom** slider on the status bar to the left for less magnification or to the right for greater magnification.

MAGNIFY A SELECTION

Select a range or object on the worksheet whose size you want to increase to fill the worksheet window (the magnification percentage will vary depending on the size of your selection).

1. In the View tab Zoom group, click **Zoom To Selection**.

   –Or–

   From the Zoom dialog box, click **Fit Selection** and click **OK**.

2. To return to a normal magnification, in the View tab Zoom group, click **100%**.

   –Or–

   Move the Zoom slider to the center (100%) position on the status bar.

NOTE

Zoom is similar to *scaling*, a feature that changes the size of a worksheet to fit on a specified number of pages. The major difference is that scaling is temporary, only affecting what prints (see "Scale Your Data Before Printing" later in the chapter).

prints data down that swath as far as there is data, and so forth. If you choose a landscape (wide) orientation, it will probably make more sense to first print pages across, then down.

1. In the Page Layout tab Sheet Options group, click the **Dialog Box Launcher**.

2. In the Sheet tab, under Page Order (see Figure 5-7), select the printing order that works best for the way you have data arranged on the worksheet.

3. Click **OK**.

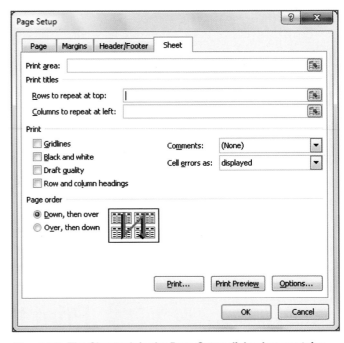

Figure 5-7: *The Sheet tab in the Page Setup dialog box contains several printing options.*

Print Comments

You can print comments in a list at the end of a worksheet, or you can print them as, and where, they appear on the worksheet.

1. In the Page Layout tab Sheet Options group, click the **Dialog Box Launcher**, and click the **Sheet** tab.

TIP

To display a comment, right-click the comment and click **Show/Hide Comments**. (See Chapter 3 for more information on working with comments.)

2. In the Print area, click the **Comments** down arrow, and choose where to print the comments.

3. Click **At End Of Sheet** to print comments on a separate page, listed by cell, author, and comment, as shown in Figure 5-8.

–Or–

Click **As Displayed On Sheet** to print comments that are shown on the worksheet.

4. Click **OK**.

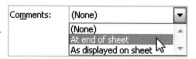

Figure 5-8: **You can print all comments on a worksheet on a separate page.**

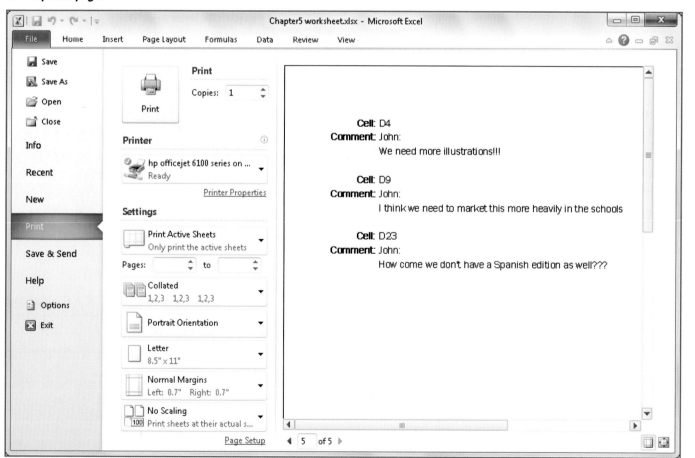

CHOOSING WORKSHEET PRINT OPTIONS

Prior to printing, you can choose several options for including or removing worksheet elements, as well as the quality of the print job. In the Page Layout tab Sheet Options group, click the **Dialog Box Launcher** to display the Sheet tab (see Figure 5-7) in the Page Setup dialog box (a few options are available directly on the ribbon).

Gridlines	Headings
☑ View	☑ View
☐ Print	☐ Print
Sheet Options	🖾

PRINT GRIDLINES

To print the lines that outline the worksheet grid of rows, columns, and cells, under Print, click **Gridlines**.

–Or–

In the Sheet Options group, under Gridlines, click **Print**.

PRINT IN BLACK AND WHITE

To save on color ink for draft prints or to otherwise print in monochrome, under Print, click **Black And White**.

PRINT USING LESS INK OR TONER

Under Print, click **Draft Quality**.

PRINT ROW NUMBERS AND COLUMN LETTERS

By default, the row numbers and column letters that define the addressing in a worksheet are not included when a worksheet prints. To include them both:

1. Under Print, click **Row And Column Headings**.

   –Or–

   In the Sheet Options group, under Headings, click **Print**.

2. Click **OK** when finished to close the Page Setup dialog box.

Use Print Areas

You can define a *print area* of a worksheet by selecting one or more ranges of cells that you want to print. Setting this area is especially useful if you print the same selected cells often. The print area is saved along with the other changes to the worksheet when the workbook is saved.

CREATE A PRINT AREA

1. Select the range of cells you want in the print area by dragging from the upper-leftmost cell to the lower-rightmost cell. To include multiple ranges, hold down **CTRL** while selecting them.

2. In the Page Layout tab Page Setup group, click **Print Area** and click **Set Print Area**. The print area is defined by a dotted line in Normal and Page Layout views, and by a blue border in Page Break Preview view.

ADD CELLS TO A PRINT AREA

1. Select the additional cells on the same worksheet you want to print.

2. In the Page Layout tab Page Setup group, click **Print Area** and click **Add To Print Area**.

REMOVE ADDED CELLS FROM A PRINT AREA

1. In the View tab Workbooks Views group, click **Page Break Preview**.

   –Or–

   Click **Page Break Preview** 🔲 on the right side of the status bar.

NOTE

The easiest way to work with print areas is to interactively select the cells you want printed and use the ribbon to set or change the print area. However, you also can edit cell references in the Sheet tab of the Page Setup dialog box or right-click the sheet in Page Break Preview view and use context menu commands.

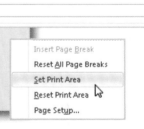

UICKSTEPS

CHOOSING WHAT TO PRINT

You have several options when deciding what portion of a workbook you want printed. You can print the entire workbook, selected sheets, an area you define, and selected pages. Most options are available in Print view. To open the Print view, shown in Figure 5-9, use any of the following methods:

Click the **File** tab, and click **Print**.

–Or–

Press **CTRL+P**.

–Or–

Click the **Print** button in the Page Setup dialog box.

PRINT THE CURRENT SHEET

1. In Print view, under Settings, click the top down arrow, and click **Print Active Sheets**.

2. Click the **Print** icon.

PRINT A SELECTION

1. Select the cells you want to print.

2. In Print view, under Settings, click the top down arrow, and click **Print Selection**.

3. Click the **Print** icon.

PRINT SELECTED SHEETS

1. Select sheets to be printed by holding down the **CTRL** key and clicking the sheet tabs at the bottom of the worksheet.

2. In Print view, under Settings, click the top down arrow, and click **Print Active Sheets**.

3. Click the **Print** icon.

Continued . . .

In either case, click **OK** in the Welcome dialog box that informs you that you can move page breaks by dragging them.

2. Drag the border of the print area to include only the cells you want in the print area.

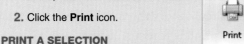

REMOVE A PRINT AREA

1. Click the sheet that contains the print area you want to remove to make it active.

2. In the Page Layout tab Page Setup group, click **Print Area** and click **Clear Print Area**.

PRINT A PRINT AREA

1. Set the print area and make the worksheet it is on active.

2. Click the **File** tab, and click **Print**.

3. Under Settings, click the top down arrow, and then click **Print Active Sheets**. The print area cells will be previewed in the right pane.

4. Click the **Print** icon.

PRINT A SHEET IN LIEU OF ITS PRINT AREA

You can choose to print an entire worksheet that contains a print area without first clearing the print area.

1. Click the **File** tab, and click **Print**.

QUICKSTEPS

CHOOSING WHAT TO PRINT *(Continued)*

PRINT ALL SHEETS

1. In Print view, under Settings, click the top down arrow, and click **Print Entire Workbook**.

2. Click the **Print** icon.

PRINT SPECIFIC PAGES

1. In the Print dialog box, under Settings, use the **Pages** spinners to set the starting and ending pages to print a range of pages,

   –Or–

   To print one page, set both **Pages** spinners to the same page number.

   –Or–

   To print from a selected page to the last page, set only the leftmost (starting) spinner to the selected page number.

2. Select which part of the workbook to print, as described previously.

3. Click the **Print** icon.

2. Under Settings, click the top down arrow, and select the **Ignore Print Area** check box at the bottom of the menu. (Remember to clear the check box when you want to print only the print area.)

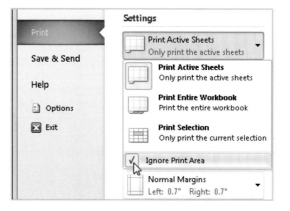

Preview the Print Job

Before your printer actually starts printing paper, you can verify what you have set up to print. Print Preview displays replicas of the printed pages your data will produce, provides a hub for most printing features, and can be used as a printing starting point, as shown in Figure 5-10.

To open Print Preview, click the **File** tab, and click the **Print** option. A preview of the printing option selected under Settings is shown in the right pane of Print view.

–Or–

Click **Print Preview** (or **Print**) in the Page Setup dialog box.

The tools on the Print Preview pane include:

- **Zoom To Page** toggles between a full-page view and a magnified view of the upper-left corner of the current page.

- **Next Page** and **Previous Page** let you navigate among multiple pages. You can also type a page number in the page text box and click **ENTER** to view a specific page.

- **Show Margins** turns off or on visible margin lines that can be dragged to the position you want.

TIP

If a worksheet has a print area, by default, it will print instead of the full worksheet, unless you've chosen to ignore it (see "Print a Sheet in Lieu of Its Print Area"). Also, if you have multiple ranges on your print area, each range will print on a separate page.

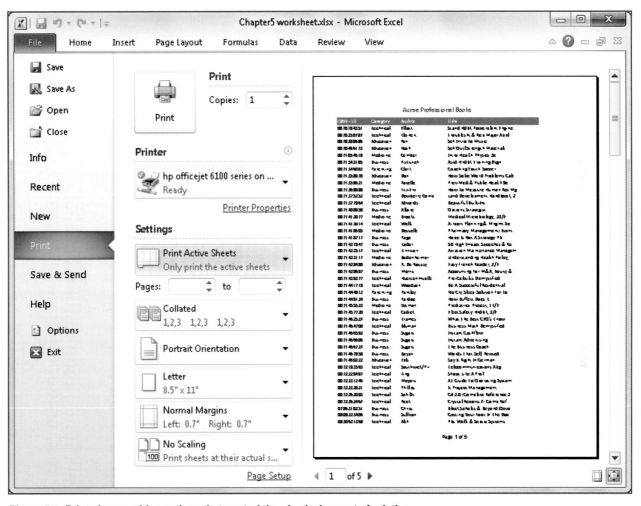

*Figure 5-9: **Print view provides options that control the physical aspect of printing.***

SET MARGINS IN PRINT PREVIEW

1. Open a worksheet in Print Preview.

2. Click **Zoom**, if necessary, to show the first page of the worksheet in full-page view.

3. Click **Show Margins**, if necessary, to show six margin lines and handles, as well as column width handles, as shown in Figure 5-11.

The printing option
selected here...

...displays in the
preview pane

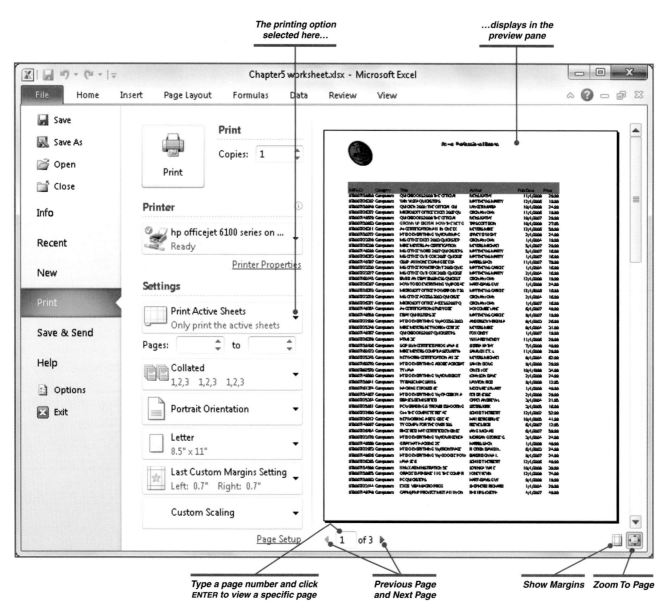

Type a page number and click
ENTER to view a specific page

Previous Page
and Next Page

Show Margins   Zoom To Page

*Figure 5-10: **Print Preview shows replicas of printer pages and provides tools to verify and modify print options before sending the job to a printer.***

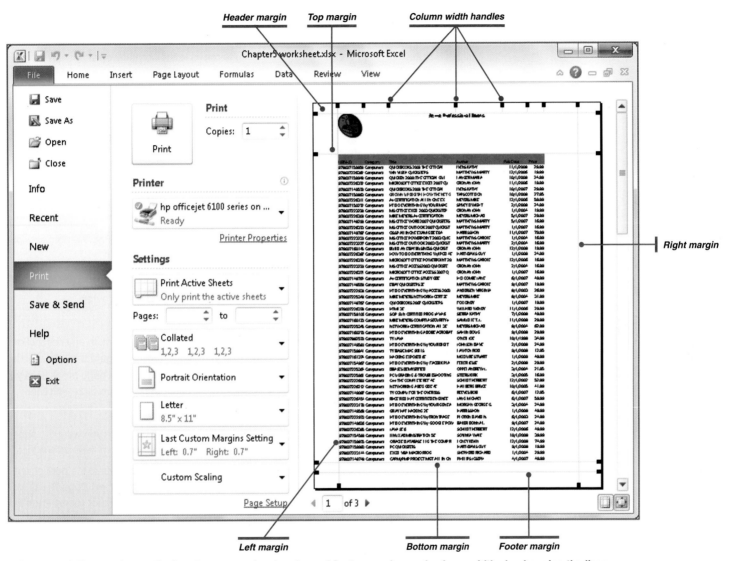

Figure 5-11: *You can interactively set page margins, header and footer margins, and column widths by dragging the lines representing margins in Print Preview.*

TIP

All pages in Print Preview use the same margin and column settings.

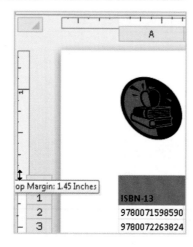

Welcome to Page Break Preview

You can adjust where the page breaks are by clicking and dragging them with your mouse.

☐ Do not show this dialog again.

OK

Breaks Background Print Titles

Insert Page Break
Remove Page Break
Reset All Page Breaks

4. Point at a line or handle until the mouse pointer becomes a cross with either horizontal or vertical arrowheads, and drag the line or handle to set a new margin or column width.

5. Click the **File** tab (or any other tab) to return to the normal worksheet view.

SET PAGE MARGINS IN PAGE LAYOUT VIEW

1. Click **Page Layout** 🔲 view on the right side of the status bar.

2. Point at the transition between dark and light areas on each end of the horizontal or vertical rulers until the mouse pointer becomes a pair of either horizontal or vertical arrowheads, and then drag the transition to increase or decrease the top, bottom, left, or right margins.

ADJUST PAGE BREAKS

You can adjust page breaks using Page Break Preview.

1. To open Page Break Preview, click **Page Break Preview** 🔳 on the right side of the status bar.

   –Or–

   In the View tab Workbook Views group, click **Page Break Preview**.

   In either case, you see the Welcome message.

2. Click **Do Not Show This Dialog Again**, if that's what you want. In any case, click **OK**. The worksheet opens in a condensed format, as shown in Figure 5-12. Dashed lines show page breaks where Excel will separate data into pages; page break lines you move or add are shown as solid lines (outer boundary lines are also solid lines).

3. Do one or more of the following:

   ● Adjust page breaks by dragging a page break line to where you want the page break. Dashed lines become solid after you move them from their default locations.

   ● Insert a page break by selecting the row below or the column to the right of where you want the new page break, right-clicking, and clicking **Insert Page Break**; or in the Page Layout tab Page Setup group, click **Breaks**, and then click **Insert Page Break**.

   ● Remove a page break by dragging it from the worksheet area to the dark gray area.

   ● Remove all page breaks you added or changed by right-clicking the worksheet and clicking **Reset All Page Breaks**; or in the Page Layout tab Page Setup group, click **Breaks**, and then click **Reset All Insert Page Breaks**.

4. To close Page Break Preview, switch to either Normal or Page Layout view by clicking their respective buttons on the status bar or in the View tab Workbook Views group on the ribbon.

Excel-defined page break

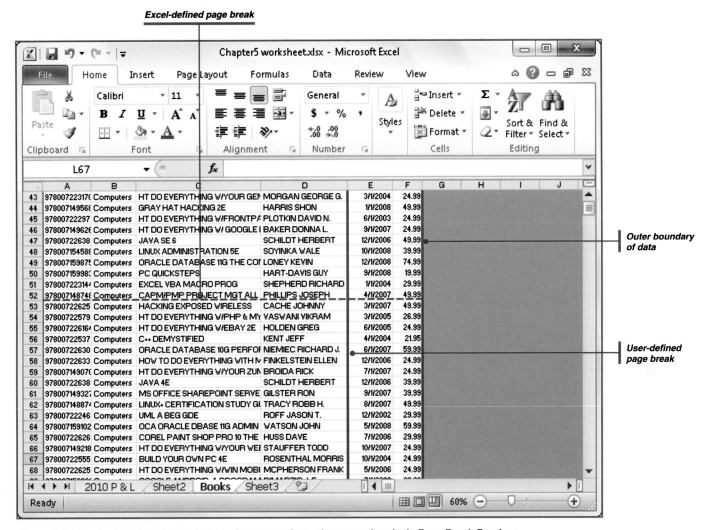

Outer boundary of data

User-defined page break

*Figure 5-12: **Dashed lines and superimposed page numbers show page breaks in Page Break Preview.***

Scale Your Data Before Printing

You can automatically adjust data on a worksheet to fit the number of pages you select or to a percentage that will print on as many pages as needed using several different options.

In the Page Layout tab Scale To Fit group, click the **Width** or **Height** down arrows, and select how many pages you want the worksheet to print. The worksheet will scale to accommodate your choice.

–Or–

Click the **Scale** spinner to increase (see text and objects larger, but fewer cells) or decrease (see text and objects smaller, but more cells) the percentage of magnification (the Width and Height option must both be set to Automatic).

Output the Print Job

You can print to printers attached to your computer or to printers on your network. You can also print to a file instead of to a printer and choose features provided by your printer manufacturer. All this is accomplished from Print view (see Figure 5-9).

Click the **File** tab, and click **Print**; or press **CTRL+P**.

CHOOSE A PRINTER

Click the **Printer** down arrow, and select a printer that is installed on your computer or on your network from the drop-down list. The printer name is displayed, and information about the printer is listed below it.

PRINT TO A FILE

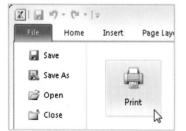

You can print your workbook information to a file instead of directly to a physical device. Print files are often used to create Adobe PDF documents (you must select a PDF printer and follow its unique instructions) or when you want to create a file of the print job to send to another computer or special remote printer.

1. Click the **Printer** down arrow, and click **Print To File** at the bottom of the menu.

2. Click **Print**.

3. In the Print To File dialog box, type the path and file name where you want the print file located, and click **OK**.

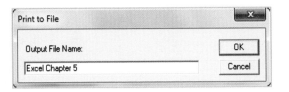

NOTE

Depending on your printer, you may have additional options available to you under Settings, such as two-sided printing and the ability to change page orientation.

SELECT PRINTER-SPECIFIC OPTIONS

Most printers have additional printing options and features besides those provided in Excel.

To display a printer's properties dialog box, as shown in Figure 5-13, click **Printer Properties** in Print view.

–Or–

Click **Options** in the Page Setup dialog box.

PRINT MULTIPLE COPIES

1. In the Print view Print area at the top, click the **Copies** spinner to reflect the number of copies you want.

2. Under Settings, verify that **Collated** is selected to print each copy from start to finish before starting to print the next copy.

–Or–

Click the **Collated** down arrow, and click **Uncollated** to print each page the number of times set in the Copies spinner before printing the next page.

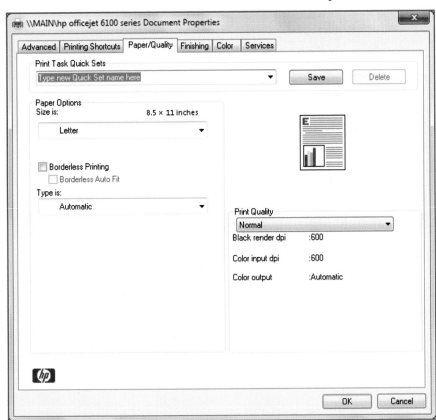

Figure 5-13: Printers have printing features in addition to those provided by Excel.

Save and View Custom Views

After you have altered print settings, changed zoom magnifications, and worked with hidden rows and columns, you can save these settings and return to them.

1. Set up a worksheet with the layout and print settings you want.

2. In the View tab Workbook Views group, click **Custom Views**.

3. In the Custom Views dialog box, click **Add**, type a name for your view, and include or exclude print, hidden, and filter settings (filtering is described in Chapter 8). Click **OK** when finished.

4. To view a saved view, click **Custom Views** in the Workbook Views group, select the view you want in the Custom Views dialog box, and click **Show**.

Chapter 6

Charting Data

In this chapter you will learn how to display worksheet data graphically in *charts*. Providing a more visual representation of data than a worksheet grid, charts show trends and comparisons at a quick glance. Figure 6-1 shows a column chart, typically used to compare the values of two or more categories, and many of the elements that can be used on a chart.

Charts in Excel quickly and easily produce a professional product that you can then modify if needed. After creating a simple chart, you can rely on Excel to provide several layout and style options, which you can use on their own or make further changes to. To fully integrate charts with the overall appearance of your workbook, many charting elements, such as color, font, and fills, take on the attributes of the current workbook theme. New to Excel 2010 are *sparklines*, mini-charts that appear in a cell so you can quickly spot

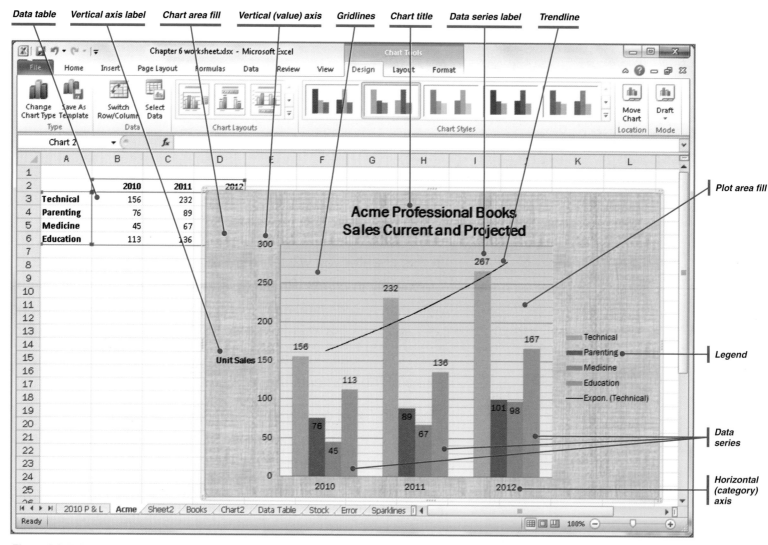

Figure 6-1: *This Excel chart demonstrates the typical collection of chart elements.*

BUILDING A CHART

Excel guides you through the process by assuming you'll move through one or more of the four tabs on the ribbon that contain chart-building tools. The tabs are essentially the steps to build a chart.

1. The **Insert** tab provides the means to initially create a chart from one of several chart types and subtypes. For many purposes, these charts are as far as you'll need to go.

2. The **Design** tab (under Chart Tools) lets you further refine the overall layout of the chart elements, change the chart type, and apply design styles.

3. The **Layout** tab (under Chart Tools) provides tools to add chart elements, such as axes, labels, and graphics. You can also add visual elements to help analyze data such as trendlines.

4. The **Format** tab (under Chart Tools) lets you fine-tune selected elements in terms of color, fills, and size.

Charts can be created in one of two forms:

● **Embedded charts** are objects that reside on a worksheet, much like a drawing or picture, along with other objects and the underlying data. The chart is enclosed within a border and can be sized and moved similar to other graphic objects.

● **Chart sheets** are workbook sheets that contain a chart separated from its underlying worksheet. These charts also can be sized and moved within the sheet, and other graphic objects, such as pictures and SmartArt (professionally designed layouts combined with text-entering capabilities), can be added to the chart sheet.

trends in data. Display options are available that allow you to hide data you may not want to display and that permit you to choose whether to show the chart on the same worksheet as its underlying data or in a separate chart sheet. These, along with other things you can do with charts, are covered in the following sections.

Create and Design a Chart

This section shows you how to create a chart and establish the basic design, or "infrastructure," of a chart. The topics in this section cover the tools involved in the first two basic steps in building a chart (see the "Building a Chart" QuickSteps).

Choose a Chart Type

Excel organizes charts into 12 types, categorized by the function they perform. Within each chart type are from 2 to 19 variations called *subtypes*. For example, the Line chart type has seven ways to display trends, as shown in Figure 6-2. In total, you have 73 chart options to choose from and a virtually unlimited number of user-defined charts you can set up as *templates* (see "Create Your Own Chart Type" later in the chapter). The main chart types are summarized in Table 6-1.

SELECT A CHART TYPE FROM A GALLERY

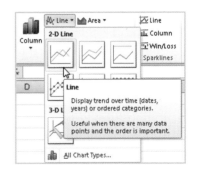

1. Select the data range that you want to chart (see Chapter 2 for information on selecting ranges and the "Selecting Data for Charting" QuickFacts in this chapter).

2. In the Insert tab Charts group, click the chart type you want (or click **Other Charts** to see more types). To see a description of the chart types or subtypes, point to a chart icon and a ScreenTip displays.

NOTE

Though you do not have to select a range of data to create a chart (you can just click a cell within the range and Excel will do its best to assume the range), if you do, the chart initially displayed by Excel will give you a more accurate view of your data.

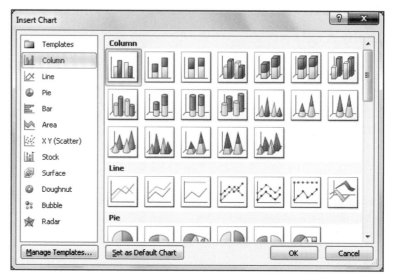

Figure 6-2: *The Insert Chart dialog box displays all chart types in one venue.*

CHART TYPE	FUNCTION
Column, Bar, Line	Compare trends in multiple data series in various configurations, such as vertical or horizontal; available in several subtypes, such as 3-D line, cylinder, cone, and pyramid
Pie and Doughnut	Display one data series (pie) or compare multiple data series (doughnut) as part of a whole or 100 percent
XY (Scatter)	Displays pairs of data to establish concentrations
Area	Shows the magnitude of change over time; useful when summing multiple values to see the contribution of each
Radar	Connects changes in a data series from a starting or center point with lines, markers, or a colored fill
Surface	Compares trends in multiple data series in a continuous curve; similar to Line chart with a 3-D visual effect
Bubble	Displays sets of three values; similar to an XY chart with the third value being the size of the bubble
Stock	Displays three sets of values, such as high, low, and closing stock prices
Templates	Charts that include formatting and unique settings that you might want to save to apply to future charts

Table 6-1: *The 12 Functional Types of Excel Charts and the user-defined Template chart type.*

3. Click the subtype you want from the respective gallery. A professionally designed chart is created and displayed on the worksheet.

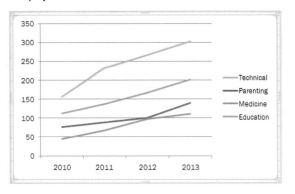

SELECT A CHART TYPE FROM A DIALOG BOX

1. Select the data range that you want to chart.

2. In the Insert tab Charts group, click the **Dialog Box Launcher** (the arrow in the lower-right corner of the group area). The Insert Chart dialog box appears (see Figure 6-2) with the default chart type selected (see "Change the Default Chart" if you want to change it).

3. Scroll through the complete inventory of Excel-provided chart types/subtypes in the large box to the right.

   –Or–

   Click a chart type in the left pane to auto-scroll to its chart subtypes.

4. To see an abbreviated description of the chart subtypes, point to a subtype icon and a ScreenTip displays.

5. Double-click the chart subtype you want. A professionally designed chart is created and displayed on the worksheet.

CREATE A CHART QUICKLY

1. Select the data range that you want to chart.

2. Press **ALT+F1** to create an embedded chart.

   –Or–

   Press **F11** to create a chart sheet.

   In either case, a chart is created using the default chart type. See "Change the Default Chart," next, for steps to change the default chart type, and see "Choose a Chart Location," later in the chapter, to switch a chart between embedded and a chart sheet.

Chart templates (referred to in pre-2007 versions of Excel as "custom types") are available in the Templates folder of the Insert Chart and Change Chart Type dialog boxes. They are customized charts that extend your inventory of available chart types on which to base a new chart. See "Create Your Own Chart Type" and the "Using Chart Templates" QuickSteps later in the chapter for more information.

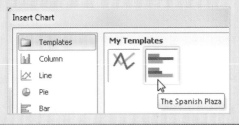

TIP

Chart sheets do not display their underlying data by default. You can add the range of cells that comprise the data, with or without legend keys. See "Display the Data Table" later in this chapter.

QUICKFACTS

SELECTING DATA FOR CHARTING

Charts are created from worksheet data. Excel makes assumptions on how to set up the plot area, assign axes, and make labels based on the data. Though you can change many of the chart elements after the chart is created and Excel will quickly reconfigure the chart, it speeds things along (and increases the likelihood of seeing what you want!) if the data is properly organized. Guidelines for setting up data for charting and assumptions Excel uses include:

- The selected data must be a rectangular *data range* or consist of multiple selections in a rectangular array.

- Text, which is used solely to create labels, should only be in the topmost row and/or the leftmost column; otherwise, text encountered within the range is charted as zero.

- Each cell must contain a *value* (or data point). Values in the same row or column are considered to be related and are called a *data series*. The first data series starts with the first cell in the upper-left area of the selected data that is not text or formatted as a date. Subsequent data series are determined by Excel, continuing across the rows or down the columns. Values are plotted on the vertical (generally, the Y, or value) axis.

- As Excel determines whether there are more rows or columns selected, it will assume the lesser number to be the data series and the greater number to be categories that are plotted on the horizontal (generally, the X, or category) axis. In Figure 6-3, three columns and four rows of data are selected; therefore, Excel plots the three years of values, each as a data series, and considers the rows to be categories.

CHANGE THE DEFAULT CHART

Excel ships with the clustered column subtype as the default chart (see Figure 6-1). You can change it to any of the Excel chart types or to one you saved as a template. (The Charts group is unavailable if your active sheet is a chart sheet, described in the previous section. Select a standard sheet to perform these steps.)

1. In the Insert tab Charts group, click the **Dialog Box Launcher**.

2. In the Insert Chart dialog box (see Figure 6-2) or the Change Chart Type dialog (same as the Insert Chart dialog box but it appears when there is already an embedded chart displayed), click the chart type you want to be the new default chart type.

3. Click **Set As Default Chart**, and click **OK**.

Choose a Chart Location

You can change where a chart is located, from an object on the worksheet (embedded chart) to a full, separate sheet (chart sheet, shown in Figure 6-4), and vice versa.

To relocate a chart:

1. Open either the worksheet that contains the embedded chart or the chart sheet whose position you want to change.

2. In the Design tab (under the Chart Tools contextual tab) Location group, click **Move Chart**.

3. In the Move Chart dialog box, click **New Sheet** to move the chart to a chart sheet. You can change the name of the chart sheet that will be created to something other than the default.

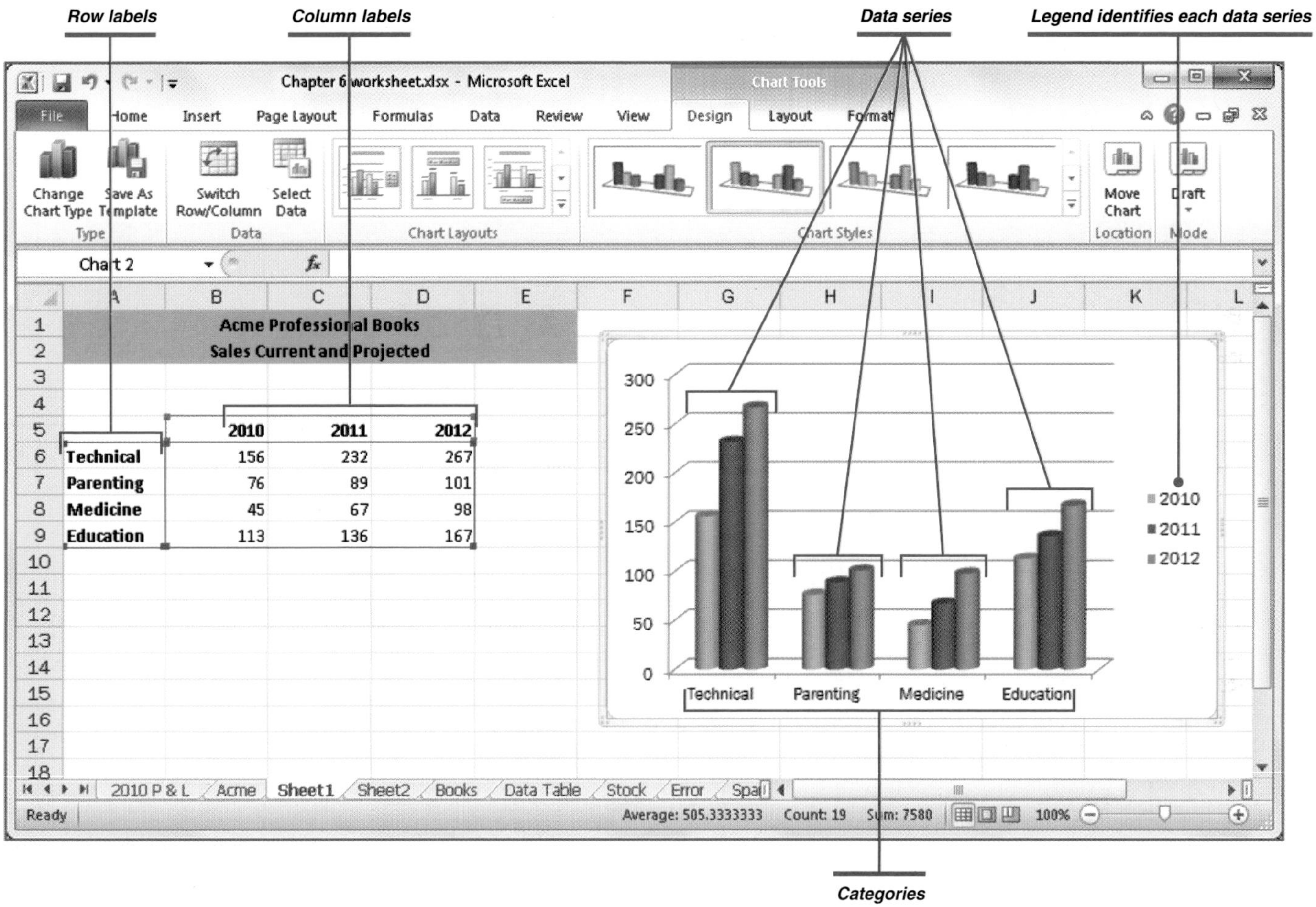

Row labels   Column labels   Data series   Legend identifies each data series

Categories

Figure 6-3: **Excel determines whether row or column labels become the plotted data series by choosing the lesser number for the data series and the greater for categories.**

–Or–

Click the **Object In** down arrow to select the sheet in the workbook where you want the chart to be added as an embedded chart.

4. Click **OK**. The chart is moved to the location you specified and removed from its original location.

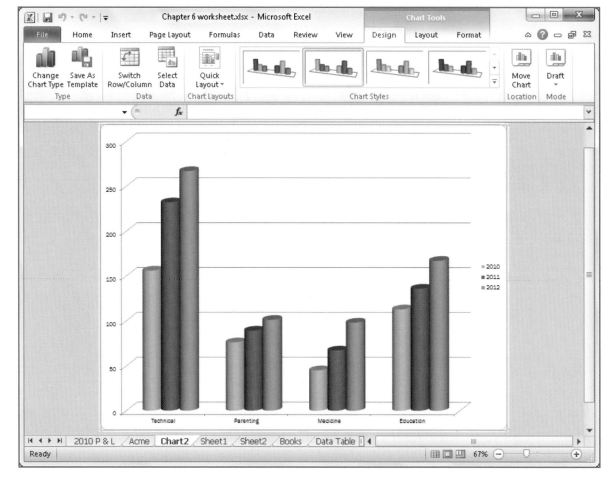

Figure 6-4: *You can create an embedded chart and easily move it to a chart sheet, shown here.*

Modify How the Data Is Plotted

Without affecting any of the underlying data, you can add or remove data
series, select the cells that identify the data series' name and the data series'
value, and change which cells are used for labels for the category (X) axis.

1. Display a worksheet with an embedded chart or open a chart sheet containing a chart.
   Click the chart to display the Chart Tools tabs.

2. In the Design tab Data group, click **Select Data**. The Select Data Source dialog box appears, shown in Figure 6-5. You can perform several actions from the dialog box.

● To change the range of data that is charted, click the **Collapse Dialog** 🔃 button at the right end of the Chart Data Range text box. Select the range and click the **Expand Dialog** 🔄 button in the shrunken Select Data Source dialog box to return to the full-sized Select Data Source dialog box.

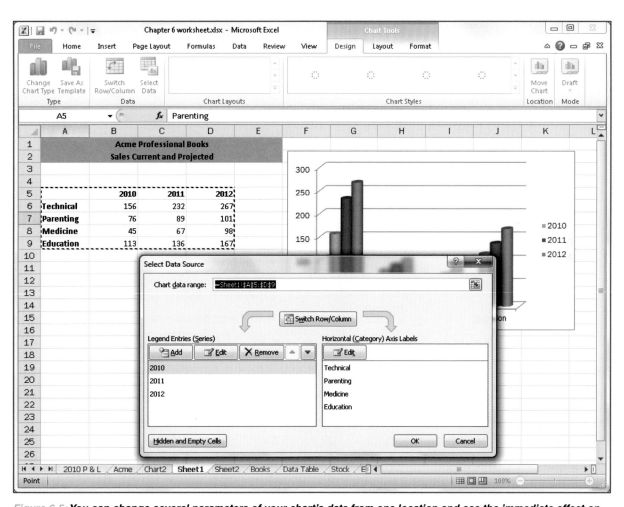

Figure 6-5: *You can change several parameters of your chart's data from one location and see the immediate effect on the chart.*

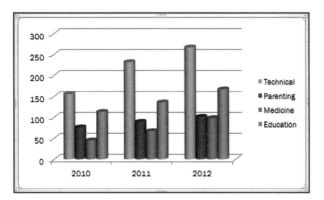

Figure 6-6: *Compare the switching of the data series and horizontal axis with the chart in Figure 6-5.*

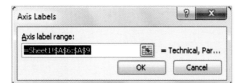

NOTE

The series name and values you choose can be from other worksheets or open workbooks. All you are really doing is adding more information to the chart that is not within your originally selected data.

–Or–

Type the range in the Chart Data Range text box.

- To switch between the row and column labels being used as the data series and horizontal (category) axis, select your data range, and click **Switch Row/Column**. (If this is all you want to do, you can click **Switch Row/Column** in the Data group without first opening the Select Data Source dialog box.) The chart changes accordingly (see Figure 6-6).

- To include more data in the chart, click **Add** in the Legend Entries (Series) pane. In the Edit Series dialog box, click the applicable **Collapse Dialog** buttons to add cells for the data series' name and its values. Click **OK** to return to the Select Data Source dialog box.

- To change existing data series, select the series you want to change, and click **Edit**. Make any changes and click **OK** to return to the Select Data Source dialog box.

- To remove a data series, select the series and click **Remove**.

- To change the order in which the data series is presented, select the data series you want to move, and click the up and down arrows to move it where you want it.

- To change the horizontal (category) axis labels, click **Edit** in the right pane. On the worksheet, select the range for the labels, and click **OK**.

- To change how empty and hidden cells are accounted for, click **Hidden And Empty Cells**. In the Settings dialog box, select the behavior you want, and click **OK**.

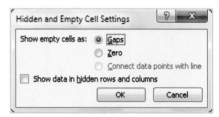

3. Click **OK** when you are finished with the Select Data Source dialog box.

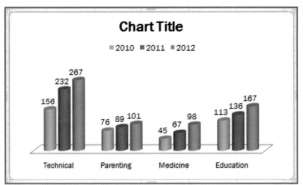

Chart Title

■2010 ■2011 ■2012

Figure 6-7: *Layouts allow you to rearrange and modify the elements on your chart with just a few mouse clicks.*

NOTE

You can change the style-related attributes of individual chart elements to provide full flexibility in how you want your chart to appear. See the applicable section under "Modify Chart Elements" for the element you want to change.

Apply a Chart Layout

A chart *layout* allows you to quickly choose how chart elements are arranged within the boundaries of the chart window. For example, the default column layout places the legend on the right of the data series. Other layouts place the legend under the title, under axis labels (see Figure 6-7), or omit it altogether. As with selecting a chart type, you can easily modify any layout by moving or changing other chart element attributes.

1. Click the chart whose layout you want to change.

2. In the Design tab (Chart Tools) Chart Layouts group, click the **More** down arrow to view the gallery of layout icons available for your current chart type.

3. Click the layout you want. The chart changes to conform to your choice.

Change a Chart's Style

Styles change the color, fill, and special effects of several chart elements (for example, the rectangles or cylinders in a column chart or the color of plot area gridlines), including the background of the chart area window. A chart's initial style is derived from the workbook's theme (see Chapter 3 for more information on themes). You can change the current style by selecting a different combination of colors and shading from a gallery (or by changing the workbook's theme).

1. Click the chart whose style you want to change.

2. In the Design tab (Chart Tools) Chart Styles group, click the **More** down arrow to view the gallery of style icons available for your current chart type (see Figure 6-8).

3. Click the style you want. The chart changes to conform to your choice.

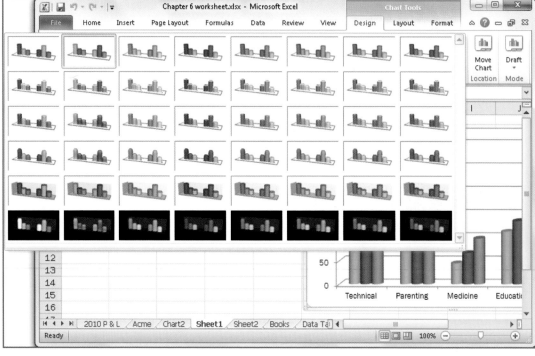

*Figure 6-8: **There is no shortage of styles for a given chart type.***

QUICK**STEPS**

SELECTING CHART ELEMENTS

You can select chart elements using the keyboard or the mouse. When selected, elements will display small circular and/or rectangular handles (for some elements, these are sizing handles; for others, they just show selections), and the selected element's name appears in the Format tab (Chart Tools) Current Selection group on the ribbon.

Acme Books

SELECT CHART ELEMENTS BY CLICKING

Place the mouse pointer over the element you want selected, and click it.

Continued . . .

Modify Chart Elements

In addition to applying broad changes through styles, layouts, and themes, Excel allows you to treat each element of a chart uniquely; that is, each has its own set of formatting and other characteristics you can apply. Once you have a basic chart displayed, you can totally redesign it by selecting and changing each of its component elements.

Add Titles

Titles help readers quickly orient themselves to the data being presented. On an Excel chart, you can have chart and axis titles.

1 2 3 4 5 6 7 8 9 10

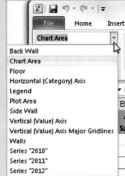

QUICKSTEPS

SELECTING CHART ELEMENTS
(Continued)

SELECT CHART ELEMENTS FROM THE RIBBON

1. Click the chart to display the Chart Tools tabs on the ribbon.

2. In the Format tab (Chart Tools) Current Selection group, click the **Chart Elements** down arrow at the top of the group.

3. Click the chart element you want selected from the drop-down list. Selection handles surround it.

SELECT CHART ELEMENTS USING THE KEYBOARD

1. Click the chart to select it.

2. Press the **UP ARROW** or **DOWN ARROW** key to cycle through the groups of elements.

–Or–

Press **RIGHT ARROW** or **LEFT ARROW** to cycle through the elements within a group.

REMOVE A SELECTION

Press **ESC**.

TIP

You can add a second category and/or value axis with its own title. A second axis is typically used when the values in one data series are proportionally different from the others and need a different scale of values. See "Add a Second Value Axis" later in the chapter.

---

1. Click the chart.

2. In the Layout tab (Chart Tools) Labels group, click **Chart Title**.

3. Click one of the options to place the chart title where you want it, or click **None** to remove it.

4. In the Labels group, next to Chart Title, click **Axis Titles**.

5. Point to either the primary horizontal or vertical axis, and click one of the options to place the respective axis title where you want it; or click **None** to remove it.

6. Select the default title text that appears on the chart ("Chart Title" or "Axis Title"), and type the title you want.

Show or Hide Axes

The primary horizontal (category) and vertical (value) axes can be displayed or not, depending on whether the information provided adds value to your chart.

1. Click the chart.

2. In the Layout tab (Chart Tools) Axes group, click **Axes**. Point to:

   - **Primary Horizontal Axis** and click one of the options to place the axis where you want it; or click **None** to remove it.

   - **Primary Vertical Axis** and click one of the options to choose a scale; or click **None** to remove it.

3. Select the horizontal or vertical axis, and click **More Primary Horizontal** (or **Vertical**) **Axis Options** at the bottom of the respective options drop-down list. Click **Axis Options** in the left pane of the Format Axis dialog box (shown in Figure 6-9) to see options related to:

   - Minimum and maximum scale values

   - Axis type (horizontal axis only); text or date

   - Locations for tick marks and where the axes intersect

   - Distance axis is from its label

4. Make any adjustments and click **Close**.

Add or Remove Gridlines

Gridlines provide a background reference to value and category axes intervals. You can choose to have a few gridlines at what Excel determines are the major intervals, such as every 10 values on a value scale of 0–100, and/or at minor intervals, such as at every other value on a value scale of 0–100, or not at all. Figure 6-10 shows minor and major gridlines.

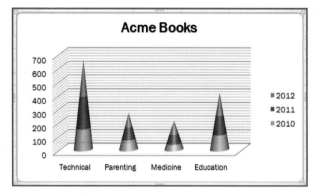

Figure 6-10: **Adding minor gridlines provides a more accurate determination of values, but they can clutter a chart.**

1. Click the chart.
2. In the Layout tab (Chart Tools) Axes group, click **Gridlines**.
3. Point to **Primary Horizontal** (or **Vertical**) **Gridlines**, and click one of the options to display major, minor, or both sets of gridlines; or click **None** to remove them.

Show or Hide a Legend

A *legend* identifies the data series in a chart. You can choose to display the legend or not and where on the chart the legend is located.

1. Click the chart.
2. In the Layout tab (Chart Tools) Labels group, click **Legend**.
3. Click one of the options to place the legend where you want it, or click **None** to remove it.

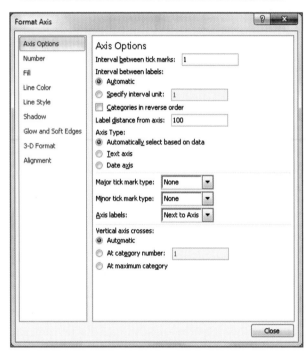

Figure 6-9: **You can modify horizontal and vertical axes to fit any unique set of data (horizontal options shown here).**

IDENTIFYING CHART ELEMENTS

It's easy to confuse which element is selected on a chart, especially on more complex charts with multiple series and axes. Excel provides several clues as to the identity of the selected element and, if applicable to the element, its value and data. Click an element to see its particulars:

- On the ScreenTip of the element
- In the Current Selection group on the Format tab (Chart Tools)
- In the Name box on the Formula bar (identifies the chart only)
- In the Formula bar (identifies the data series)
- Color-coded on the worksheet (identifies the data range)

TIP

You can move the legend anywhere within the chart area by dragging it with your mouse.

TIP

After data labels are displayed on your chart, you can edit any label by clicking it twice slowly. Do not double-click it, or you will open its Format dialog box.

TIP

Unlike earlier versions of Excel, which had discrete limits, in Excel 2010, the number of data points in a data series is limited only by the memory available on your computer.

Add Data Labels

The value of a data series can be interpolated using the vertical (value) axis and gridlines, but if you want the values shown directly on the plot area, you can add them.

1. Click the chart.

2. In the Layout tab (Chart Tools) Labels group, click **Data Labels**.

3. Click **Show** to place data labels on the chart, or click **None** to remove them.

4. Click **More Data Label Options** at the bottom of the drop-down list. Click **Label Options** in the left pane of the Format Data Labels dialog box to see additional options.

- Under Label Contains, select whether to display a name instead of a value.

- Select **Include Legend Key In Label** to provide a color-coded rectangle near each data series that corresponds to the legend label.

- Click the **Separator** down arrow, and click the character you want to separate multiple labels.

5. Click **Close**. (Figure 6-11 shows a chart with several data label possibilities.)

Display the Data Table

You can add the underlying worksheet data, or *data table*, to the chart area.

1. Click the chart.

2. In the Layout tab (Chart Tools) Labels group, click **Data Table**.

3. Click one of the options to place the data table below the chart, with or without legend keys, or click **None** to remove it.

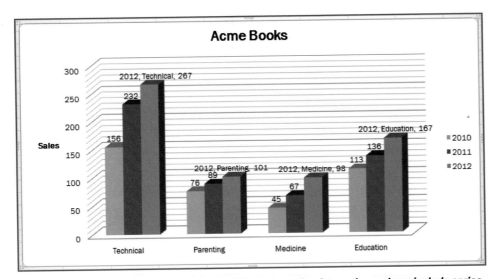

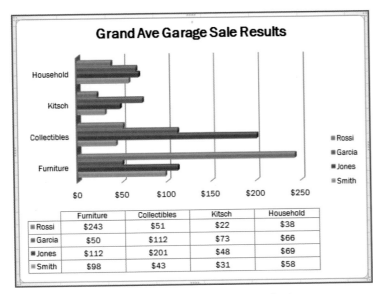

Figure 6-12: *A chart's data table can be added to a chart.*

4. Click **More Data Table Options** at the bottom of the drop-down list. Click **Data Table Options** in the left pane of the Format Data Table dialog box to determine whether you want horizontal, vertical, or outline borders. Clear each check box if you don't want any borders.

5. Click **Close**. The data table is added to the chart area below the plot area (see Figure 6-12).

Create Your Own Chart Type

After you have applied formatting and added or removed chart elements, your chart may not resemble any of the standard or even custom chart types provided by Excel. To save your work so that you can build a similar chart at another time:

1. Build the chart and then select it.

2. In the Design tab (Chart Tools) Type group, click **Save As Template**.

3. In the Save Chart Template dialog box, name the chart (the file name becomes the chart's name), and click **Save**. The chart is saved in a Charts folder within your Microsoft Templates folder and will be available in the Insert Chart and Change Chart Type dialog boxes in their respective Templates folders (see "Choose a Chart Type" earlier in the chapter).

Add a Second Value Axis

When you have a data series that contains values (or data points) with disproportional or different types of values, you might need to create a second value axis to keep the scaling meaningful.

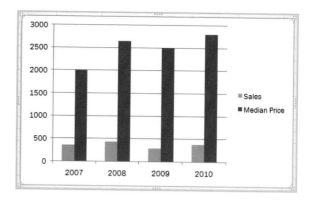

QUICKSTEPS

USING CHART TEMPLATES

When you create your own chart type, you are saving the layout, design, and formatting of a chart as a template. You can have more templates by adding them from your installation discs, or you can install them from outside sources, such as Office.com.

ADD CHART TEMPLATES FROM EXCEL

If you do not have chart templates available to you other than those you saved, they were not installed when Excel was set up. You can change your program configuration to add prebuilt templates.

1. In Windows 7/Vista, click **Start** and then click **Control Panel**.

2. From a view of Control Panel categories, under the Programs category, click **Uninstall A Program**.

—Or—

From a list of control panels, click **Programs And Features**.

3. In the Uninstall Or Change A Program pane, shown in Figure 6-13, select your Microsoft Office/Excel installation program, and click **Change**. Follow the prompts to add features to your Excel installation.

VIEW THE NAMES OF YOUR TEMPLATES/ CUSTOM CHARTS

To view the names of your custom charts and imported templates:

1. Open either the Create Chart (new charts) or Change Chart Type (existing charts) dialog box by clicking the Insert tab Charts group **Dialog Box Launcher**.

Continued . . .

1. Create a column chart with two data series using one of the methods described earlier in the chapter.

2. Right-click one of the data series (this will be the series that changes from a column to a line), and click **Format Data Series**.

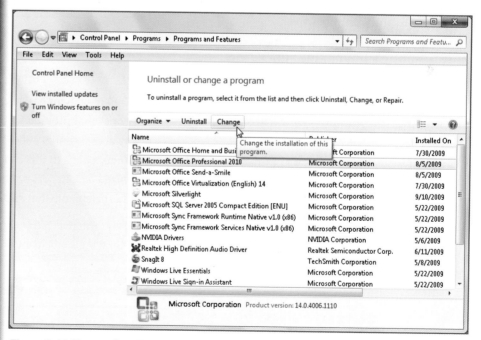

Figure 6-13: **You can install chart templates by changing your Excel installation parameters in the Programs And Features Control Panel.**

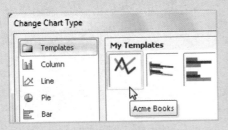

USING CHART TEMPLATES *(Continued)*

2. Click the **Templates** folder, and point to each template icon. A ScreenTip appears in a few seconds displaying the template's name, that is, the file name it was given when it was saved.

CREATE A CHART FROM A TEMPLATE

You apply the attributes of a custom chart type saved as a template as you do other chart types.

For new charts: Select the data you want used in the chart, and click the Insert tab Charts group **Dialog Box Launcher**. In the Insert Chart dialog box Templates folder, double-click the template you want to apply. A new chart will be created using the custom attributes.

–Or–

For existing charts: Select the chart and click the Insert tab Charts group **Dialog Box Launcher**. In the Change Chart Type dialog box Templates folder, double-click the template you want to apply. The custom attributes are applied to the existing chart.

3. In the Format Data Series dialog box, click **Series Options**. Under Plot Series On, click **Secondary Axis**. Click **Close**.

4. In the Design tab (Chart Tools) Type group, click **Change Chart Type**. Click one of the line charts, and click **OK**. The two-data series column chart is converted to a column-line combination chart with a second value axis (see Figure 6-14).

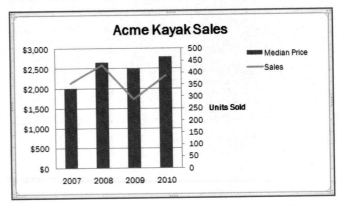

Figure 6-14: **Two value axes allow you to combine two different data series on one chart to ascertain relationships.**

Format Chart Elements

Each chart element has an associated Format dialog box with one or more categories that provide formatting options. Several of the chart elements have identical or a similar set of formatting options (unique options are described in other sections in this chapter). Table 6-2 shows the formatting options, organized by categories that display in the individual Format dialog boxes, and the chart elements that apply.

You can format a chart element by simply double-clicking it, or you can use one of several methods using the ribbon and context menus.

1. Click the chart.

2. In the Layout tab (Chart Tools), click the element whose formatting you want to change from the Labels, Axes, or Background groups. Click the **More *element* Options** command at the bottom of each drop-down list.

–Or–

FORMATTING OPTIONS	DESCRIPTION	APPLY TO
Fill	Provides options for gradient, picture, or texture fill, as well as color choices, degrees of transparency, and gradient options	Axis, chart area, data labels/series, legend, markers, plot area, titles, walls/floors
Line	Offers solid or gradient lines, as well as color choices, degrees of transparency, and gradient options	Axis, chart area, data labels/series, error bars, gridlines, legend, markers, plot area, titles, trendlines, walls/floors
Line Style	Provides options for width, dashed, and compound (multiple) lines, as well as styles for line ends and line joins	Axis, chart area, data labels/series, error bars, gridlines, markers, legend, plot area, titles, trendlines, walls/floors
Shadow	Provides preset shadow styles and controls for color, transparency, size, blur, angle, and distance	Axis, chart area, data labels/series, legend, plot area, titles, trendlines, walls/floors
Glow and Soft Edges	Provides hazy and/or less defined edges and corners	Axis, chart area, data labels/series, error bars, gridlines, legend, plot area, titles, trendlines, walls/floors
3-D Format	Adds 3-D dimension to shapes; provides top, bottom, material, and lighting presets and controls for depth contours and color	Axis, chart area, data labels/series, legend, plot area, titles, walls/floors
3-D Rotation	Provides angular rotation and perspective adjustments, as well as positioning and scaling controls	Walls/floors
Number	Provides the same number formats as the Format Cells Number tab, such as currency, accounting, date, and time	Axis, data labels
Alignment	Vertically aligns, rotates, and stacks text	Axis, data labels, titles, legends
Properties	Defines how the chart is moved and sized in relation to adjoining cells, and provides sheet protection settings	Chart area
Alt Text	Allows a title and description of the chart to be read from the computer for visually impaired users who have set up their Windows 7 Ease Of Access control panel to do so	Chart area

Table 6-2: **Chart Element Formatting Options**

NOTE

Graphics (including shapes, pictures, clip art, and text boxes) can be easily added to charts and formatted. See Chapter 7 for more information on working with graphics.

Select the element, and in the Format tab (Chart Tools) Current Selection group, click **Format Selection**.

–Or–

Right-click the element and click **Format *chart element***.

In any case, a Format dialog box appears similar to the one shown in Figure 6-15.

3. Select and/or adjust the formatting options, and click **Close**.

UICKSTEPS

WORKING WITH CHARTS

Charts are highly flexible, and you can easily change several of their characteristics.

RESIZE A CHART

1. Click the chart. Eight sizing handles (sets of faint dots in the corners and middle of each side) appear on the expanded border of the chart area.

2. Point to a sizing handle. The mouse pointer becomes a double-headed arrow.

3. Drag to increase or decrease the chart size. The plot area changes accordingly.

POSITION A CHART

You can move a chart to other programs by other means (the Cut and Move Chart commands), but to adjust its location within the Excel window, it's generally easier to simply drag it into the position you want.

1. Click the chart.

2. Point to the chart border (but not to a sizing handle). The mouse pointer becomes a cross with four arrowheads.

3. Drag the chart into the position you want.

REMOVE A CHART

When removing a chart, make sure you click or right-click the chart area, not a chart element (verify this by clicking the **Format** tab (Chart Tools) and seeing Chart Area displayed in the Current Selection group).

Click the chart area, and press **DELETE**.

–Or–

Right-click the chart area, and click **Cut**.

INSERT A CHART SHEET

1. Right-click the worksheet tab to the right of where you want the new chart sheet, and click **Insert**.

Continued . . .

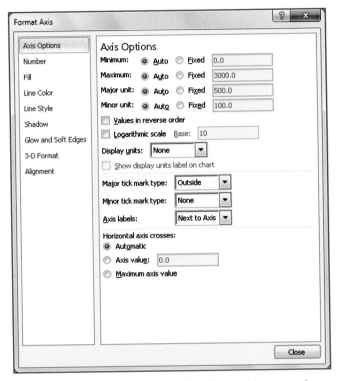

Figure 6-15: **You can get very detailed when making manual formatting changes.**

Use Charts

Charts can be moved, copied, printed, and enhanced with shapes, pictures, and text, and analyzed with trendlines, standard deviation indicators, and—new to Excel 2010—sparklines.

Add Charts Elsewhere

Charts used within Office 2010 programs (Microsoft Excel, Microsoft Word, and Microsoft PowerPoint) appear and behave almost identically, allowing you to easily share information among the three programs.

WORKING WITH CHARTS *(Continued)*

2. In the Insert dialog box General tab, double-click the **Chart** icon. The chart sheet is inserted and is named "Chart *x*."

3. Add a chart to the new chart sheet. (See "Choose a Chart Location" and "Add Charts Elsewhere" in this chapter for ways to move and copy charts.)

REVERT A CHART'S STYLING

Sometimes you can get carried away with visual customizations and want to start over with a basic appearance. You can quickly remove styling changes and reset a chart or individual elements to match the attributes of the workbook's theme.

1. Click the chart or chart element you want to revert.

2. In the Format tab (Chart Tools) Current Selection group, click **Reset To Match Style**.

   –Or–

   Right-click the chart and click **Reset To Match Style**.

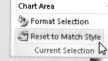

NOTE

When charts are copied or moved within Excel (except when using the Picture paste option), a relationship is maintained with their underlying worksheet data. Charts and underlying data tables in the same workbook are updated according to your calculation settings in the Excel Options Formulas and Advanced areas. When charts and their underlying data are in different workbooks, updates occur just as when they are in the same worksheet—if all workbooks are open. Charts in closed workbooks are updated when you next open them.

MOVE AND COPY A CHART WITHIN EXCEL

You can relocate both embedded charts and charts that have been placed on their own chart sheets. Any changes to the underlying data will be updated in the chart, according to calculations options selected for the workbook (see Chapter 4 for more information on recalculating).

1. Right-click the chart and click **Cut** to move it.

   –Or–

   Click **Copy** to copy the chart.

2. Right-click the upper-leftmost cell where you want the chart, either in the same or another workbook, and click one of the three paste options:

- **Keep Source Formatting** copies the theme and formatting from the worksheet where the chart originated.

- **Use Destination Theme** applies the theme of the destination worksheet to the chart.

- **Picture** takes a snapshot of the chart in the originating worksheet and pastes it as a graphic in the destination worksheet. Chart data and elements lose their association with the originating worksheet.

USE CHARTS IN WORD AND POWERPOINT

Excel is primarily a data collection and analysis program; Word and PowerPoint present data and other information. You can use Office 2010 to achieve the best of both worlds by using Excel to collect, retain, and manipulate the data and copying the charts to Word and PowerPoint for use in documents and presentations. You have several options as to the relationship between the data in Excel and the charts in other programs.

1. In Excel, right-click in a blank area of the chart, and click **Copy** (or use one of several alternative copying techniques).

2. Open Word 2010 or PowerPoint 2010. Click where you want the Excel chart inserted, and in their respective Home tab Clipboard group, click the **Paste** down arrow.

TIP

Besides copying and pasting Excel charts into Word and PowerPoint, you can copy charts into many other programs using the paste option available within each program. The results will be similar to using the Picture paste option, that is, a static snapshot of the chart.

3. Click one of the paste options, as described next. The chart will appear in Word or PowerPoint as it did in Excel, shown in Figure 6-16.

- **Keep Source Formatting** copies the chart as it appears in Excel.

- **Use Destination Theme** resets the chart's styling to match the current theme in Word or PowerPoint, providing a more unified look.

A familiar set of charting tools awaits your pasted chart in Word or PowerPoint

Figure 6-16: **Charts are easily copied from Excel to Word and PowerPoint, where you can link to the data and use charting tools to modify the formatting.**

TIP

In the vein of "too much of a good thing," your formatting can become so onerous that the speed at which the chart refreshes, or redraws, itself can be adversely affected, especially when linked to other programs. To compensate for this sluggishness, you can display your charts in Draft mode, which increases the refresh rate by removing screen-intensive formatting, such as chart area fills. To change modes, on the Design (Chart Tools) tab, click the **Draft** down arrow in the Mode group, and select the mode (Draft or Normal) and whether to apply a mode to all charts.

- **Link And Keep Source Formatting** copies the chart with the formatting, styles, and themes from the Excel workbook and maintains a link with the source workbook so that changes made to the data are updated in the Word or PowerPoint chart as well (assuming the link isn't broken by removing the workbook or deleting the data). Updates are made automatically when both source and destination documents are opened, unless default settings have been changed.

- **Link And Use Destination Theme** copies the chart and applies the theme of the destination document or slide and maintains a link with the source workbook so that changes made to the data are updated in the Word or PowerPoint chart as well (assuming the link isn't broken by removing the workbook or deleting the data). Updates are made automatically when both source and destination documents are opened, unless default settings have been changed.

- **Picture** inserts the chart as a standalone picture. No changes to the structure are allowed by the destination program, and no data updates are provided by Excel.

Analyze Charts

"Past performance does not guarantee future results," as the saying goes, but Excel can analyze plotted data to predict possible trends, show differences in data series, point out high-low values (see Figure 6-17), and show errors. However, not all analysis tools are available for all chart types. Table 6-3 shows which tools are available for specific chart types. The more common analysis tools are described next.

ANALYSIS CHARTING TOOLS	AVAILABLE CHART TYPES AND SUB-TYPES
Trendlines	Column, Bar, Line, 2-D, Stock, XY, Bubble (no stacked charts)
Drop Lines	Area, Line
High-Low Lines	2-D Line
Up/Down Bars	Line, Stock (added by default to stock charts)
Error Bars	Column, Line, Stacked, Bar, Area, XY, Stock, Bubble

*Table 6-3: **Available Analysis Charting Tools***

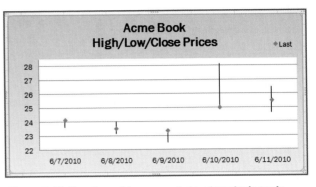

Figure 6-17: *Excel provides several visual analysis tools specific to chart types.*

ADD A TRENDLINE

Trendlines interpret a data series and make projections for the existing data or project the current trend into the future (see Figure 6-1). To add one or more trendlines to your chart:

1. Click a data series in the chart that you want analyzed.

2. In the Layout tab (Chart Tools) Analysis group, click **Trendline** and click the type of trendline you want to apply. An addition is made to the legend, identifying the trendline.

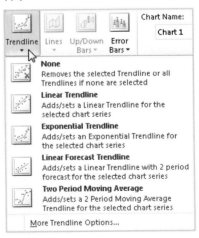

3. Repeat step 2 to add additional trendline types.

4. To fine-tune trendlines, double-click the trendline you want to change.

 –Or–

 Right-click the trendline and click **Format Trendline**.

5. In the Format Trendline dialog box, click **Trendline Options**. Change any parameters, including type, the name as it appears in the legend, and forecast periods (Figure 6-1 shows a trendline with a one-period forecast). Click **Close** when finished.

SHOW ERRORS

You can add indicators that show the margin of error of your data series, as shown in Figure 6-18.

1. Click a data series in the chart that you want to add error bars to.

 –Or–

 If you want to add error bars to all series, do not select any.

> **NOTE**
>
> Standard error and standard deviation are measures of spread (typically from the mean) used in statistical analysis.

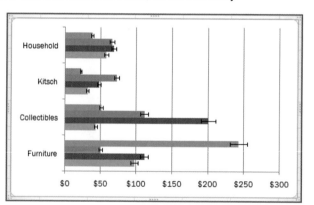

Figure 6-18: **These error bars show the margin of error to be plus or minus 5 percent of each data series value.**

2. In the Layout tab (Chart Tools) Analysis group, click **Error Bars** and click the type of error bar that you want to apply.

3. To fine-tune error bars for a data series, double-click the error bar for the data series you want to change.

 –Or–

 Right-click the error bar, and click **Format Error Bars Options**.

4. In the Format Error Bars dialog box, click *Horizontal* or *Vertical* **Error Bars** (which option you see depends on the attitude of the error bars/chart type). Change any parameters, including the amount of the error bar, whether the error bar represents a plus/minus amount, and whether the ends are capped or not.

5. Click **Close** when finished.

Print a Chart

You can print a chart, along with data and other worksheet objects (see Chapter 5), or you can choose to print just the chart, as described here.

1. Select the embedded chart or a chart located on a chart sheet.

2. Click the **File** tab, and click **Print**. Under Settings, the **Print Selected Chart** option is chosen by default. Select a printer and any additional printing options. Click **Print** when ready.

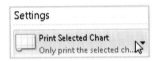

Settings

Print Selected Chart
Only print the selected ch...

Create Sparklines

As the name implies, sparklines add some dazzle to your work. Without having to navigate to other areas of a worksheet or workbook to view full-sized charts in order to visually interpret data, sparklines provide a convenient, albeit small, way to easily show background data in a *single cell*.

UICKSTEPS

WORKING WITH SPARKLINES

You know Microsoft believes it is on to something big when it devotes a new contextual tab to a feature, as is the case for sparklines in Excel 2010. Much like with conventional charting, there are a variety of options to display, format, and use sparklines.

Continued . . .

![clock icon] **QUICKSTEPS**

WORKING WITH SPARKLINES (Continued)

CHANGE THE SPARKLINE TYPE

You can easily switch between the two similar sparkline types, Line and Column ▬ ■ ▬ ■ , in order to convey your data in more meaningful ways (the third Sparkline type, Win/Lose, similar to the 100% stacked column chart, has a more specific usage and doesn't lend itself well to changing to other types).

1. Select your current sparkline.
2. In the Design (Sparkline Tools) tab Type group, click **Line** or **Column** to change the selected sparkline.

DISPLAY KEY VALUES

You can easily identify key values in a sparkline.

1. Select the sparkline.
2. In the Design (Sparkline Tools) tab Show/Hide group, select the check box next to the type of data point you want to identify on the sparkline (highest/lowest points, first/last points, negative points, or—only relevant to Line sparklines— markers (shown next), which show the placement of each value in the range on the line.)
3. Remove identifying points and markers by clearing their respective check boxes.

FORMAT SPARKLINES AND MARKERS

You can select the color for sparklines, markers, and points, as well as change the weight for line sparklines.

1. Select the sparkline or a group of sparklines.
2. To quickly see several combinations of sparklines and points/markers color combinations, click the **More** down arrow in the Design (Sparkline Tools) tab Style group, and select one of the combinations (points/markers are only shown if you have them selected in the Show/Hide group).

Continued . . .

For example, if you wanted to show price performance for a series of stocks in a presentation, you could put a sparkline next to each stock's name, as shown in Figure 6-19. As with standard charting features, once you have a sparkline created, Excel provides several formatting options to change the appearance and style of your sparklines.

Sparklines are created very simply from existing data.

1. Open a worksheet that contains the data you want to show as one or more sparklines. Arrange your worksheet so that you have a blank column where you want the sparklines to appear.

2. In the Insert tab Sparklines group, click the type of sparkline you want. In all cases, the Create Sparklines dialog box appears.

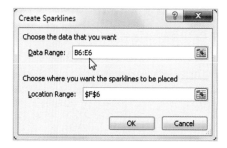

3. Select the data range you want to include in the sparkline. (I find it works best to select the first row of a range.) The range displays in the Data Range box.

4. Click **Collapse Dialog** 🔲 next to Location Range, and click the cell where you want the sparkline for the first row. Click **OK**. A sparkline appears in the cell.

QUICKSTEPS

WORKING WITH SPARKLINES (Continued)

–Or–

Use the Sparkline Color ✎ ▾ and Marker Color
■▾ tools in the Style group to select individual
colors for the specific sparkline features.

3. To change the weight of sparkline lines, click the
Sparkline Color down arrow, click **Weight**, and
select the weight/thickness of your line.

CHANGE AXIS PARAMETERS

You can modify how the horizontal and vertical sparkline
axes are used to present your data.

1. Select the sparkline or a group of sparklines.

2. In the Design (Sparkline Tools) tab Group group,
click **Axis**. A menu of options provides several
variations on how to plot your data.

3. Select the option you want, or click one of the
Custom Value choices to set your own parameters.

REMOVE SPARKLINES

You can remove individual sparklines as well as sparkline
groups.

- To remove an individual sparkline, select the
sparkline, and in the Design (Sparkline Tools) tab
Group group, click **Clear**.

- To remove several selected sparklines or sparkline
groups, select the sparklines (use **CTRL+CLICK**
for noncontiguous sparklines) or select the group.
In the Design (Sparkline Tools) tab Group group,
click the **Clear** down arrow, and choose the
applicable clear option.

5. Point to the **Fill** handle in the lower-right corner of the sparkline cell, and drag down
the column the number of rows in your range. When you release the mouse button,
sparklines are applied to the other cells, much like dragging a formula uses relative
addressing to copy a formula to adjacent cells (see Figure 6-19).

4th Qtr	Total Yr
$39,876	$137,590
$6,082	$23,276
$16,983	$63,987
$28,721	$109,330
$91,662	$334,183

Horizontal Axis Options

✓ General Axis Type

Date Axis Type...

Show Axis

Plot Data Right-to-Left

Vertical Axis Minimum Value Options

✓ Automatic for Each Sparkline

Same for All Sparklines

Custom Value...

Vertical Axis Maximum Value Options

✓ Automatic for Each Sparkline

Same for All Sparklines

Custom Value...

NOTE

Sparklines created by defining a location range, either
in the Create Sparklines dialog box or by dragging a fill
handle, are grouped together within
a blue border. See the "Working with
Sparklines" QuickSteps for information
on ungrouping sparklines.

$39,876	
$6,082	
$16,983	
$28,721	
$91,662	

Clear ▾

Clear Selected Sparklines

Clear Selected Sparkline Groups

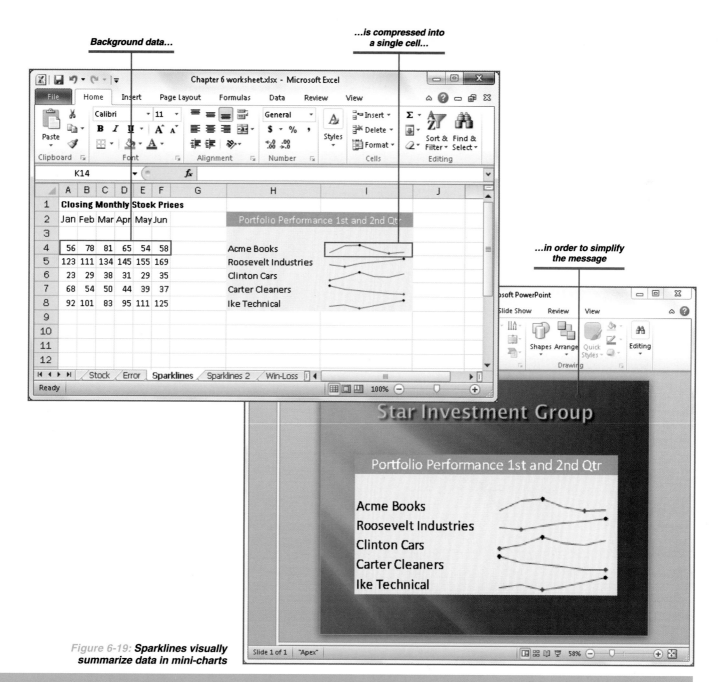

Background data...

...is compressed into a single cell...

...in order to simplify the message

Figure 6-19: **Sparklines visually summarize data in mini-charts**

Chapter 7
Working with Illustrations

Over the years Excel (as well as its other Microsoft Office brethren) has evolved from being a one-trick pony (spreadsheets, in the case of Excel) to being a multifaceted program that incorporates the tools and features of what used to be the niche of other programs into its own. This expansion of features is no better demonstrated than in the use of graphic elements to add life, clarity, and just some plain fun to the staid world of numbers and calculations. Under the umbrella of *illustrations*, Excel provides several different approaches to allow you to add visually enhancing media to your worksheets. You can simply insert pictures such as photos, select from an exhaustive library of clip art from Office.com, or insert your own screen captures; or, you can add prebuilt designs in the form of various shapes or add structured collections of graphics called SmartArt.

UNDERSTANDING ILLUSTRATIONS

The term *illustrations* is a catch-all name for the several types of graphics that you can use in Excel (it also happens to be the name of the group on the Insert tab where they can be found). Illustrations include the following:

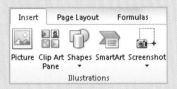

- **Pictures** are separate files, typically photos, in formats such as .jpg, .gif, and .bmp.

- **Clip art** consists of separate files, generally small drawings and icons, located in collections on your computer or found on Office.com.

- **Shapes** are prebuilt, simple graphics of common building-block drawings such as circles, lines, arrows, flowchart elements, and callouts. Integrated with shapes is WordArt, a tool to add graphic artist–type effects to associated text.

- **SmartArt** are shapes that have been enhanced and grouped together with text elements to provide prebuilt templates to demonstrate common interrelations such as processes, cycles, and hierarchies.

- **Screenshots** are graphic "captures" of what is displayed on your screen, such as windows, toolbars, and portions of Web pages. (The illustrations in this book are mostly screen captures).

Continued . . .

Of course, once the illustrations are on your worksheet, you have at your disposal a deep set of formatting, image enhancing, and other customization tools.

In this chapter you will learn how to insert, modify, format, and manage illustrations, as well as how to arrange, resize, and position them.

Add Illustrations

The first step to adding visual enhancements to your worksheet (and sometimes the last) is to simply insert the illustration.

Add Shapes

Shapes are initially added to the worksheet from the Insert tab. Once positioned on your worksheet, you can easily change the shape to any other shape in the gallery.

ADD A SHAPE

1. In the Insert tab Illustrations group, click **Shapes** to open the full shapes gallery. The shapes gallery displays dozens of shape icons, divided into several categories, as shown in Figure 7-1.

2. Click the shape you want. Your mouse pointer turns into a small cross.

3. Drag your cross pointer to the approximate location and size you want. In the case of the freeform drawing shapes, see the "Working with Curves" QuickSteps.

4. Release the mouse button when finished. The shape is surrounded by a selection border and handles (see "Working with Illustrations" later in the chapter for information on selecting shapes and using handles), and is filled with a color determined by the workbook's theme (see Chapter 3 for more information on working with themes).

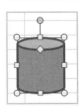

UNDERSTANDING ILLUSTRATIONS

(Continued)

Excel 2010 continues the trend of recent Office releases that blur the distinction between various types of graphics and makes working with them a more unified experience. The result is a tightly integrated grouping that shares similar formatting, sizing, and other attributes. No need to wonder what sort of illustration you are working on—simply select the illustration, and contextual tabs are displayed on the ribbon, providing quick access to many galleries of prebuilt designs, styles, and other tools. You can achieve more control by changing the component elements of these prebuilt offerings (such as fill, outline, and special effects), or you can use a common Formatting dialog box that lets you modify the formatting attributes in fine detail.

NOTE

After you have at least one shape selected on your worksheet, the contextual Format tab (Drawing Tools) is displayed on the ribbon. From here, you can access the primary tools for working on shapes, as well as insert additional shapes from its Insert Shapes group.

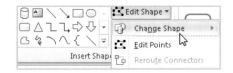

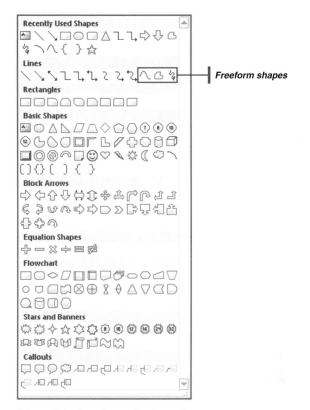

Figure 7-1: **There is no shortage of shapes you can choose from.**

CHANGE FROM ONE SHAPE TO ANOTHER

You can easily switch shapes once you have inserted one on a worksheet. There is no need to delete your initial choice and start over.

1. Click the shape to select it.

2. In the Format tab (Drawing Tools) Insert Shapes group, click **Edit Shape** and click **Change Shape**. The same shapes gallery displays as you saw when you inserted a shape (see Figure 7-1).

3. Click the new icon you want to use. Any formatting you may have applied to the original shape is retained, and the shape assumes the new look.

QUICKSTEPS

WORKING WITH CURVES

Freeform tools are available to draw curved shapes.

CREATE A CURVE

Open the shapes gallery from the Insert tab Illustrations group or the Format tab (Drawing Tools) Insert Shapes group. The freeform tools are located on the right end of the Lines category (see Figure 7-1).

- Click **Curve** and click the cross pointer to establish the curve's starting point. Move the pointer and click to set an inflection point, and then continue to move the pointer and click to create other curvatures. Double-click to set the end point and complete the drawing.

- Click **Freeform** and use a combination of curve and scribble techniques. Click the cross pointer to establish curvature points, and/or drag the pencil pointer to create other designs. Double-click to set the end point and complete the drawing.

- Click **Scribble** and drag the pencil icon to create the shape you want. Release the mouse button to complete the drawing.

ADJUST A CURVE

1. Right-click the curve and click **Edit Points**. Black rectangles (*vertices*) appear at the top of the curvature points.

Continued . . .

Add Text

You can add text to an existing shape or within its own shape (text box). You can use standard editing and formatting tools to modify text used in shapes (see Chapter 2). You can also apply WordArt styling to add some zing to your text (see "Add WordArt Styling to Text" later in the chapter for WordArt styling and formatting techniques).

ADD TEXT TO A SHAPE

Text added in this way is integral to the shape. If you have more than a few words or phrases to add, a separate text box (described next) may prove easier to work with.

1. Right-click the shape that you want to add text to (you cannot add text in this way to a shape that is filled with a picture).

2. Click **Edit Text**. An insertion bar is added to the approximate middle of the shape.

3. Start typing text. The text wraps to subsequent lines as necessary and is contained within a text area that conforms to the shape, with margins separating the text from the edges of the shape.

4. Highlight the text to edit it. A selection box surrounds selected text.

5. To format the text, point at the selected text. A faint mini-toolbar displays above it. Move the mouse pointer over the toolbar to gain full use of its tools.

–Or–

Use the text tools on the Home tab to apply the formatting you want.

In either case, see Chapter 2 for information on the individual text formatting tools you can use.

WORKING WITH CURVES *(Continued)*

2. Select a vertex and a dumbbell-shaped curve handle appears.

3. Drag the ends of the curve handle to develop the degree of curve you want.

4. Change any other vertex, and click outside the curve when finished.

ADD CURVATURE POINTS

1. If there are no vertices on the shape, right-click the curve and click **Edit Points**.

2. Right-click the edge of a curve where you want the point, and click **Add Point**. Then drag the point or its curve handles as needed to form the curve you want.

REMOVE LINES IN A CLOSED CURVE

Right-click the line you want removed, and click **Delete Segment**. (You may need to first right-click any line in an open curve and click **Close Path** for the Delete Segment option to be available.)

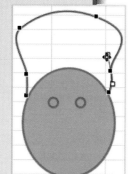

TIP

To fit text into a text box that extends beyond the boundaries of the text box, right-click the text box, and click **Format Shape**. Click **Text Box** in the left pane, and under Autofit, click the **Resize Shape To Fit Text** check box. Click **Close**.

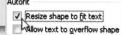

ADD A TEXT BOX

A text box is simply a shape that contains text. You can move, size, or rotate the text box as you can with other shapes.

1. In the Insert tab Text group, click **Text Box**.

–Or–

In the Insert tab Illustrations group, click **Shapes** and click the **Text Box** icon (leftmost in the first row) in the Basic Shapes group.

The mouse pointer turns into an elongated cross.

2. Click in the approximate location where you want the text box (the mouse pointer changes to a standard crosshairs), and drag across and down the worksheet. Release the mouse button when you have the text box the approximate size you want.

3. Start typing text. The text wraps to subsequent lines as necessary and is contained within the sides of the text box, extending beyond the bottom of the border if necessary.

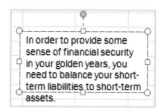

4. Highlight the text you want to edit.

5. To format the text, point at selected text, and a faint mini-toolbar displays above it. Move the mouse pointer over the toolbar to gain full use of its tools.

–Or–

Use the text tools on the Home tab to apply the formatting you want.

In either case, see Chapter 2 for information on the individual text formatting tools you can use.

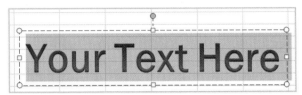

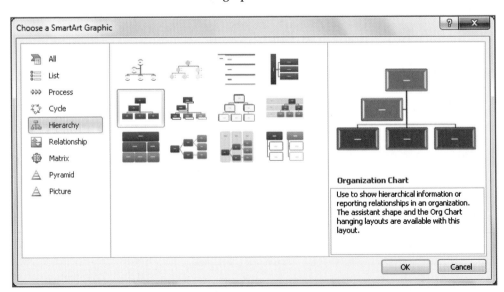

Figure 7-2: *In just two clicks, you can add a text box with WordArt applied.*

ADD WORDART

1. In the Insert tab Text group, click **WordArt** and click an initial style to apply to your text, shown in Figure 7-2. A text box with sample text displays on your worksheet.

Your Text Here

2. Type your text. See "Add WordArt Styling to Text" later in the chapter to apply additional WordArt styling.

Use SmartArt

Excel provides predefined shapes for inserting many flexible and professional-looking diagrams and connecting symbols. Figure 7-3 shows the categories of SmartArt shapes that are available, including a description of the selected graphic.

Figure 7-3: *SmartArt shapes offer you many choices for adding professional and complex collections of shapes to your worksheets.*

To choose between the categories, you must be clear on what you are trying to show, what structure best displays the data, and how much data there is to display (some of the shapes do not hold a lot of text).

To insert a SmartArt shape:

1. In the Insert tab Illustrations group, click **SmartArt**. The Choose A SmartArt Graphic dialog box appears (see Figure 7-3).

2. Click the category on the left, and then select a shape in the middle. When you click a shape, a display of it is previewed on the right.

3. When you find the shape you want, select it, and click **OK** to close the dialog box and insert the shape. The SmartArt Tools tabs, Design and Format, are now available, as shown in Figure 7-4.

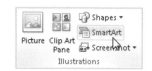

Figure 7-4: *Using the SmartArt Tools Design and Format tabs, you can change the color, layouts, and styles of SmartArt shapes, as well as add or remove shape elements.*

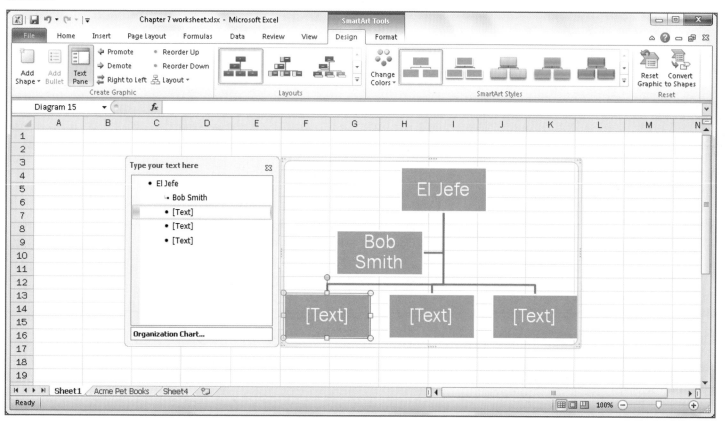

4. In the Type Your Text Here text box, click a bullet and type your text. As you type, the
   text will be recorded in the appropriate shape.

   –Or–

   Click the text box directly, and type your text. The text will size to fit the shape.

Insert Pictures

You can browse for picture files or use the Clip Art task pane to assist you.

BROWSE FOR PICTURES

1. Select the cell where you want the upper-leftmost corner of the picture. (Don't be too
   concerned with the exact placement; you can easily move the image where you want it.)

2. In the Insert tab Illustrations group, click **Picture**. The Insert Picture dialog box appears
   (see Figure 7-5).

3. Browse to the picture file you want, and select it. Click **Insert**. The image displays
   on the worksheet, as shown in Figure 7-6. (See the "Using Handles and Borders to
   Change Illustrations" QuickSteps later in the chapter to see how to move and resize
   the picture.)

SEARCH FOR PICTURES

1. Select the cell where you want the upper-leftmost corner of the picture.

2. In the Insert tab Illustrations group, click **Clip Art**. The Clip Art task pane opens, similar
   to Figure 7-7, on the right side of the Excel window.

NOTE

The Format tab (SmartArt Tools) contains many tools to change the shape, such as Shape Fill, Shape Outline, and Shape Effects. See "Format Illustrations and Text" later in the chapter for information on formatting techniques. However, the Shapes group is a bit unique. It allows you to make selected graphic elements larger or smaller, or to change the shape. If your graphic is styled in 3-D, you can edit it in 2-D in order to resize or move it.

NOTE

"Clip Art task pane" is a bit of misnomer. It is used to search for and organize conventional clip art (drawing) files, but also handles other media files, such as photos, sound, and video. In this section, clip art and/or photo files are referred to as "pictures." To complicate the terminology a bit more, screen captures, described in "Take Screenshots" later in the chapter, also have picture formatting properties, though they are not saved as individual files, and thus are not included in this section.

Details pane   Preview pane   Change the size of thumbnails   Use to display/hide preview pane

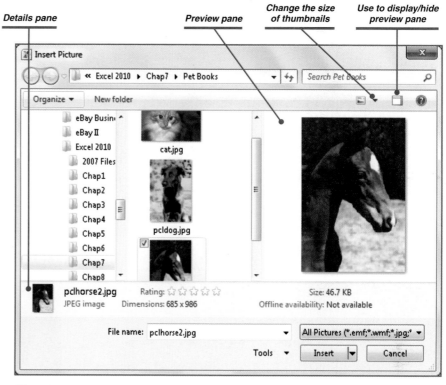

Figure 7-5: **Windows 7 displays picture files as thumbnails so you can select, preview, and review image details.**

TIP

If you do not see thumbnails of your picture files in the Insert Picture dialog box, or if you want to change the size of the ones you do see, click the **Change Your Views** down arrow on the dialog box toolbar (see Figure 7-5), and click the size of icons you want. To view/hide the details and/or preview panes in Windows 7, click **Organize**, click **Layout**, and select/unselect the applicable panes.

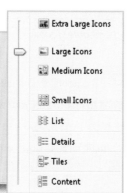

3. In the **Search For** text box, type a keyword, such as people or pet.

4. Click the **Results Should Be** down arrow, and deselect all file types *except* **Illustrations** and **Photographs**.

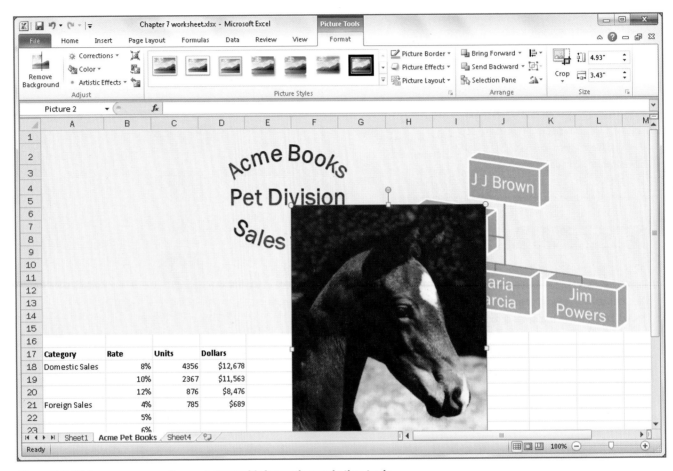

Figure 7-6: **Pictures appear on the worksheet with formatting and other tools.**

TIP

You can change the location and size of a task pane, such as the Clip Art task pane. To move the task pane, drag the pane's title bar to where you want the pane. To size the task pane, point to its border, and drag the double-headed arrow to increase or decrease the pane to the size you want (if the task pane is "docked" on either the left or right side, you can only drag the side closest to the worksheet).

5. Click **Go**. In a few moments, thumbnails of the search results will appear (see Figure 7-7).

6. Click a thumbnail to insert it on your worksheet.

   –Or–

   Point to a thumbnail, click its down arrow, and click **Insert**.

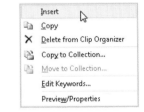

Insert
Copy
Delete from Clip Organizer
Copy to Collection...
Move to Collection...
Edit Keywords...
Preview/Properties

Figure 7-7: *The Clip Art task pane helps you find pictures and then organize them.*

ADD PICTURES FROM OFFICE.COM

1. Select the cell where you want the upper-leftmost corner of the picture.

2. In the Insert tab Illustrations group, click **Clip Art**. The Clip Art task pane opens.

3. Click the **Find More At Office.com** link at the bottom of the task pane. Assuming you have an active Internet connection, you are connected to the Microsoft Office Images page, shown in Figure 7-8.

4. Use the **Search** box to locate the selection of pictures you're looking for, or click one of the pictures highlighted on the page. The picture is shown in an enlarged view along with characteristics of the image and options to acquire it.

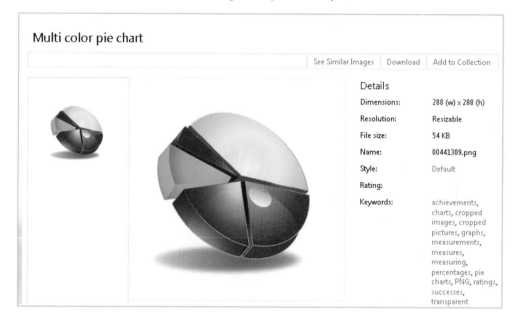

Take Screenshots

Screenshots (also called screen captures and screen grabs) allow you to copy a portion of what you see on your screen, be it an icon, window, or the entire screen. In Excel, you can select any open windows to capture (except for Excel itself), or you can drag a selection rectangle across whatever area of the screen you want.

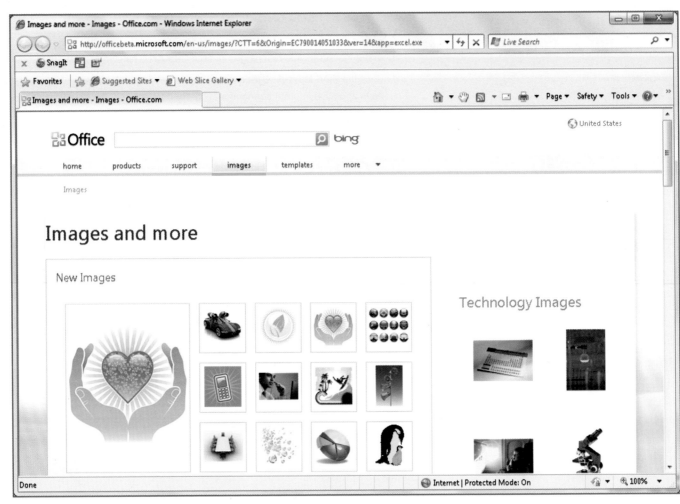

*Figure 7-8: **Office.com offers additional illustration files for free download.***

The capture is placed on your worksheet and can be modified using the Picture Tools formatting features.

1. Minimize the Excel window, and arrange your desktop with the program(s), window(s), and objects you want to capture.

2. Restore the Excel window, and in the Insert tab Illustrations group, click **Screenshot**.

USING PICTURES

Pictures, unlike shapes, are individual files with extensions such as JPG, GIF, and WMF that are stored on your computer or are available from other sources, such as a network, DVD, or the Internet. Pictures are photos produced by digital cameras or scanners, or clip art consisting of images created in drawing programs such as Abode Illustrator or Microsoft Paint. Table 7-1 lists the picture file formats supported by Excel.

Although pictures have attributes that are unique to their file format origin (for example, brightness and contrast), they also can be combined into shapes as a fill, thereby conforming to the size and outline of the shape. In this case, the graphic will have two Format tabs: one to accommodate the shape and one for the picture. In addition, screenshots taken from within Excel share the same Picture Tools formatting tools (see "Take Screenshots" later in the chapter). While it all can sound confusing, in practice, it's quite simple. Select the object, and Excel will provide the appropriate tools.

FILE TYPE	EXTENSION
Windows Bitmap	BMP, RLE, DIB
Computer Graphics Metafile	CGM
Enhanced Windows Metafile/Compressed Enhanced Windows Metafile	EMF/EMZ
Encapsulated PostScript	EPS
FlashPix	FPX
Graphics Interchange Format	GIF, GFA
Joint Photographic Experts Group	JPG, JPEG, JFIF, JPE
Macintosh PICT/Compressed Macintosh PICT	PCT, PICT/PCZ
Portable Network Graphics	PNG
Tagged Image File Format	TIF, TIFF
Windows Metafile/Compressed Windows Metafile	WMF/WMZ
WordPerfect Graphics	WPG

Table 7-1: **Picture File Formats Supported by Excel**

3. From the Available Screen Shots area, select one of your open windows.

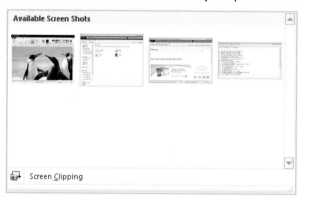

–Or–

Click **Screen Clipping**. Use the large black cross to drag across the area you want, as shown in Figure 7-9, and release the mouse button when finished.

In both cases, the image you selected is displayed on your worksheet surrounded by selection handles.

TIP

When doing manual screenshots, drag over a slightly larger area than what you're looking to capture. You can more easily crop the picture to a smaller, precise size after it's on your worksheet than you can add more image back in.

Drawing Tools	Picture Tools
Format	Format

Figure 7-9: *Screenshots are a powerful tool, allowing you to use your screen to provide visual additions to your worksheet.*

Working with Illustrations

You can perform several actions on illustrations, such as size, move, rotate, and combine with other illustrations, to get them into just the right position and configuration you need to accentuate your Excel data. (By "illustrations," I'm talking about everything that is in the Insert tab's Illustrations group, including pictures, clip art, shapes, SmartArt, and screenshots.)

Select, View, and Delete Illustrations

How you select an illustration depends on whether you're working with single or multiple illustrations on a worksheet. When you select multiple illustrations, you can perform actions that affect them all as a group.

CAUTION

There are a number of places in Excel (Picture Tools group and several dialog boxes, for example) where you can choose to reset a picture or shape to a previous state. Particularly for pictures, they can be reset to a state several actions from the most recent one. It's safer to click **Undo** on the Quick Access toolbar (above the File tab) to cancel the most recent action or click the **Undo** down arrow and select how far back you want to cancel from the list.

Group Objects	ome
Rotate Object	
Resize Object	Frar
Crop Picture	**B**
Resize Object	

To keep the selected illustrations as a group, see the "Combining Illustrations by Grouping" QuickSteps later in the chapter. In addition, you can hide illustrations from view.

SELECT A SINGLE ILLUSTRATION

Select a single illustration by clicking it. Handles will appear around the illustration that allow you to perform interactive changes (see the "Using Handles and Borders to Change Illustrations" QuickSteps).

SELECT MULTIPLE ILLUSTRATIONS

Hold down **CTRL** and click each illustration.

–Or–

1. Select an illustration and, in its contextual Format tab Arrange group, click **Selection Pane**. The Selection And Visibility task pane displays on the right side of the worksheet, listing all illustrations on the worksheet, as shown in Figure 7-10.

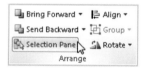

2. Hold down **CTRL** and click the illustrations you want selected. Close the task pane when finished.

HIDE AND SHOW ILLUSTRATIONS

Depending on your audience, you might want to show or hide visual enhancements (to give a clear view of the data and speed printing) you add to a worksheet. You can easily choose which ones you want to be visible.

1. Open the Selection And Visibility task pane (see the previous procedure).

2. By default, all illustrations are visible, denoted by the "eye" icon to the right of each illustration listed in the pane (you may need to horizontally expand the task pane to see the eye icon). Click the **eye** icon for any illustrations you want to be hidden.

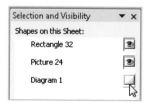

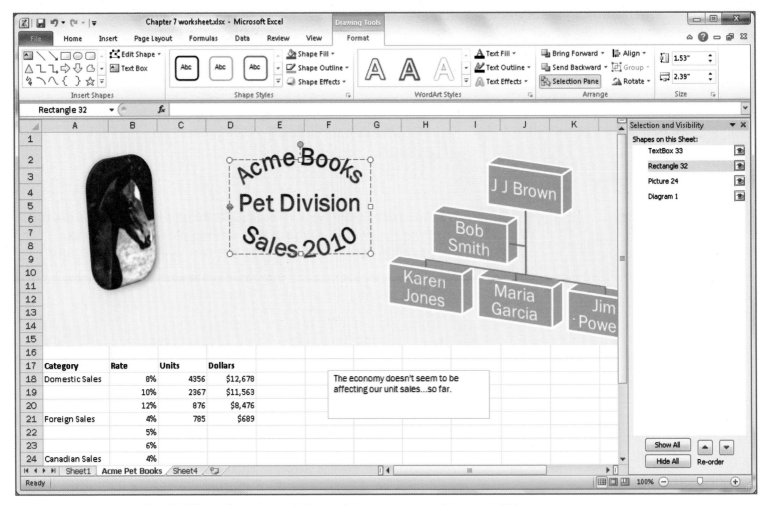

Figure 7-10: *You can see a list of all illustrations on a worksheet, select one or more, and choose to hide any.*

–Or–

To hide all illustrations, click **Hide All** at the bottom of the task pane.

3. To view hidden illustrations, click the empty check boxes next to the illustrations you want to become visible. The eye icon returns.

–Or–

To view all hidden illustrations, click **Show All** at the bottom of the task pane.

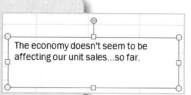

The economy doesn't seem to be affecting our unit sales...so far.

QUICKSTEPS

USING HANDLES AND BORDERS TO CHANGE ILLUSTRATIONS

Once illustrations are selected, you can interactively perform several useful actions by using the handles that surround the illustration (see Figure 7-11).

MOVE AN ILLUSTRATION

1. Point to any area on the border of the illustration other than a handle. The mouse pointer changes to a cross with arrowheads on each end.
2. Drag the illustration to the location you want.

ROTATE AN ILLUSTRATION

Drag the green dot clockwise or counterclockwise. The green dot stays in place until you release the mouse button. Hold down **SHIFT** when dragging to rotate in 15-degree increments.

CHANGE AN ILLUSTRATION'S PERSPECTIVE

If the illustration supports interactive adjustment, a yellow diamond adjustment handle is displayed.

Drag the **yellow diamond** to achieve the look you want.

Continued . . .

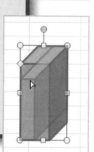

DELETE AN ILLUSTRATION

Click the illustration you want to delete, and press **DELETE**.

Crop Pictures

Pictures can be *cropped* (or trimmed) by removing area from the sides, either interactively or precisely.

CROP BY DRAGGING

1. Select the picture.
2. In the Format tab (Picture Tools) Size group, click **Crop** . Cropping marks replace the standard handles surrounding the picture.

Change perspective   Rotate the illustration   Change size in two dimensions

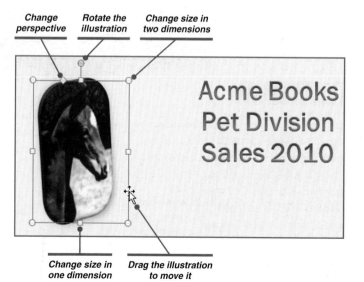

Acme Books Pet Division Sales 2010

Change size in one dimension   Drag the illustration to move it

Figure 7-11: **A selected illustration displays several handles that allow you to interactively change it.**

UICKSTEPS

USING HANDLES AND BORDERS TO CHANGE ILLUSTRATIONS (Continued)

RESIZE AN ILLUSTRATION

Drag one of the round corner sizing handles surrounding the illustration—or at either end of it, in the case of a line—in the direction you want to enlarge or reduce the size of the illustration in two dimensions.

–Or–

Drag a square sizing handle on the sides of the illustration in the direction you want to enlarge or reduce the size of the illustration in one dimension.

TIP

Hold down **SHIFT** when dragging a corner sizing handle or corner cropping mark to make proportional changes to the height and length.

TIP

To size or rotate an illustration more precisely, select the illustration and, in the Format tab Size group, click the **Height** and **Width** spinners to adjust the illustration's size. Alternatively, click the Size group **Dialog Box Launcher**. Under Size And Rotate, use the applicable spinners to make precise adjustments to rotation and size. Under Scale, select **Lock Aspect Ratio** to scale the illustration proportionally. Click **OK** when finished.

3. Place your mouse pointer over a cropping mark. Drag corner cropping marks inward to reduce the picture in two dimensions; drag a side cropping mark inward to reduce the picture in one dimension (drag a cropping mark outward to add white space to the picture). The mouse pointer turns into a cross.

4. Release the mouse button when the cutting line(s) is where you want it.

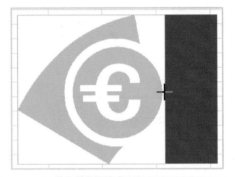

5. To remove the cropping marks and turn cropping off, click **Crop** in the Size group or press **ESC**.

CROP TO FIT A SHAPE

1. Select the picture.

2. In the Format tab (Picture Tools) Size group, click the **Crop** down arrow, and click **Crop To Shape**.

3. In the shapes gallery (see Figure 7-1), click the shape that you want the picture to assume. You can quickly create some interesting designs.

Size

Size and rotate

Height:	1.22"	Width:	1.05"
Rotation:	343°		

Scale

Height:	100%	Width:	100%

☑ Lock aspect ratio

☐ Relative to original picture size

TIP

To quickly size, crop, rotate, or change positions in a stack, right-click the picture. A box of tools appears above or below the standard context menu.

2.24"	
3.25"	

Position Illustrations

While illustrations can be positioned by simply dragging them, Excel also provides a number of other techniques that help you adjust where an illustration is in relation to other illustrations and objects on the worksheet.

MOVE ILLUSTRATIONS INCREMENTALLY

Select the illustration or group (see the "Combining Illustrations by Grouping" QuickSteps), and press the arrow key (for example, **UP ARROW**) in the direction you want to move it in small increments.

REPOSITION THE ORDER OF STACKED ILLUSTRATIONS

You can stack illustrations by simply dragging one on top of another.

Right-click the illustration you want to change, and point to **Bring Forward** (see Figure 7-12). Then:

- Click **Bring Forward** to move the illustration up one level (same as Bring To Front if there are only two illustrations in the stack).
- Click **Bring To Front** to move the illustration to the top of the stack.

–Or–

Right-click the illustration you want to change, and point to **Send Backward**. Then:

- Click **Send Backward** to move the illustration back one level (same as Send To Back if there are only two illustrations in the stack).
- Click **Send To Back** to move the illustration to the bottom of the stack.

ALIGN ILLUSTRATIONS

You can align illustrations to your worksheet's gridlines and use the lines as an aligning tool, as well as align illustrations to one another.

- Select an illustration and in the Format tab Arrange group, click **Align**. Click **Snap To Grid** at the bottom of the menu to turn it on. When you move an illustration near a gridline, it will "snap" to the line.

- To align illustrations with one another, select the illustrations and in the Format tab Arrange group, click **Align** and click one of the vertical or horizontal alignment options on the menu.

TIP

You can use the Selection And Visibility pane to re-order stacked illustrations. Display the pane by clicking **Selection Pane** in the Format tab Arrange group. Select the object you want to re-order by clicking it on the worksheet or by clicking its name in the Shapes On This Sheet list. Click the **Bring Forward** or **Send Backward** re-order button at the bottom of the pane.

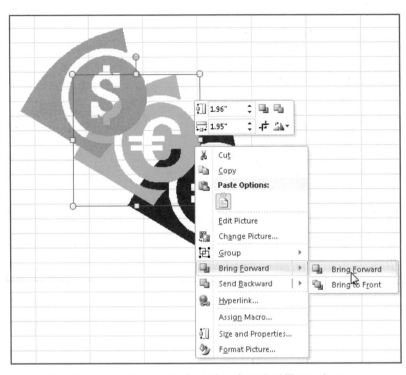

Figure 7-12: *You can easily change the order of stacked illustrations.*

QUICKSTEPS

COMBINING ILLUSTRATIONS BY GROUPING

You can combine illustrations for any number of reasons, but you typically work with multiple illustrations to build a more complex drawing. To prevent losing the positioning, sizing, and other characteristics of these components, you can group them so that they are treated as one illustration.

GROUP ILLUSTRATIONS

1. Select the illustrations to be grouped by clicking the first one and then holding down **CTRL** while selecting the others.

Continued . . .

EVENLY SPACE ILLUSTRATIONS

1. Select three or more illustrations, and in the Format tab Arrange group, click **Align**.

2. Click **Distribute Horizontally** or **Distribute Vertically**, depending on how you want the illustrations oriented.

Format Illustrations and Text

This section describes how you can apply formatting. Start by being efficiently lazy, using themes (see Chapter 3) and styles provided on the ribbon. Next, make any adjustments to the constituent attributes of the style. Finally, delve into the details provided by a common formatting dialog box.

COMBINING ILLUSTRATIONS BY GROUPING *(Continued)*

2. Right-click any of the selected illustrations, and click **Group**. Click **Group** again on the flyout menu. A single set of selection handles surrounds the perimeter of the illustrations. Coloring, positioning, sizing, and other actions now affect the illustrations as a group instead of individually (see Figure 7-13).

UNGROUP ILLUSTRATIONS

To separate a group into individual illustrations:

Right-click one of the grouped illustration, click **Group**, and click **Ungroup** on the flyout menu. Selection handles appear on each of the illustrations that made up the group.

RECOMBINE A GROUP AFTER UNGROUPING

After making a modification to an illustration that was part of a group, you don't have to reselect each component shape to reestablish the group.

Right-click any illustration that was in the group, click **Group**, and click **Regroup** on the flyout menu. A group selection border and handles surround the originally grouped illustrations.

NOTE

To cover every conceivable option for each type of illustration in Excel would fill up a book all by itself. The examples provided in this section are not exhaustive; rather, they illustrate the methodology you can apply to formatting other types of illustrations and text you will use.

Figure 7-13: **Grouping lets you treat multiple selected illustrations as one illustration.**

Use Styles

The ribbon (assuming your Excel window is at a sufficient width) displays styling samples for pictures, shapes, and WordArt. With a click or two, you can apply a professional-looking design (and then spend all the time you saved working on formulas!).

1. Select the illustration you want to apply a style to.

2. In the Format tab (the tab will be unique to Pictures, Shapes, or SmartArt tools), point to the style examples on the ribbon, shown in Figure 7-14. The illustration or text will change to reflect the style attributes.

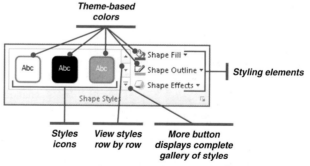

Figure 7-14: **Styling options for shapes allow you to make quick choices or provide tools for more hands-on work.**

3. When you find a style that's close to want you want, click the style icon in the particular Styles group (click the **More** button to see the complete gallery, or click the row-by-row buttons).

QUICKSTEPS

CHANGING A PICTURE'S ATTRIBUTES

In Excel, you can use several tools to format the picture, instead of the shape that contains it. These tools are available in the Format tab (Picture Tools) Adjust group.

CORRECT LIGHTING AND CLARITY

1. Click the picture to select it.

2. In the Adjust group, click **Corrections** to view a gallery of options that allow you to sharpen, soften, and adjust brightness and contrast by percentages that are greater than or less than the original setting. Point to the effects to see the changes on your picture. Click the effect you want.

3. To adjust corrections more precisely, click **Picture Correction Options** at the bottom of either gallery, and adjust the percentage of the desired effect by dragging its slider, typing a percentage, or using the respective spinner to find the value you want. Click **Close** when finished.

Continued . . .

Apply Styling Elements to Pictures

You can alter the appearance of an inserted picture by changing key elements, such as its overall shape (by converting it to SmartArt shapes); the color, weight, and style of a border or outline; and special effects, such as mirroring.

CHANGE A PICTURE'S BORDER

1. Click the picture to select it.

2. In the Format tab (Picture Tools) Picture Styles group, click **Picture Border**. The standard Office color gallery opens, along with options to change the border outline. (You will have to reopen the Picture Border menu each time you make one of the following selections.)

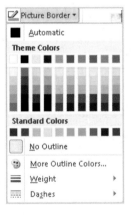

3. Click **Weight** and point to the border thickness options. The outline on your picture will change according to where your mouse pointer is placed. Click the weight you want to apply it to your picture.

4. Click **Dashes** and point to the line style you want, solid or dashed. The outline on your picture will change according to where your mouse pointer is placed. For more line options, click **More Lines**. Click the line style you want to apply it to your picture.

5. Point to a color on the color gallery, and see the immediate effect on the border. Click a color icon from Theme Colors (this changes according to the workbook theme applied) or Standard Colors, or click **More Outline Colors** for more options. (Chapter 3 describes the various color options available from the color gallery in detail.)

QUICKSTEPS

CHANGING A PICTURE'S ATTRIBUTES *(Continued)*

RECOLOR A PICTURE

You can change the color of a picture by applying an overall solid tint. For example, you can change a colored or black-and-white photo to sepia or grayscale.

1. Click the picture to select it.

2. In the Adjust group, click **Color** to view a gallery of tinting options. Point to the effects to see the changes on your picture. Click the effect you want.

APPLY FILTERING EFFECTS

As in dedicated graphic programs, you can apply one of several filters to a picture to give professional results.

1. Click the picture to select it.

2. In the Adjust group, click **Artistic Effects** to view a gallery of filtering options. Point to the effects to see the changes on your picture. Click the effect you want.

REMOVE A PICTURE'S BACKGROUND

You can accentuate the main focal point of a picture by removing its background.

1. Click the picture to select it.

2. In the Adjust group, click **Background Removal**.

COMPRESS A PICTURE

You can decrease the file size of a picture to save storage space or allow for faster online transmission.

1. Click the picture to select it.

2. In the Adjust group, click **Compress Pictures** .

3. Choose whether to apply this to the selected picture or to all pictures on the worksheet (clear the check box) and which resolution you want. Click **OK** when finished.

Continued . . .

ADD EFFECTS TO PICTURES

To add some pizzazz to your pictures, you can apply special effects that add three-dimensional and other eye-catching elements (see Figure 7-15).

1. Click the picture to select it.

2. In the Format tab (Picture Tools) Picture Styles group, click **Picture Effects**.

3. Click one of the effects' categories, and point to the options in the gallery. The picture will change according to where your mouse pointer is placed. Click the effect you want to apply (you can apply multiple effects).

Figure 7-15: **Your imagination is the only limit when working with multiple special effects.**

QUICKSTEPS

CHANGING A PICTURE'S ATTRIBUTES *(Continued)*

CHANGE A PICTURE

You can swap one picture for another, preserving formatting changes, or you can reset a picture to its original formatting.

1. Click the picture to select it.

2. In the Adjust group, click **Change Picture** 🖼️ to switch the selected picture's formatting for another picture.

   –Or–

   Click **Reset Picture** 🖼️ to remove all applied formatting.

CONVERT A PICTURE TO A SMARTART SHAPE

Typically, pictures are rectangular in shape, conforming to conventions of uniformity, balance, and function. You can create some rather interesting and creative variations of these images by changing the original outline to one of dozens of prebuilt SmartArt shapes. See "Use SmartArt" earlier in the chapter for information on working with SmartArt shapes.

1. Click the picture to select it.

2. In the Format tab (Picture Tools) Picture Styles group, click **Picture Layout**. A gallery of SmartArt shapes displays.

3. Click the SmartArt that interests you. The selected picture assumes the shape(s) of the SmartArt, as shown in Figure 7-16. (Some shapes are more conducive to assuming a picture than others.)

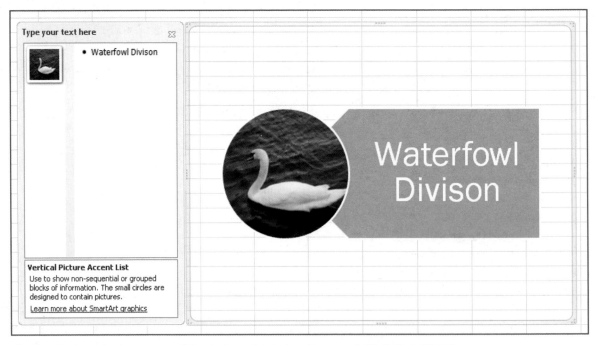

Figure 7-16: **SmartArt becomes stylish art when pictures are incorporated into SmartArt shapes.**

Change a Shape's Fill

By default, shapes are filled with a color or with a combination of colors, determined by the workbook's theme. You can change the fill color and do much more with textures, gradient fills, and even by using a picture.

CHANGE FILL COLOR

1. Click the shape to select it.

2. In the Format tab (Drawing Tools) Shape Styles group, click **Shape Fill**. A gallery of color options and other fill choices is displayed.

3. Point to a color on the color gallery, and see the immediate effect on the fill. Click a color icon from Theme Colors (they will change according to the workbook theme applied) or Standard Colors, or click **More Fill Colors** for more options. (Chapter 3 describes the various color options available from the color gallery in detail.)

USE A PICTURE

1. Click the shape to select it.

2. In the Format tab (Drawing Tools) Shape Styles group, click **Shape Fill** and click **Picture**. The Insert Picture dialog box appears.

3. Browse to locate the picture you want, select it, and click **Insert**. The picture will be inserted into the background of the shape.

SET GRADIENTS AND TEXTURES

A gradient fill flows one or more colors within a shape, from lighter to darker shades, in varying directions, transparency, and other attributes. A texture provides a consistent weave or other pattern in varying colors and designs.

1. Click the shape to select it.

2. In the Format tab (Drawing Tools) Shape Styles group, click **Shape Fill**.

3. Click **Gradient** or **Texture** to see the respective galleries.

4. If you need more control over either fill, click **More Gradients** or **More Textures** at the bottom of the respective galleries.

NOTE

Inserting a picture into a shape's fill achieves the same result as applying a shape to a picture. In either case, you can take a rectangular picture and change its boundaries.

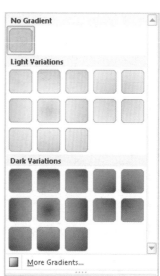

5. In the Format Shape dialog box, click **Fill** in the left pane, and click **Gradient Fill** or **Picture Or Texture Fill** to access detailed options, as shown in Figure 7-17.

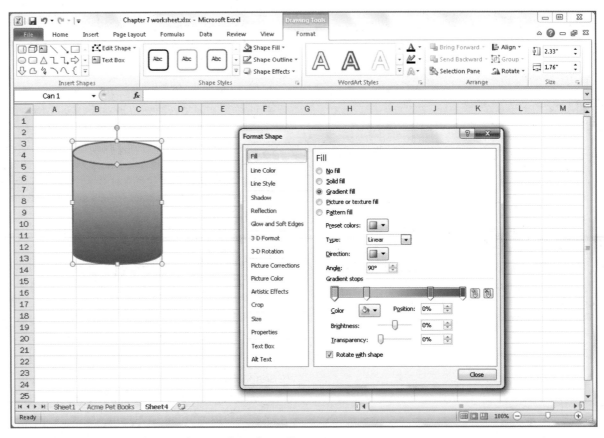

Figure 7-17: **You can get quite exact in your shape formatting.**

Add WordArt Styling to Text

WordArt styling used to be confined to text solely created by WordArt. In Excel 2007, and now in 2010, you can apply WordArt effects, such as transforming text to follow a curved path, to all text used in shapes. WordArt provides an easy and effective graphic artist's professional touch (see Figure 7-18).

Figure 7-18: ***WordArt effects can make a graphic artist out of you!***

1. Select the text to which you want to apply WordArt styling (text can be in a shape, text box, or directly from WordArt). See "Add Text" earlier in the chapter.

2. In the Format tab (Drawing Tools) WordArt Styles group, click a style to apply a prebuilt style.

Text fill

Text outline

Text effects

More button

–Or–

Click **Text Fill** or **Text Outline** to apply color and other styling to the respective elements of the text (see "Change a Picture's Border" and "Change a Shape's Fill" earlier in the chapter for information on available options).

Shadow ▶

Reflection ▶

Glow ▶

–Or–

Click **Text Effects** to view a menu of galleries that offer an abundance of special effects you can apply. Point to any option to view the effect on your text.

Bevel ▶

3-D Rotation ▶

3. Click the effect you want.

Transform ▶

TIP

To remove WordArt from a shape, select the shape and click the **More** button in the WordArt Styles group. Click **Clear WordArt** at the bottom of the gallery.

Make Detailed Formatting Changes

The Format Shape and Format Picture dialog boxes are the gateway for you to "tweak" formatting attributes to very fine detail. Shapes and pictures share a common set of formatting categories, although a particular shape or picture might not have all options available (see Figure 7-19).

To access the Format dialog box, right-click the shape or picture, and click **Format Shape** or **Format Picture**.

–Or–

Click the **Dialog Box Launcher** in the Shape Styles or Picture Styles group.

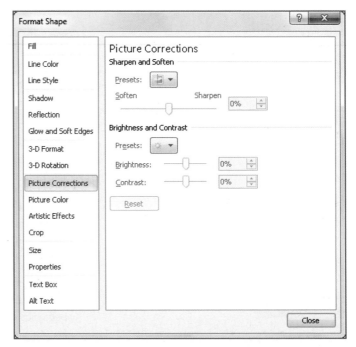

Figure 7-19: *Shapes and pictures share a common dialog box, but not all options.*

How to...

Chapter 8
Managing Data

Excel, as you've seen in other chapters, "excels" at calculating and displaying information. An often-overlooked aspect of what Excel has to offer is how well it works with more structured data. *Tables*, referred to as "lists" in early releases, contain related data that's independent of other information on the worksheet (see the "Understanding Excel Tables" QuickFacts). This chapter shows you how to create tables, how to work with them, and how to manage and organize data. In addition, you will learn how to validate data entered into a table, organize data by sorting it, retrieve just the data you want by setting up filters, and condense data by outlining and grouping. (See Chapter 10 for methods to acquire data from external sources.)

8

UNDERSTANDING EXCEL TABLES

Excel provides the ability to work with data in *tables*. Tables, like databases, consist of columns of similar data—the names of all the salespeople in a company, for example. Each salesperson covers a certain region, so this table would also need a Territory column. Each salesperson has a cell phone number; each has projected sales targets and actual sales, and so forth. You could say each salesperson has a collection of information pertaining just to them. In an Excel table, each row in the worksheet contains this collection of unique data—unique in the sense that while two or more salespeople might call Washington their territory, each row contains data for only one salesperson.

	A	B	C	D	E
1	**Last Name**	**First Name**	**Territory**	**Qtr Sales**	**Mobile**
2	Jones	Tom	Oregon	$6,876	(425) 555-4321
3	Smith	John	Washington	$4,567	(425) 555-2121
4	Garcia	Maria	Washington	$3,475	(425) 555-1212

When you work with cells in or adjacent to a table, Excel automatically "comes to the table" with several tools and features to eliminate mouse clicks and keystrokes, and basically make your work in tables easier, faster, and more efficient.

In the days before Microsoft had a database product, such as Access or SQL (Structured Query Language) Server, an Excel *list* provided basic database functions. From its database roots, you may see database terms used when referring to tables—for example, in database terminology, columns are called *fields*, rows are called *records*, and the table itself is generally called a *datasheet*. So you can call a series of rows of related data that is organized into categories, a table, a list, a datasheet, or even (sometimes) a database.

Build Tables

Tables are easily created, allowing you to add new data from existing data (see Chapter 10 for information on importing data from external sources) or add data from scratch. In either case, once Excel recognizes data is within a table, it makes assumptions that help you to view, enter, format, and use the data in calculations.

Create a Table

Excel 2010 makes creating a table easier than ever. However, before you designate a range of data to be a table, you might want to consider reorganizing your data to better work with table features.

- **Column headings** (or *labels*) should be formatted differently from the data so that Excel can more easily differentiate one from the other. All data in a column should be similar. Avoid mixing dates and other number formats with text.

- **Clean up the data range** by eliminating any blank rows or columns within the range and removing extra spaces in cells.

- **Display all data** by showing any rows or columns you might have hidden. Hidden data can be inadvertently deleted.

- **Place values to be totaled** in the rightmost column. Excel's Total Row feature creates a total row, which you can toggle off or on, when it recognizes data that can be summed in the last column.

CREATE A BLANK TABLE

1. On the worksheet where you want to create a table, drag to create a range comprising the approximate number of columns and rows you think you need for your data (you can add or remove some afterwards).

2. In the Insert tab Tables group, click **Table**. The Create Table dialog box displays your selected range, and the range is outlined within a selection border.

TIP

Use the Borders button ▦ ▾ in the Home tab Font group to add a border that separates column headings from data instead of spacing or other separation techniques.

3. Click **OK**. The table is created (see Figure 8-1) with placeholder column headers that you can edit to fit your data, alternating row colors for better data differentiation, an AutoFilter down arrow to access easy filtering and sorting of data (see "Create an AutoFilter" later in the chapter for information on using filters), and a sizing arrow. In addition, a Design tab provides access to table-related tools.

Column header placeholders   *AutoFilter*   *Table-related tools*

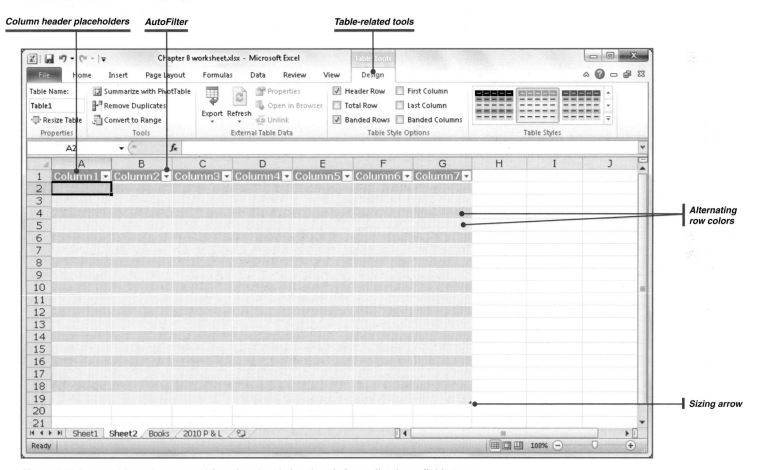

Alternating row colors

Sizing arrow

Figure 8-1: ***A new table makes several functional and visual tools immediately available to you.***

UICKSTEPS

ADDING ROWS AND COLUMNS TO A TABLE

Tables are easily resized by adding rows and columns.

ADD ROWS TO THE END OF THE TABLE

Click the lower rightmost cell in the table (containing the sizing arrow), and press **TAB**. When you complete the entry, the sizing arrow moves to the next row below.

–Or–

Type in an empty row that is adjacent to the end of the table. The table will "annex" the row, unless the last row is empty or the last row is a total row.

–Or–

Drag the sizing arrow downward over the rows you want to add.

ADD COLUMNS TO THE SIDES OF A TABLE

Type in an empty column that is adjacent to the right side of the table. The table will "annex" the column.

–Or–

Drag the sizing arrow to the right over the columns you want to add.

| $ 34.95 | |
| $ 24.95 | |

ADD ROWS AND COLUMNS WITHIN A TABLE

1. Click in the column within the table to the right of or in the row below where you want to add more cells.

2. In the Home tab Cells group, click the **Insert** down arrow, and, depending on where you want the cells added, click **Insert Table Rows Above** or **Insert Table Columns To The Left**.

   –Or–

1. Right-click the column within the table to the right of or the row below where you want to add more cells.

2. Click **Insert** and click **Table Columns To The Left** or **Table Rows Above**, depending on where you want the cells added.

CREATE A TABLE FROM EXISTING DATA

1. Select the data you want to be included within a table.

2. In the Insert tab Tables group, click **Table**. The Create Table dialog box appears, and the range is outlined within a selection border.

3. Assuming your data is organized with column headers in the first row, select the **My Table Has Headers** check box, if Excel doesn't already recognize them. Click **OK**. The table is created in a way similar to that shown in Figure 8-1, except the column headers are created from the first row, as shown in Figure 8-2.

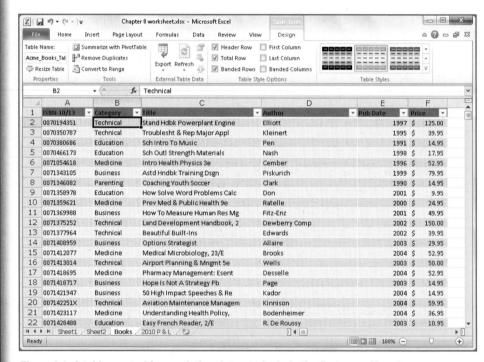

Figure 8-2: **A table created from existing data can include the first row of headers.**

TIP

Quickly create a table by selecting a range and pressing **CTRL+L**. Select whether the first row contains column headers, and click **OK**.

CAUTION

To select rows and columns to be inserted or deleted, do not use (click) the numbered row headers and lettered column headings provided by Excel. Doing so will delete the entire row or column, including any data outside the table border. Instead, select just the portion of a row or column in the table by placing your mouse pointer just to the right of the left border of the leftmost cell or just below the top border of the topmost cell. When the pointer changes to a selection arrow, click to select one row or one column, or drag to select adjacent rows.

3	0071408959
4	0830621369
5	9780072229387
6	9780072947755
7	9780071486620
8	9780071496261

NOTE

If the last column contains data that cannot be summed, the Total row is still added and a count of the values in the column is displayed instead of a sum.

TIP

A feature of tables is that when you scroll through data beyond what's visible in the sheet window, the column headers replace the lettered Excel column headings at the top of the sheet (see Figure 8-3).

Delete Rows and Columns Within a Table

1. Click in the column or row within the table that you want to delete.

2. In the Home tab Cells group, click the **Delete** down arrow, and click **Delete Table Rows** or **Delete Table Columns**, depending on what you want removed.

–Or–

1. Right-click the column or row within the table you want to delete.

2. Click **Delete** and click **Table Columns** or **Table Rows**, depending on what you want removed.

Add a Total Row

Excel provides a nifty feature that sums the last column in a table and automatically creates a Total row at the bottom of the table. The Total row lets you perform other calculations on any of the columns in the table.

SUM THE LAST COLUMN

1. Select a cell in the table to display the Design tab (Table Tools), and select that tab.

2. Select the **Total Row** check box in the Table Style Options group. The rightmost column is summed within a new row, with the word "Total" in the leftmost cell, as shown in Figure 8-3.

3. To remove the Total row, click the **Total Row** check box to deselect it.

PERFORM FUNCTIONS IN A COLUMN

1. Add a Total Row (see "Sum the Last Column").

2. In the Total row at the bottom of the table, click the cell at the bottom of a column whose values you want to calculate. A down arrow appears to the right of the cell.

3. Click the cell's down arrow, and select the function you want performed (see Figure 8-3). The result is displayed in the cell.

Selecting Total Row...

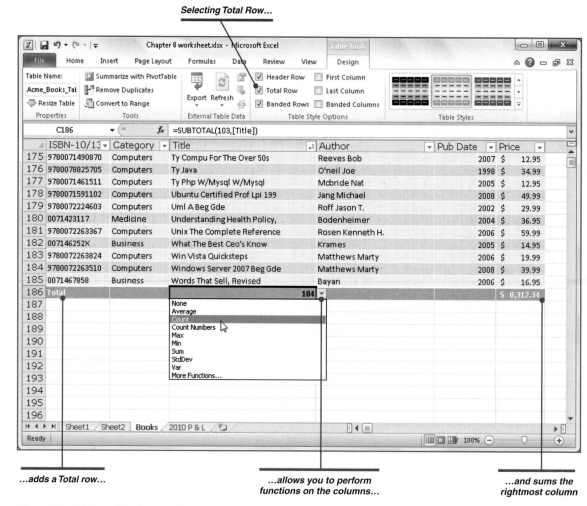

...adds a Total row...

...allows you to perform
functions on the columns...

...and sums the
rightmost column

Figure 8-3: **Adding a Total row performs several functions.**

TIP

If you don't see style examples on the ribbon in the
Design tab (Table Tools) Table Styles group,
increase the width of the Excel window until you
do. Otherwise, click **Quick Styles** to open the full
gallery of style examples.

Quick
Styles
Table Styles

Apply Styles to a Table

By default, table rows are banded in alternating shades from colors drawn from
the workbook theme, with the header and possible total rows in a darker shade.
You can apply a Quick Style, modify table elements, or create a style of your own.

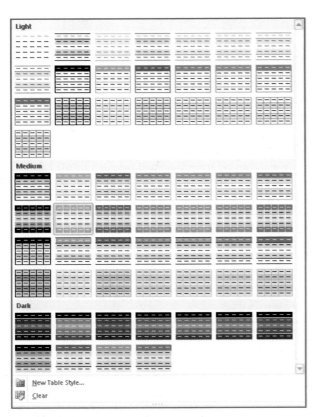

Light

Medium

Dark

New Table Style...

Clear

Figure 8-4: *The fastest way to style a table is to start with one of the several style samples.*

APPLY A QUICK STYLE TO A TABLE

1. Click a cell in the table to select it.

2. In the Design tab (Table Tools) Table Styles group, point to the style examples on the ribbon.

   –Or–

   Click the row-by-row buttons.

   –Or–

   Click the **More** button to see the complete gallery (as shown in Figure 8-4).

   In all cases, pointing to a Quick Style icon will change the table to reflect the style attributes.

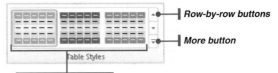

Row-by-row buttons

More button

Table Styles

Quick Styles on ribbon

3. When you find a style that's close to what you want, click the **Quick Style** icon in the particular Styles group (Light, Medium, or Dark).

CHANGE TABLE ELEMENTS

You can modify a table to show or hide elements that make the table data easier to view.

1. Click a cell in the table to select it.

2. In the Design tab (Table Tools) Table Styles Options group, select or deselect the option you want (Header Row and Total Row options are covered earlier in this chapter).

   - **Banded Rows/Banded Columns** displays alternating colors of rows and columns, respectively (the default is banded rows).

   - **First Column/Last Column** highlights the respective column in a darker shade.

CREATE YOUR OWN TABLE STYLE

You can save any changes you make to a Quick Style and have it available for future formatting within the same workbook.

1. Apply a Quick Style and the styling options available on the Design tab (Table Tools), as described in "Apply a Quick Style to a Table."

QUICKSTEPS

WORKING WITH TABLES

Tables provide a few features unique to themselves.

REVERT A TABLE TO A RANGE

1. Click a cell in the table.

2. In the Design tab (Table Tools) Tools group, click **Convert To Range**. Click **Yes** to confirm that you want to convert the table to a normal range.

REMOVE DUPLICATES

You can delete rows (or records) that contain duplicate values on a column-by-column basis.

1. Click a cell in the table.

2. In the Design tab (Table Tools) Tools group, click **Remove Duplicates**. The Remove Duplicates dialog box appears, shown in Figure 8-5.

3. If your data does not have headers, deselect the **My Data Has Headers** check box.

4. To check for duplicate values in all columns, click **OK**.

   –Or–

   Click **Unselect All** and select the columns you want checked for duplicate values. Click **OK**.

   In either case, any row with a duplicate value is deleted from the table (see accompanying Caution).

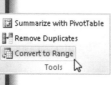

Summarize with PivotTable
Remove Duplicates
Convert to Range
Tools

CAUTION

Removing duplicate values removes each row, or record, within a table. To ensure that you can recover data you might inadvertently delete, click the **Name Box** down arrow on the left of the Formula bar, and click the table name to select the table. Right-click the selected table, and click **Copy**. Paste the table to an empty area on the same or another worksheet.

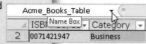

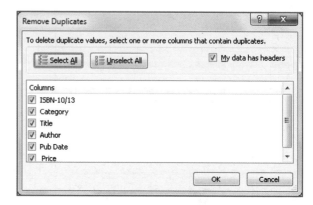

Figure 8-5: **You can choose on a column-by-column basis to remove rows that contain duplicate values.**

2. Click the **More** button in the Table Styles group, and click **New Table Style**. The New Table Quick Style dialog box appears, as shown in Figure 8-6.

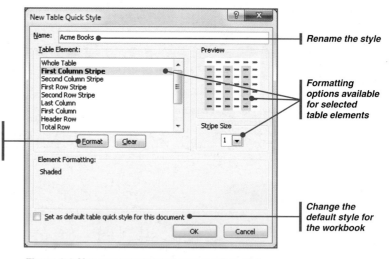

Figure 8-6: **You can create your own custom style to apply to other tables in the workbook.**

TIP

When referencing table data in a formula, use the Name Manager and AutoComplete to make life easier. In the Formulas tab Defined Names group, click **Name Manager**. Select your table (listed as Table *x*), and click **Edit**. Rename the table to something more meaningful, click **OK**, and close the Name Manager. You can now use the table name, column names, and other arguments in formulas. For example, to reference a column sum in that table, type =SUM(*tablename*[*columnname*]). For the table name, after the open parenthesis, type the first few letters of the table name, and double-click the table from the AutoComplete list. For the column name, type the opening bracket. A list of the table column headers appears. Double-click the column header you want, type a closing bracket and parenthesis, and press **ENTER**. The sum of values in the column is returned.

G	H	I
=Sum(Acme_Books_Table[		
SUM(**number1**, [number2], ...)	ISBN-10/13	
	Category	
	Title	
	Author	
	Pub Date	
	Price	
	#All	
	#Data	
	#Headers	
	#Totals	
	@ - This Row	

CAUTION

Do not select column or row headers when setting up data validation, since they are probably formatted as text and might cause compatibility problems with numbered data. In fact, Excel won't let you access the Data Validation dialog box if you do.

3. In the Name box, select the default name, and type a name of your own.

4. Select the table element to which you want to apply formatting (you can select different stripe sizes at this time if you select that element), and then click **Format**.

5. Select formatting options in the Format Cells dialog box (see Chapter 3 for more information on using the Format Cells dialog box), and click **OK**.

6. Repeat steps 4 and 5 for any other table elements you want to format, choose whether to make this table style your default (see Figure 8-6), and click **OK**. Your new table style is available at the top of the Quick Table Styles gallery.

REMOVE STYLING FROM A TABLE

1. Click a cell in the table to select it.

2. In the Design tab (Table Tools), click the **More** button in the Table Style Options group.

3. Click **Clear** below the gallery. All table style formatting is removed from the table (individual formatting, such as bolding or selected cell fills, is not removed).

Validate Data

To prevent data entry errors, you can set validation criteria. Excel checks the entered data against the criteria you set and disallows the entry if the validation conditions are not met. You can use data validation in any cell on the worksheet; however, due to the quantity of data typically entered in a table, using data validation over an entire table is highly recommended.

In addition, you can choose to have Excel display a message when a user selects a validated cell, and you can choose to have Excel display an error message when an attempt is made to enter invalid data in the cell.

CREATE A VALIDATION

1. Select the cells you want validated. Typically, you would select a column (see the Caution).

2. In the Data tab Data Tools group, click **Data Validation**. The Data Validation dialog box appears with the Settings tab displayed, as shown in Figure 8-7.

3. Click the **Allow** down arrow, and select the validation criteria to use.

4. Click the **Data** down arrow, and select the comparison operator to use.

Data Validation

`=E4`

5. Type minimum/starting and maximum/ending values in the applicable text boxes, or locate them on the worksheet using the **Collapse Dialog** button. If using values on the worksheet, click the **Expand Dialog** button to return to the dialog box.

6. Click **OK** to apply the validation.

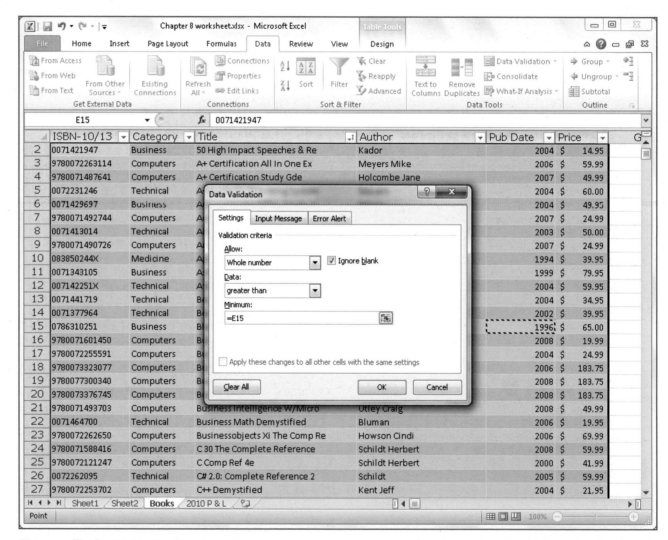

Figure 8-7: **The Data Validation dialog box provides comparison criteria you can use to establish conditions for data entry.**

QUICKSTEPS

LOCATING VALIDATION DATA

Excel easily identifies data you've selected to be validated, as well as data that doesn't fit validation criteria you've set.

FIND VALIDATED DATA

In the Home tab Editing group, click **Find & Select**, and click **Data Validation**. Data on the worksheet you had previously selected for data validation is highlighted.

FIND INVALIDATED DATA

In the Data tab Data Tools group, click the **Data Validation** down arrow, and click **Circle Validation Criteria**. To remove the circles, again click the **Data Validation** down arrow, and click **Clear Validation Circles**.

2003	$	26.99
2005	$	183.75
2008	$	24.95

–Or–

Look for green error indicators in the upper-left corner of affected cells ` $ 183.75 `. Click the cell to view the Smart tag and a tooltip providing the source of the error. Click the Smart tag down arrow, and click **Display Type Information** to see an explanation of the validation.

TIP

Verify that data validation has been removed by doing the first set of procedures in the "Locating Validation Data" QuickSteps.

REMOVE VALIDATION CRITERIA

1. Select the cell(s) whose validation you want to remove. See the "Locating Validation Data" QuickSteps to help you locate the validated cells.

2. In the Data tab Data Tools group, click **Data Validation**.

3. In the Data Validation dialog box Settings tab, click **Clear All** and then click **OK**.

CREATE A DATA ENTRY MESSAGE

You can forestall data entry mistakes by providing a message, similar to a tooltip, with information about a selected cell.

2003	$	26.99
2005	$	183.75
2008	$	
2007	$	
2006	$	
2007	$	

Price Range
This price is above our target!!!

1. Set up a validation (see "Create a Validation), or select the range for an existing validation.

2. In the Data tab Data Tools group, click **Data Validation** and click the **Input Message** tab.

3. Verify that the **Show Input Message When Cell Is Selected** check box is selected.

4. Type a title for the message and the message itself in their respective text boxes.

5. Click **OK** when finished. When a user selects a cell to enter data, or selects an existing cell with invalid data, a tooltip-type message will be displayed with the text you provided.

CREATE AN ERROR MESSAGE

When you (or anyone else!) try to add data that doesn't meet a cell's validation criteria, Excel returns a generic message box that informs you of your error. You can modify the type of alert that is displayed and the text that appears.

1. Set up a validation. See "Create a Validation."

2. In the Data tab Data Tools group, click **Data Validation** and click the **Error Alert** tab.

3. Verify that the **Show Error Alert After Invalid Data Is Entered** check box is selected.

4. Click the **Style** down arrow, and select the severity of the alert. The alert's associated icon is displayed below the selected style.

5. Type a title for the alert and the message itself in their respective text boxes.

6. Click **OK** when finished. When a user tries to complete an entry with data that doesn't meet the validation criteria, the alert you created will pop up, as shown in Figure 8-8.

TIP

You can create a message to appear when *any* cell is selected, not just those that have validation conditions applied—although comments are typically used for that purpose. See Chapter 3 for information on adding comments to a cell.

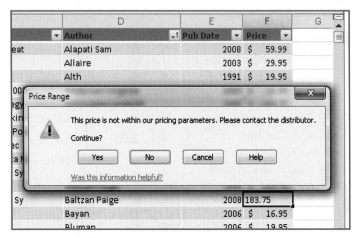

Figure 8-8: *You can create custom error messages to alert users that they are trying to enter invalid data.*

Organize Data

Data in a worksheet is often entered in a manner that doesn't lend itself well to being viewed or to being able to find specific data that you want. Excel provides several tools to assist you in organizing your data without permanently changing the overall structure of the worksheet. You can sort data on any column based on several criteria, filter data to view just the information you want to see, and outline data to streamline what you see.

Sort Data by Columns and Rows

You can sort data based on several criteria, such as:

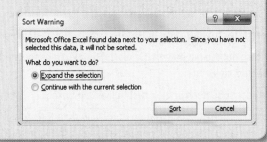

TIP

You can sort data anywhere on a worksheet. However, when sorting outside of a table, you have to be careful to correctly select the data that you want sorted, or run the risk that related data becomes disassociated (data in one column might change, while the data in the rest of the columns remains the same). If this is what you intend, you can do it, but Excel will point it out to you.

- **Ascending** or **descending** order according to the values in one or more columns. Excel sorts numbers "smallest to largest" and dates "oldest to newest," considered "ascending," as well as their reverses.

- **Fill Color** or **Font Color** in a selected cell

- **Cell icons** attached to cells

- **Custom lists**, such as month or day names

All data in the selected range (or table) is realigned so that the data in each row remains the same, even though the row might be placed in a different order than it was originally. You can also sort on dates and days of the week, and use values tabled by rows instead of columns.

NOTE

Sorting in Excel is determined by a specified *sort order*. For example, numbers in an ascending sort are sorted before letters; combined number and letter (*alphanumeric*) values are sorted next; logical values with False, then logical values with True; error values; and finally, any blanks.

PERFORM AN ASCENDING/DESCENDING SORT

1. Click a cell in the range or table.

2. In the Data tab Sort & Filter group, click **Sort *ascending*** ↕ (the name changes according to the data type selected) to sort from smaller to larger numbers, newest to oldest dates, or from A to Z. (See the accompanying Note on sort orders.)

   –Or–

   Click **Sort *descending*** ↕ to sort from larger to smaller numbers, oldest to newest dates, or from Z to A.

SORT BY COLOR AND ICONS

1. Right-click a cell in the column that contains a color or a conditional formatting icon set by which you want to sort the range or table (see Chapter 4 for more information on conditional formatting).

2. Click **Sort** and click whether you want the data sorted based on the fill color, font color, or icon in the selected cell. The range or table is sorted, similar to what is shown in Figure 8-9.

SORT BY MULTIPLE CRITERIA

You can nest levels of sorting criteria to refine a sort based on multiple criteria. For example, you could first sort a table

	A	B	C	D	E	F
1	ISBN-10/13	Category	Title	Author	Pub Date	Price
2	9780073052335	Computers	Sys Analysis & Design Meth 7e	Whitten Jeffrey L.	2005	$ 178.75
3	9780072958867	Computers	Dbase Sys Concepts 5e	Silberschatz Abraham	2005	$ 154.75
4	9780072465631	Computers	Dbase Mgt Sys	Ramakrishnan Raghu	2002	$ 143.75
5	9780073019338	Computers	Software Engineering	Pressman Roger S.	2004	$ 145.75
6	0070194351	Technical	Stand Hdbk Powerplant Engine	Elliott	1997	$ 125.00
7	0071375252	Technical	Land Development Handbook, 2	Dewberry Comp	2002	$ 150.00
8	9780073323077	Computers	Business Driven Information Sy	Baltzan Paige	2006	$ 183.75
9	9780073376745	Computers	Business Driven Technology	Baltzan Paige	2008	$ 183.75
10	9780077300340	Computers	Business Driven Information Sy	Baltzan Paige	2008	$ 183.75
11	0071455523	Medicine	Prediatrics Pretest, 11/E	Yetman	2006	$ 24.95
12	0071441719	Technical	Be A Successful Residential	Woodson	2004	$ 34.95
13	9780072263787	Computers	Html 3e	Willard Wendy	2006	$ 29.99
14	9780071601276	Computers	Comptia Security All In One Ex	White Gregory B.	2009	$ 59.99
15	0071413014	Technical	Airport Planning & Mngmt 5e	Wells	2003	$ 50.00
16	9780072229981	Computers	Solaris 10 The Comp Ref	Watters Paul	2005	$ 52.99
17	9780071591027	Computers	Oca Oracle Dbase 11g Admin Exa	Watson John	2008	$ 59.99

Sheet1 Sheet2 **Books** 2010 P & L

Ready   100%

Figure 8-9: Using color or cell icons makes it easy to quickly bring data into view.

8

based on a category of books, then the year they were published, and then by list price within each year.

1. Click a cell in the range or table you want to sort.

2. In the Data tab Sort & Filter group, click **Sort**.

   –Or–

   In the Home tab Editing group, click **Sort & Filter**, and click **Custom Sort**.

   –Or–

   Right-click a cell in the range or table you want to sort, click **Sort**, and click **Custom Sort**.

   In any case, the Sort dialog box appears, shown in Figure 8-10.

3. If sorting data outside a table, select or deselect the **My Data Has Headers** check box, depending on whether your range has column headings or not.

4. Click the **Sort By (Column)** down arrow, and select the column of primary importance in determining the sort order.

5. Click the **Sort On** down arrow, and click the criteria you want to sort on.

6. Click the **Order** down arrow, and click whether the sort is ascending or descending. Or click **Custom List** to sort on a prebuilt list or one of your own.

7. Click **Add Level** to create another set of sorting options (Figure 8-10 shows two levels). Repeat steps 4–6 for the next set of criteria to be sorted. Continue building sorting levels as deep and detailed as you need, using the following available tools:

   - Select a level and click **Copy Level** to create a copy of a previous level and minimize repetitious entries.

   - Select a level and click **Delete Level** to remove a level from the list.

   - Click the **Move Up** and **Move Down** arrows to re-order the priority of multiple levels.

8. Click **OK**. The data is sorted based on your criteria (see Figure 8-11).

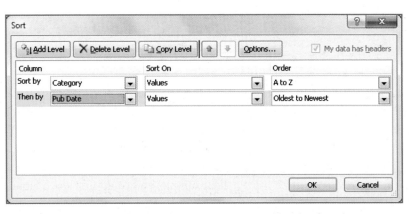

Figure 8-10: *The Sort dialog box allows you to set up 64 levels of sorting.*

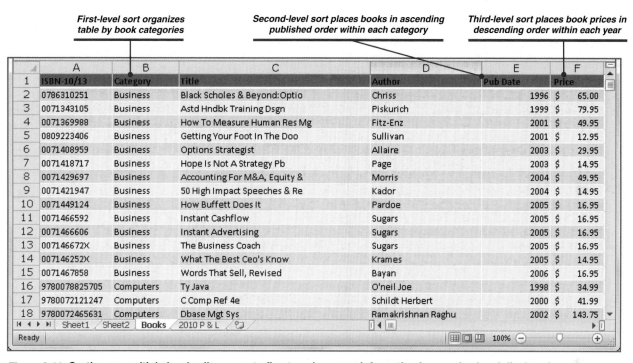

First-level sort organizes table by book categories

Second-level sort places books in ascending published order within each category

Third-level sort places book prices in descending order within each year

	A	B	C	D	E	F
1	ISBN-10/13	Category	Title	Author	Pub Date	Price
2	0786310251	Business	Black Scholes & Beyond:Optio	Chriss	1996	$ 65.00
3	0071343105	Business	Astd Hndbk Training Dsgn	Piskurich	1999	$ 79.95
4	0071369988	Business	How To Measure Human Res Mg	Fitz-Enz	2001	$ 49.95
5	0809223406	Business	Getting Your Foot In The Doo	Sullivan	2001	$ 12.95
6	0071408959	Business	Options Strategist	Allaire	2003	$ 29.95
7	0071418717	Business	Hope Is Not A Strategy Pb	Page	2003	$ 14.95
8	0071429697	Business	Accounting For M&A, Equity &	Morris	2004	$ 49.95
9	0071421947	Business	50 High Impact Speeches & Re	Kador	2004	$ 14.95
10	0071449124	Business	How Buffett Does It	Pardoe	2005	$ 16.95
11	0071466592	Business	Instant Cashflow	Sugars	2005	$ 16.95
12	0071466606	Business	Instant Advertising	Sugars	2005	$ 16.95
13	007146672X	Business	The Business Coach	Sugars	2005	$ 16.95
14	007146252X	Business	What The Best Ceo's Know	Krames	2005	$ 14.95
15	0071467858	Business	Words That Sell, Revised	Bayan	2006	$ 16.95
16	9780078825705	Computers	Ty Java	O'neil Joe	1998	$ 34.99
17	9780072121247	Computers	C Comp Ref 4e	Schildt Herbert	2000	$ 41.99
18	9780072465631	Computers	Dbase Mgt Sys	Ramakrishnan Raghu	2002	$ 143.75

Sheet1 / Sheet2 / **Books** / 2010 P & L

Ready   100%

Figure 8-11: **Sorting on multiple levels allows you to fine-tune how your information is organized and displayed.**

SORT DATA BY ROWS

1. Click a cell in the range you want to sort. (The range cannot be an Excel-defined table.)

2. In the Data tab Sort & Filter group, click **Sort**.

3. Click **Options** (see Figure 8-10). The Sort Options dialog box appears.

4. In the Orientation area, click **Sort Left To Right**. Click **OK**.

5. In the Sort dialog box, the Sort By element will change from "Column" to "Row." Perform steps 3–8 in "Sort by Multiple Criteria."

QUICKSTEPS

REMOVING FILTERS

What happened to my data? Nothing, actually. When you apply filters, your data doesn't permanently disappear. Filtering only hides data that doesn't fit the criteria you select. You can return to the view of your data before you applied a filter.

REMOVE A FILTER FROM A COLUMN

1. Click the **AutoFilter** down arrow next to the column heading.
2. Click **Clear Filter From** *columnname*.

REMOVE FILTERS FROM ALL COLUMNS IN A RANGE OR TABLE

In the Data tab Sort & Filter group, click **Clear**. Filters are removed from the data, although AutoFilter down arrows are retained in the column headers.

TURN OFF AUTOFILTER

In the Data tab Sort & Filter group, click **Filter**. AutoFilter is turned off, and the AutoFilter down arrows are removed from column headers.

TIP

You can apply filters to only one range or table on a worksheet at a time, but you can apply filters to more than one column in a range or table. Actually, you can nest filters by filtering on multiple columns, similar to sorting. For example, you could filter a table of books by category and then filter that list by author, displaying only those books by a given author with a certain category.

Create an AutoFilter

Filtering data allows you to quickly hide potentially thousands of rows (records) of data that you don't need at the moment so that only those rows of data that you want to see are displayed. The quickest and easiest way to filter data is to have Excel add AutoFilter to your column headings.

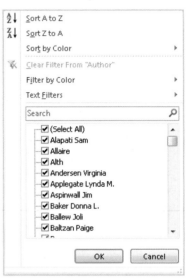

1. Click a cell in the range or table where you want to filter data.
2. If AutoFilter down arrows are not to the right of each column heading, in the Data tab Sort & Filter group, click **Filter** to add them.
3. Click the **AutoFilter** down arrow in the column that contains the values to which you want to apply a filter.
4. Decide what you want to filter from the menu, and follow the appropriate steps in the following sections.

FILTER BY COLUMN VALUES

1. On the Filter menu, click **Select All** in the values list to remove the check marks next to all values in the column.
2. Select the values whose rows you want to display. Click **OK**.

FILTER BY EMPTY CELLS

The Blanks option is only displayed if the column has at least one blank cell.

1. On the Filter menu, click **Select All** to remove the check marks next to all values in the column.
2. Select **(Blanks)** at the bottom of the values list. Click **OK**.

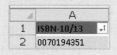
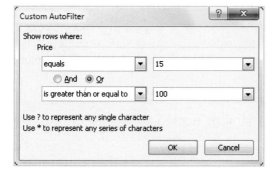

FILTER BY CELL FILL

The Filter By Color option is available in columns that have at least one cell filled with a color or texture.

On the Filter menu, click **Filter By Color**, and click the color you want to filter by.

–Or–

Click **No Fill** to display only those rows that do not have a fill.

FILTER BY NUMERIC VALUES

Excel provides several "quick" criteria you can choose from to quickly filter your data (most of these options simply open the Custom Filter dialog box prefilled with the criteria you chose).

1. On the Filter menu, click **Number Filters**. A list of criteria options is displayed.

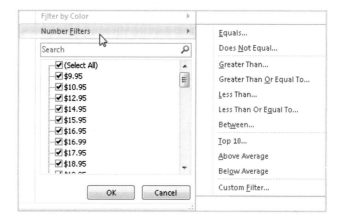

2. Click the comparison you want to filter by, type or select a value, and click **OK**. (Clicking **Above Average** or **Below Average** immediately performs the filter; clicking **Top 10** opens a dialog box, where you can filter for top or bottom values or percentages.) Figure 8-12 shows a filter on a book table of prices between $10 and $15.

–Or–

1. Click **Custom Filter** at the bottom of the Numeric Filters submenu to display the Custom AutoFilter dialog box, where you can add a second comparison to the criteria.

Filtered column indicator

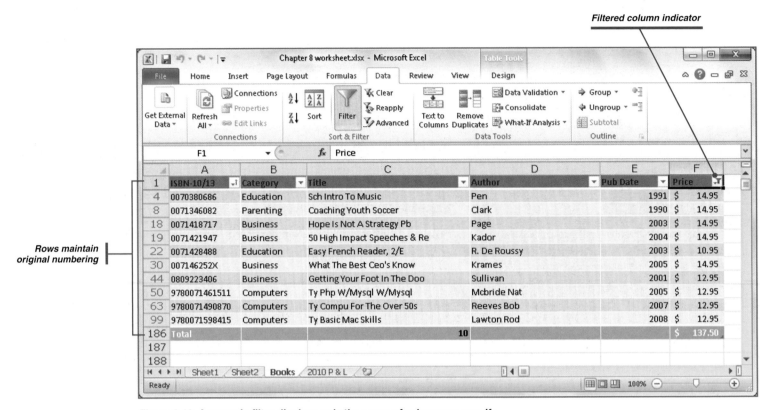

Rows maintain
original numbering

Figure 8-12: *A numeric filter displays only the range of values you specify.*

2. Click the first comparison operator down arrow, and select an operator. Type or
   select the value you want the operator to act upon. (See "Use Wildcards in Criteria"
   later in the chapter for information on using wildcards to represent single or multiple
   characters.)

3. Click **And** or **Or** to apply a logic operator.

4. Click the second comparison down arrow, select an operator, and then type or select
   its corresponding value.

5. Click **OK** when finished.

SETTING UP CRITERIA AND EXTRACT RANGES

Before you perform an advanced filter to copy the results to a range outside your data range, you need to set up the criteria and extract ranges with column headers that match the column headers in the data range. For example, in a table containing several columns of book data, you could set up your *criteria* range to filter on "Cronan John" in the Author column and extract only information from the title, published date, and price columns into a separate range on either the same worksheet or a different one. In this case, your criteria range would include the Author label in one cell and "Cronan John" in the cell below it. Your extract range would include three columns: Title, Pub Date, and Price. When dragging the extract range, include the labels and as many rows as might be necessary. Also, copy the labels from the data range to the criteria and extract ranges by using Copy and Paste to reduce text entry errors (spoken from personal experience!).

Criteria:	Author		
	Cronan John		
Extract:	Title	Pub Date	Price

Use Advanced Filtering

You can set up an advanced filter when the criteria are located elsewhere than the table or data range. You can then have the results copied to a separate range on the worksheet. In addition, you can use wildcards in setting up your comparison criteria.

FILTER BASED ON EXTERNAL CRITERIA

1. Click a cell in the table, or select the range where you want to filter data.

2. In the Data tab Sort & Filter group, click **Advanced**. The Advanced Filter dialog box appears.

3. In the List Range text box, verify the range. If you need to make changes, click the **Collapse Dialog** button 📷, reselect the range, and click the **Expand Dialog** button 📖.

4. In the Criteria Range text box, click the **Collapse Dialog** button, select the cell that contains your criteria, and click the **Expand Dialog** button.

5. Click **Filter The List, In-Place** if you want the entire rows of data that meet the filter to display on the current worksheet, displacing the original table/range (similar to a standard filter). Click **Clear** in the Sort & Filter group to return the worksheet to its original state.

   –Or–

   Click **Copy To Another Location** to extract the filter results to a range elsewhere, consisting of as many columns of data as you want. In the Copy To text box, click **Collapse Dialog**, select the range where you want the filter results copied (see the "Setting Up Criteria and Extract Ranges" QuickFacts), and click the **Expand Dialog** button.

6. Click **OK** when finished. The data your criteria specified is copied to your extract range (see Figure 8-13).

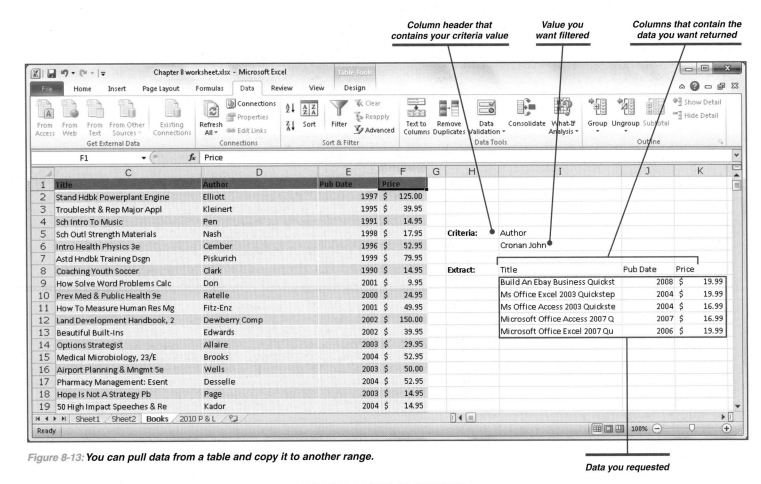

Column header that contains your criteria value

Value you want filtered

Columns that contain the data you want returned

Data you requested

Figure 8-13: **You can pull data from a table and copy it to another range.**

USE WILDCARDS IN CRITERIA

You can use *wildcard* comparison criteria to help you find data.

- Type an asterisk (*****) as a placeholder for any number of missing characters. For example, typing *son finds Robinson, Dobson, and bison.

- Type a question mark (**?**) as a placeholder for a single character. For example, typing Jo?n finds John and Joan.

- Type a tilde (**~**) before an asterisk, question mark, or tilde to find words or phrases containing one or more asterisks, question marks, and tildes. For example, typing msdos~~ finds msdos~.

NOTE

Auto Outlining is not available for Excel tables. To use Auto Outlining in tables, first convert them to a range. You can manually group selected columns and rows in tables by using the Group command.

Outline Data Automatically

You can display only summary rows and columns by outlining a range and hiding the details. The mechanics of creating the automatic outline involve just a few clicks; however, there are a few things you should do to your data in advance of applying an automatic outline.

- **Column headings** should be in the first row if you are outlining by row; **row headings** should be in the first column if you are outlining by column.

- **Similar data** should be in the columns or rows you are outlining, and the data must be set up as a hierarchical summary.

- **Blank rows or columns** should be removed.

- **Sort the data** to get it into the groupings you want.

- **Create total or summary rows and columns** that sum the detail rows above or the detail columns to the left or right.

When you are ready to outline your data:

1. Click a cell in the range you want to outline.

2. In the Data tab Outline group, click the **Group** down arrow, and click **Auto Outline**. An outlining bar and outlining symbols are added either across the column headers and down the row headers, as shown in Figure 8-14, or across just one of the headers—depending on the structure of your data.

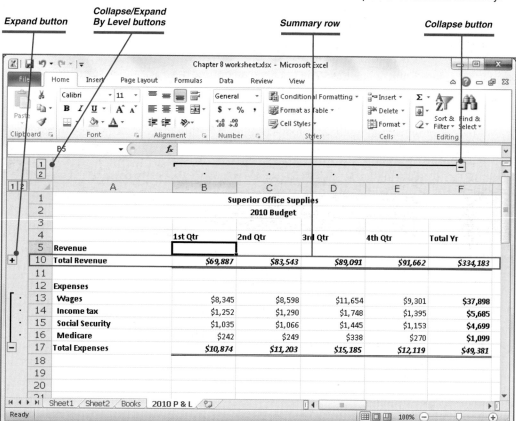

Figure 8-14: **Excel provides outlining tools to collapse and expand data by rows and columns.**

USING OUTLINES

Outlines are manipulated using a set of symbols on the row and column bars, as well as using commands in the Outline group (see Figure 8-15).

COLLAPSE ROWS AND COLUMNS

Click the **Collapse** symbol next to a group of rows or columns.

EXPAND COLLAPSED ROWS AND COLUMNS

Click the **Expand** symbol next to a hidden group of rows or columns.

COLLAPSE OR EXPAND ALL ROWS AND COLUMNS

1. Select the range where you want to show or hide all rows and columns.

2. In the Data tab Outline group, click **Show Detail** or **Hide Detail** .

COLLAPSE OR EXPAND BY LEVELS

Excel determines how many sets (or *levels*) of detail and summary data are in your outline and displays symbols you can use to expand and collapse accordingly.

Click the level symbols appropriate for the level of detail and summary data you want to see or hide.

REMOVE A GROUP

1. Select the rows or columns you want to ungroup.

2. In the Data tab Outline group, click **Ungroup**. (If you grouped by both rows and columns, select which to ungroup, and click **OK**.)

REMOVE AN AUTO OUTLINE

1. Select a cell in the outline.

2. In the Data tab Outline group, click **Ungroup** and click **Clear Outline**.

–Or–

Click the **Group** button (to the left of the down arrow). Click whether to group by rows or columns, and then click **OK**.

In either case, see the "Using Outlines" QuickSteps for ways to manipulate your data.

Outline Data by Manually Grouping

Grouping data allows you to create an outline of your data by selecting rows and columns that can be collapsed and hidden. You generally use this manual method of outlining when your data doesn't have the summary rows or columns used by the automatic outlining feature to recognize where to hide details.

1. Select the first set of rows or columns you want to be able to collapse and expand.

2. In the Data tab Outline group, click **Group**. An outlining bar is added to the left of the row headers or above the column headers, depending on whether rows or columns were selected.

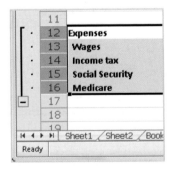

3. Repeat steps 1 and 2 for as many sets of rows or columns as you want to include in the outline.

Add Subtotals

You can add subtotals to your data grouping, assuming your data is properly set up (see the rules in "Outline Data Automatically" earlier in the chapter).

1. Select the range for which you want to add subtotals. If your data is not set up properly, Excel will provide suggestions you can use to get it in order.

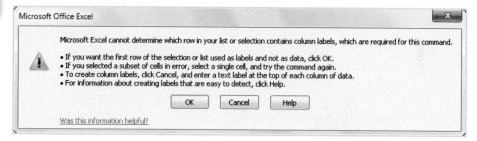

2. In the Data tab Outline group, click **Subtotal**. The Subtotal dialog box appears.

3. Click the **At Each Change In** down arrow, and select which column the subtotals will be grouped on.

4. If you want to subtotal based on something other than a Sum, click the **Use Function** down arrow, and select the function you want.

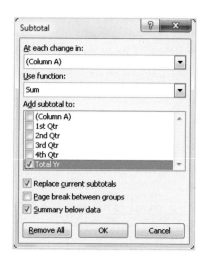

5. In the Add Subtotal To list, select which columns will receive subtotals.

6. Select whether you want any of the features provided by the check boxes, and click **OK**.

Add Styles to an Outline

Excel can quickly recognize summary rows and columns, and can add styling to differentiate them from other data.

1. Expand the outline to show any collapsed rows or columns.

2. Click a cell within the data range you want to add styling to (bolding, font, and font size changes).

3. In the Data tab, click the **Outline Dialog Box Launcher** (the small arrow in the lower-right corner).

4. In the Settings dialog box, select the **Automatic Styles** check box, and click **Create**. Bolding is applied to summary rows and/or columns, as well as other theme styling, shown in Figure 8-15.

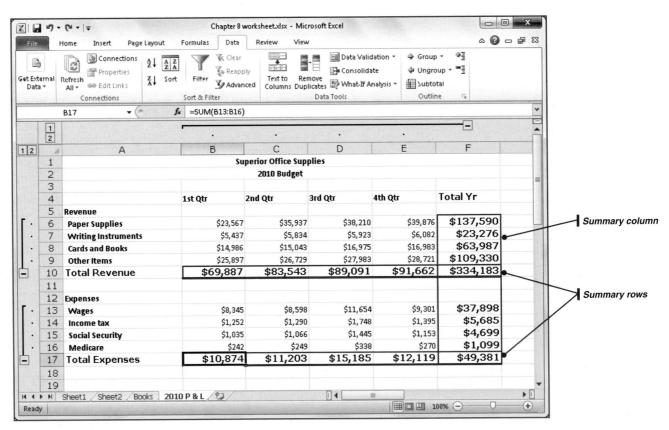

Figure 8-15: *You can automatically add styling to summary rows and columns.*

How to...

Chapter 9

Analyzing and Sharing Data

Previous chapters have shown you how to work with data in Excel, be it viewing, calculating, presenting, printing, or organizing. The one key element that hasn't yet been touched upon is how to analyze and interpret these collections of data to help us better extract meaningful conclusions and results. To this end, Excel provides several advanced tools for manipulating your data to arrive at results that you want to achieve and for reorienting your data to give you different perspectives on how it is presented and interpreted. And along with this greater appreciation for the data you have amassed within your Excel worksheets, there is an even greater need to protect it, especially when it is shared with others. This chapter will show you how.

9

Get the Results You Want

Excel provides several tools to help you find out how to arrive at a result by changing the underlying data. *Goal Seek* fills this requirement on a limited and temporary basis. *Scenarios* provide means to save and compare different sets of values that you can run to see how they affect your result. The most powerful feature in this suite of what-if analysis tools is an upgraded *Solver*, an add-in program that extends the capabilities of Goal Seek and scenarios.

Use Goal Seek

With Goal Seek, you choose a cell whose results are derived from a formula that uses the values in other cells. By seeing the change required in the value in one of the referenced cells, you see what it would take to achieve the result. To provide the answer you are looking for, Goal Seek requires three inputs:

- **Set Cell** is the cell address for the result you want. The Set Cell must contain a formula.
- **To Value** is the value (the goal) you want the formula in the Set Cell to achieve.
- **By Changing Cell** is the cell address for the value that you want to change in order to achieve the To Value (goal) you want. This cell must contain a value, not a formula, and must be referenced in the To Value's formula.

4	1st Qtr	2nd Qtr	3rd Qtr	4th Qtr	Total Yr
5					
6	$23,567	$35,937	$38,210		=SUM(B6:E6)

1. On a worksheet, enter a formula in a cell that will be your Set Cell.

2. Enter values needed in the formula in cells, one of which you'll chose to be the By Changing Cell.

3. In the Data tab Data Tools group, click **What-If Analysis**, and click **Goal Seek**.

4. In the Goal Seek dialog box, select the cell that will be the Set Cell. The cell will be surrounded by a blinking border.

5. In the To Value text box, type the new value you want the Set Cell to be.

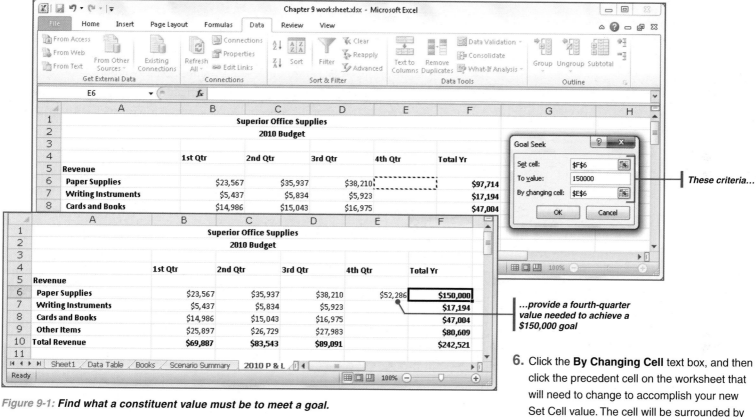

These criteria...

...provide a fourth-quarter value needed to achieve a $150,000 goal

Figure 9-1: Find what a constituent value must be to meet a goal.

6. Click the **By Changing Cell** text box, and then click the precedent cell on the worksheet that will need to change to accomplish your new Set Cell value. The cell will be surrounded by a blinking border, as shown in Figure 9-1.

7. Click **OK**. The Goal Seek Status dialog box appears and shows that a solution was found. The cells will change value (see Figure 9-1).

8. Click **OK** to accept the changes to your worksheet.

–Or–

Click **Cancel** to return the worksheet to its original values.

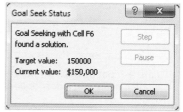

TIP

If you click **OK** in the Goal Seek Status dialog box and change the values on your worksheet, you can revert to the original values by clicking the **Undo** button on the Quick Access toolbar.

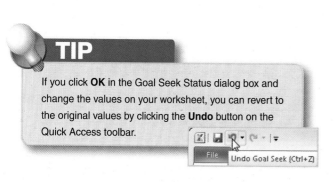

Compare Alternatives Using Scenarios

You use *scenarios* to create a set of situations where you can change the values for various cells, save the changed values, and evaluate how the scenarios compare against one another in a side-by-side summary report. For example, if you wanted to see how changes to upcoming fourth-quarter revenue might affect your year-end profit, you could create a scenario for each entry on the worksheet that you wanted to change.

IDENTIFY CHANGING CELLS

1. Name the cells whose values you will be changing by clicking a cell and typing a name in the Name Box at the left end of the Formula bar (see Chapter 2). Press **ENTER**. (It will be more meaningful to see descriptive names in the Scenario Values dialog box.)

2. Repeat for the other cells that you will be changing.

CREATE A SCENARIO

1. In the Data tab Data Tools group, click **What-If Analysis**, and click **Scenario Manager**. In the Scenario Manager, click **Add**. The Add Scenario dialog box appears, similar to what is shown in Figure 9-2.

2. In the Scenario Name text box, name the scenario according to the type of changes it contains—for example, Revenue, Low Wages, or Current Values.

3. Click the **Changing Cells** text box, and then click the first cell where you will change a value. Hold down **CTRL** while clicking any other cells whose values you'll want changed in this scenario. Move the dialog box or click the **Collapse Dialog** button if the dialog box is in your way. Expand the dialog box by clicking either **Close** or **Expand Dialog**.

4. In the Comment text box, edit the text by selecting the default text and entering your own.

5. Leave the **Prevent Changes** check box selected, unless you want the changes to replace the current values on the worksheet.

6. Click **OK**. If one of your selected cells contains a formula, you will be told that formulas in those cells will be replaced by constant values when you show the scenario. Click **OK** to continue.

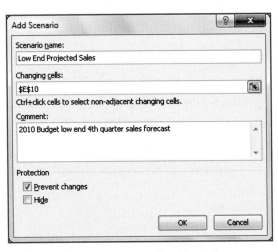

Figure 9-2: Set up each scenario with a unique name, changing cells, and a description.

7. Click **Add** to continue adding more scenarios.

–Or–

In the Scenario Values dialog box, change the values for one or more of the listed changing cells, and click **OK**.

RUN A SCENARIO

1. Open the Scenario Manager, if necessary. Select the scenario you want to run, and click **Show**, or double-click the scenario, as shown in Figure 9-3. The changing cells on your worksheet display any changed values, and any affected formulas recalculate and provide updated results.

2. To return your worksheet to its original state, close the Scenario Manager dialog box, and then click **Undo** on the Quick Access toolbar.

EDIT A SCENARIO

1. Open the Scenario Manager (see Figure 9-3), if necessary, and select the scenario you want to edit. Click **Edit**.

Figure 9-3: **The Scenario Manager provides a one-stop location to list, change, and run scenarios.**

2. In the Edit Scenario dialog box, change the name, add or remove changing cells, edit comments, and choose whether to change the protection status. Click **OK**.

3. In the Scenario Values dialog box, make any changes to the values for the changing cells. Click **OK**.

4. To delete the scenario, select it in the Scenario Manager, and click **Delete**.

COMPARE SCENARIOS

1. Open the Scenario Manager, if necessary, and click the **Summary** button.

2. In the Scenario Summary dialog box, leave the default option, **Scenario Summary**, selected.

3. Click the **Result Cells** box, and then click the first cell where you want to see the result of the change(s) you made in scenarios.

4. If there is more than one results cell you want to see, type a comma (,) after the previous results cell before you click the subsequent cell.

5. Click **OK** when finished. A new worksheet named "Scenario Summary" is added to the workbook, similar to that shown in Figure 9-4.

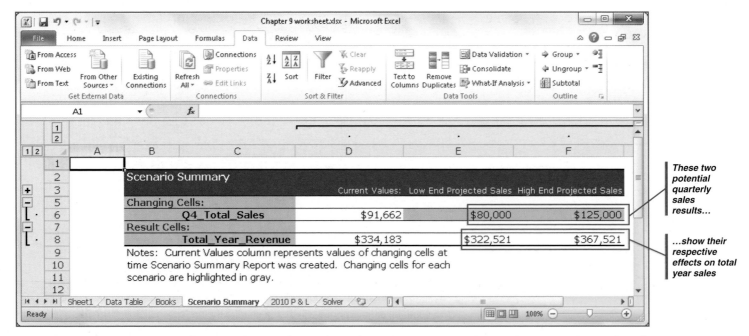

Figure 9-4: *The Scenario Summary lists changing cells from all scenarios and shows how each scenario changes the results cells.*

USING A ONE-VARIABLE COLUMNAR DATA TABLE

A quick and easy way to see how changing values will affect the results of a formula is to use a *data table*, shown in Figure 9-5. In this example, you would like to quickly see the effects on your retirement income based on several withdrawal rates from your 401(k) account.

1. Set up a column of values that represents a variable in a formula or function.

2. Place the formula or function that uses the variable in the cell to the right and above the first cell in the column of values.

3. Select the range consisting of the column of values and the column that contains the formula.

Increasing withdrawal rate...	Increasing $$$ per year
	$40,000
4.50%	
5.00%	
5.50%	
6.00%	

4. In the Data tab Data Tools group, click **What-If Analysis**, and click **Data Table**.

5. In the Data Table dialog box, click the **Column Input Cell**, and then click the cell that contains the variable. The cell reference is placed in the dialog box. Click **OK**.

The data table substitutes the values in the column for the variable in the formula and inserts the results in the column next to the column of values.

Data Table
Row input cell:
Column input cell: $B$6
OK   Cancel

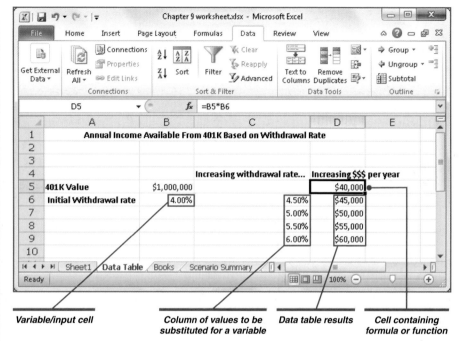

Variable/input cell   Column of values to be   Data table results   Cell containing
                           substituted for a variable   formula or function

Figure 9-5: *Data tables allow you to substitute values for variables in an easy-to-understand tabular format.*

Use Multiple Variables to Provide a Result

Solver is Excel's more sophisticated tool for providing an answer to what-if problems. Figure 9-6 shows an example worksheet where Solver could be used. Begin using Solver by identifying the following cells and parameters:

- **Objective cell** is the cell that contains a formula that you want to maximize, to minimize, or to return a specific value.

- **Changing variable cells** are related, directly or indirectly, to the objective cell-by-cell references, and Solver will adjust them to obtain the result you want in the target cell.

- **Constraints** are limitations or boundaries you set for cells that are related, directly or indirectly, to the objective cell.

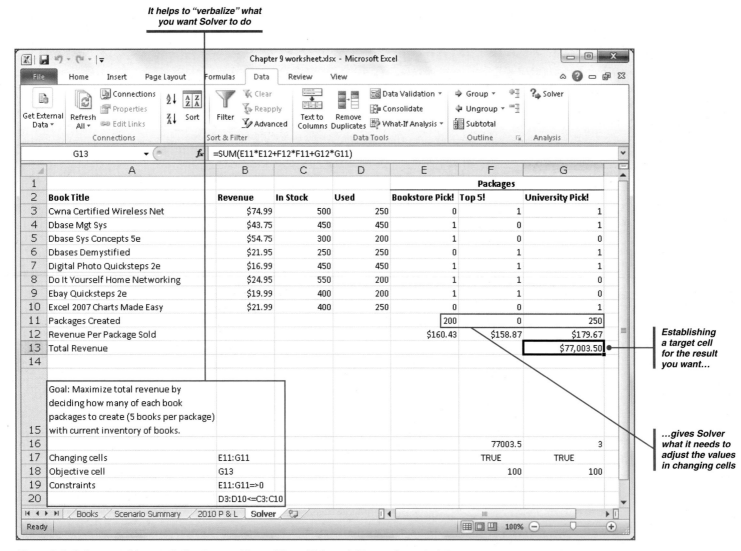

It helps to "verbalize" what you want Solver to do

Establishing a target cell for the result you want...

...gives Solver what it needs to adjust the values in changing cells

Figure 9-6: *Solver provides a solution to a problem with multiple variables and constraints.*

INSTALL SOLVER

1. Click **File**, click **Options**, and click **Add-Ins** in the left pane.

2. In the Excel Options Add-Ins dialog box, Solver Add-In is listed among the Inactive Application Add-Ins. Verify that **Excel Add-Ins** is displayed in the Manage box at the bottom of the dialog box. If not, select it. In either case, click **Go**.

3. In the Add-Ins dialog box, select **Solver Add-In**, and click **OK**. You might see a message informing you that Solver is not currently installed and giving you the opportunity to install it. Click **Yes**. You also might need your Microsoft Office CD or path to a network installation location to complete the installation.

4. After the installation is complete, a new Analysis group is added to the Data tab and the Solver add-in is added as an active application to the Excel Options dialog box.

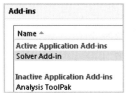

Figure 9-7: *Setting the objective cell, indicating what cells are to be changed by Solver, and listing constraints in the Solver Parameters dialog box provides all that's needed to run Solver.*

SET UP SOLVER

1. In the Data tab Analysis group, click **Solver**. The Solver Parameters dialog box appears, as shown in Figure 9-7.

2. Click in the **Set Objective** text box, and either type the address of the cell in which you want to see the result or click that cell on the worksheet. (If the dialog box is in your way, click the **Collapse Dialog** button, and then click the cell. Click **Expand Dialog** to return to the full-size Solver Parameters dialog box.) The objective cell must contain a formula.

3. In the To area, select what type of value you want the target cell to return: maximized (Max), minimized (Min), or a value you enter (Value Of).

4. Click in the **By Changing Variable Cells** text box. Type the address of the first cell whose value you want Solver to adjust, or click that cell on the worksheet. Hold down **CTRL** while clicking any other cells whose values you want Solver to adjust.

5. If you have constraints, click **Add** to open the Add Constraint dialog box.

   - Click the **Cell Reference** text box. Type the cell reference that will be subject to your constraint, or select that cell reference on the worksheet.

   - Click the operators' down arrow to see a list of comparison operators, and select the one that matches your constraint. Choosing int (whole numbers) or bin (1 or 0) places integer or binary, respectively, in the Constraint text box.

   - Click **Add** to create another constraint, or click **Cancel** if you are done adding constraints. The constraints are displayed in the Subject To The Constraints list box.

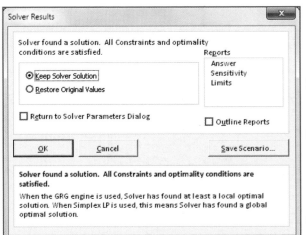

Figure 9-8: *When Solver finds a solution, it reports to you that it has satisfied all constraints.*

6. Keep the default settings in the dialog box, and click **Solve**. The Solver Results dialog box lets you know that a solution was reached, similar to what is shown in Figure 9-8. (If there's in error in your setup, you will also receive notification of this.)

Save Solver Results and Settings

You can save the work you do in Solver in several ways.

SAVE VALUES

After running a Solver problem, in the Solver Results dialog box, click **Keep Solver Solution**. The values produced by Solver are added to the worksheet, replacing your original numbers. Save the worksheet by pressing **CTRL+S**.

SAVE AS A SCENARIO

You can save different sets of changing-cells values as scenarios, whose results you can then compare (see "Compare Scenarios" earlier in the chapter).

1. In the Solver Results dialog box, click **Save Scenario**. The Save Scenario dialog box appears.

2. Type a descriptive name for the scenario, and click **OK**.

3. In the Data tab Data Tools group, click **What-If Analysis**, and click **Scenario Manager** to view and work with saved Solver and other scenarios.

SAVE SOLVER SETTINGS AS A MODEL

You can save the settings you've created in Solver as a *model*. These settings are copied onto the worksheet and are made available for you to run at a later time. You can have more than one Solver model saved per worksheet.

1. In the Solver Parameters dialog box, enter your settings and click **Load/Save**.

9

2. In the Load/Save Model dialog box, accept or change the range on the worksheet to where the Solver settings will be copied. Click **Save**. Each constraint evaluation and other cells containing parameters of the model are displayed, as shown in Figure 9-9.

3. Click **OK**.

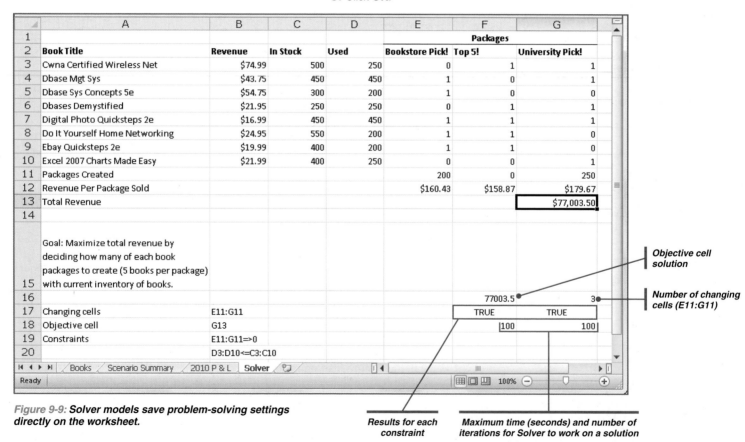

Figure 9-9: *Solver models save problem-solving settings directly on the worksheet.*

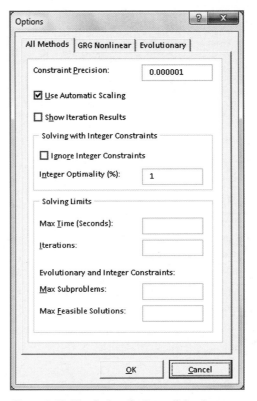

QUICKSTEPS

CHANGING SOLVER SETTINGS

In the Data tab Analysis group, click **Solver**. Perform the following procedures in the Solver Parameters dialog box.

CHANGE OBJECTIVE OR VARIABLE CELLS

Make changes to cell references in the Set Objective cell and By Changing Variable Cells areas by typing in the text boxes or clicking cells on the worksheet. Change what the objective cell is to be equal to.

CHANGE CONSTRAINTS

1. Select the constraint you want to change, and click **Change**.

2. Make changes in the Change Constraint dialog box, and click **OK**.

START ANEW

To remove all previous settings in the Solver Parameters dialog box, click **Reset All**.

SET ADVANCED OPTIONS

Click **Options**. Before changing options in the Options dialog box, shown in Figure 9-10, ensure you understanding the rationale for doing so.

Figure 9-10: *The Solver Options dialog box provides settings that typical users will seldom need to change.*

Work with PivotTables

PivotTables are Excel's "Swiss Army knife" solution for comparing and analyzing data, especially in larger worksheets. Excel helps you create the initial PivotTable report and lets you quickly make changes that pivot the table, rearranging the data for different solutions. In addition, you can create charts (*PivotCharts*) that graphically show the results of a PivotTable report.

NOTE

As shown in Figure 9-11, you can use a PivotTable to analyze external data. If you are unfamiliar with importing external data, see Chapter 10. You can also consolidate data from multiple ranges.

QUICK**FACTS**

UNDERSTANDING PIVOTTABLE TERMS

PivotTables can be daunting at first. Knowing the terminology found in the PivotTable Field List will get you started on a good footing.

- **Field** is a substitute term used for the column header label(s) in the table or range where your data is located.
- The **Report Filter** box holds fields that filter the PivotTable.
- The **Row Labels** box allows you to display each category of that item in its own row. Typically, these items are descriptive and identifying, not numerical—for example, Country, Salesperson, and Title.
- The **Column Labels** box allows you to display each category of the item in its own column. Typically, these items are descriptive and identifying, not numerical—for example, Population, Sales, and Pages.
- The **Values** box allows you to sum or otherwise perform calculations and display the results. Typically, these items are numerical and capable of being counted, summed, and calculated.

Create a PivotTable

A PivotTable allows you to take a large amount of data and automatically rearrange it so that you can more easily understand and compare it.

1. Select a cell in a range whose data you want to use in the PivotTable. In the Insert tab Tables group, click **PivotTable**.

   –Or–

   Click a cell in a table whose data you want to use in the PivotTable. In the Design tab (Table Tools) Tools group, click **Summarize With PivotTable**.

   In either case, the Create PivotTable dialog box appears, shown in Figure 9-11.

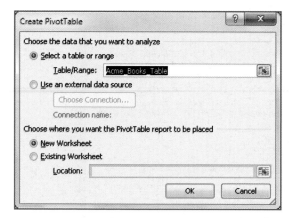

*Figure 9-11: **You need to supply minimal information to start a PivotTable.***

2. Modify the range you want included in the PivotTable, if needed, or click **Use An External Data Source** (see Note).

3. Click **New Worksheet** to have Excel create a new worksheet for the report.

   –Or–

   Click **Existing Worksheet** and click the worksheet tab and upper-left cells for where you want the PivotTable report to begin.

4. Click **OK** when finished. The Excel window changes in three major ways (see Figure 9-12): the framework of a PivotTable is inserted where you specified, a field list task pane is displayed on the right side of the worksheet window, and Options and Design tabs (PivotTable Tools) are added to the ribbon.

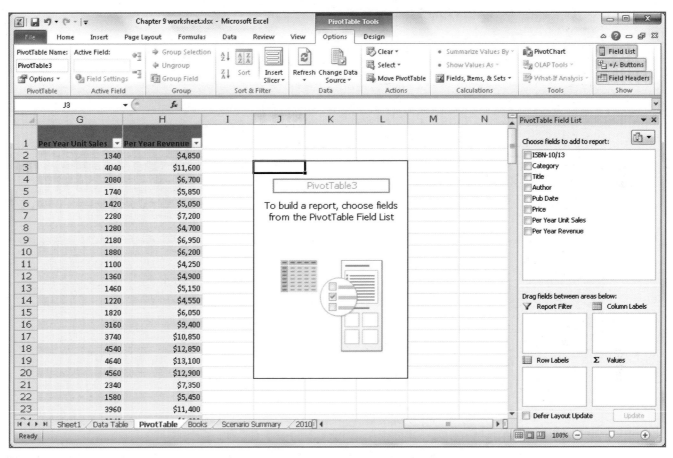

Figure 9-12: Excel provides an Options tab and a task pane to facilitate your work with PivotTables.

You can easily change how you want data categorized in the PivotTable. For example, the data in the Pub Date column in Figure 9-13 is formatted as numbers, and Excel initially places it in the Values area of the task pane. Since I want to use it as row labels, I simply drag it from the Values area to the Row Labels area, and the PivotTable is instantly reoriented.

Create the PivotTable Layout

1. Create an initial PivotTable (see the previous procedure).

2. Click the check box next to a *field* (or column header from your table or range) from the PivotTable Field List at the top of the task pane. Depending on the type of data contained in the field, Excel will assign it to an area at the bottom of the task pane. Start by selecting fields that contain data that you want to display as row labels (see Figure 9-13). You can include more than one field in a box, and you can deselect a field's check box to remove it from an area.

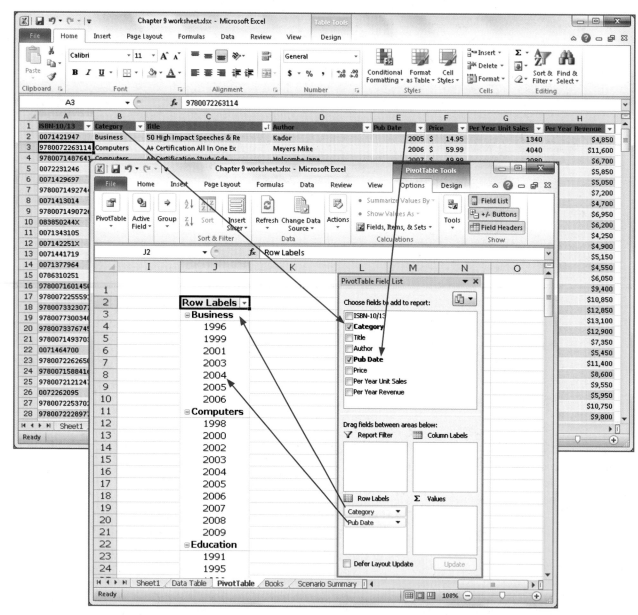

Figure 9-13: *Start a PivotTable by selecting the fields to be used as row or column labels.*

3. Next, select a field that provides the initial summary information you are looking for. If the field contains numbers or formulas, Excel will initially place it in the Values area. This is the start of a meaningful PivotTable, as shown in Figure 9-14.

4. See your data in a different aspect by dragging a row label to the Column Labels area (or vice versa).

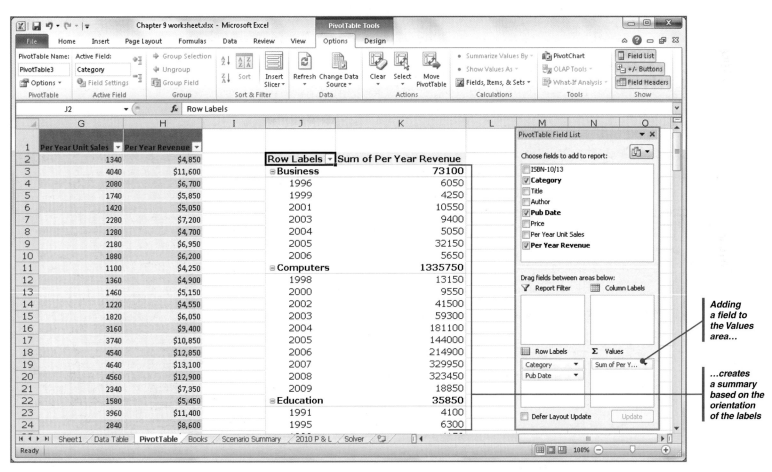

*Figure 9-14: **This sample PivotTable shows sales summarized by authors within a category using row labels.***

–Or–

Click the field icon down arrow of the field you want to move, and click one of the direction options.

Figure 9-15 shows how the data in the PivotTable in Figure 9-14 changes when a field is moved from a row label to a column label. This is where a "Pivot Table" gets its name.

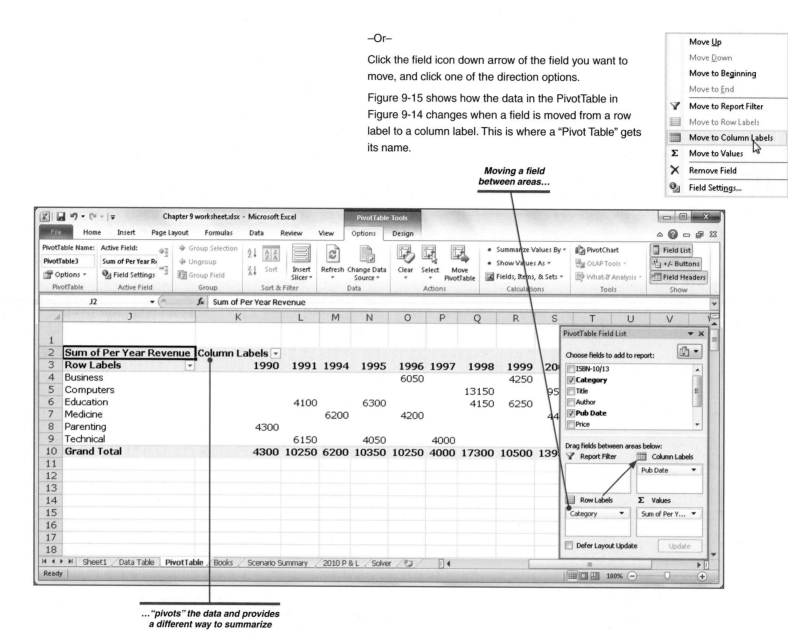

*Moving a field
between areas...*

*..."pivots" the data and provides
a different way to summarize*

Figure 9-15: *By simply moving a field between the Row Labels and Column Labels areas, you can change the summary to columnar year-by-year totals.*

Use Slicers

Slicers, new to Excel 2010, are filters that float over the worksheet and allow you to quickly view only selected data in a PivotTable. Figure 9-16 shows two slicers that have been added next to a PivotTable (you can display a slicer for each field in your PivotTable). Each slicer, representing the initial possible values within a field, can be quickly changed to filter only the data you want to see, by you and by Excel. In Figure 9-16, I selected to view the book sales revenue for a single author.

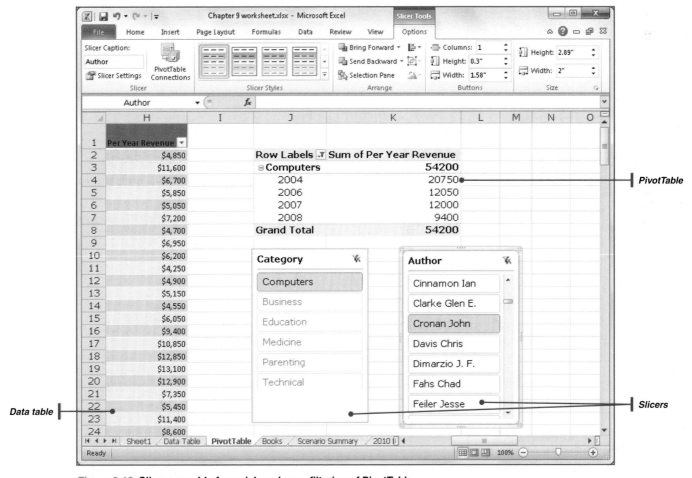

Figure 9-16: *Slicers provide for quick and easy filtering of PivotTables.*

TIP

To return a PivotTable to its original configuration after applying and/or removing slicers, select a cell in the PivotTable. In the Options tab (PivotTable Tools) Actions group, click **Clear** and then click **Clear Filters**.

QUICKSTEPS

USING PIVOTTABLES

PivotTables can utilize many features that are employed in tables, outlines, and in general worksheet usage. Access these features on the Options tab (PivotTable Tools) or by right-clicking specific PivotTable elements and selecting them from the context menu. Here is a sampling of the options you have available to you.

Start by selecting a cell in the PivotTable.

SORT AND FILTER PIVOTTABLES

1. Click the **AutoFilter** down arrow of the orientation header (Row Labels or Column Labels) you want to sort or filter the data on.

2. Click the **Select Field** down arrow (only available if you have nested fields or labels), and click the field to sort or filter by.

Continued . . .

Since this author (yours truly) only writes books in one category (Computers), Excel filtered out all the nonapplicable categories of book types and only presented the pertinent category and its revenue numbers. If I selected multiple authors that sold books in other categories, those categories and values would also be displayed. Good stuff! Also, slicers can be customized through styles, sorting, size, and other parameters.

INSERT SLICERS

1. Click anywhere in the PivotTable.
2. In the Options tab (PivotTable Tools) Sort & Filter group, click **Insert Slicer**.
3. In the Insert Slicers dialog box, select the fields you want represented by slicers. Click **OK**.

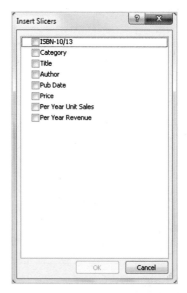

3. Click one of the sort or filter options on the menu at the top (see Chapter 8 for more information on sorting and filtering).

–Or–

Click the field you want to sort by directly on the PivotTable, and use the Sort & Filter group on the Options tab for the same sorting options.

HIDE OR SHOW THE PIVOTTABLE FIELD LIST TASK PANE

In the Options tab (PivotTable Tools) Show group, click **Field List** to hide the task pane. Click it a second time to redisplay the task pane.

APPLY CALCULATIONS TO VALUES

You can choose from several calculated methods to change how your values are interpreted. For example,

Continued . . .

---

4. Drag the border or a blank area of the slicer to move the slicer close to the PivotTable (you might have to scroll your worksheet horizontally toward the left to find the inserted slicers).

APPLY AND REMOVE SLICER FILTERS

Initially, all values in the slicer are selected.

1. Click a value button to filter on one value.

   –Or–

   Use the **CTRL+CLICK** or **SHIFT+CLICK** technique to select multiple noncontiguous or contiguous values to filter, respectively.

2. Use step 1 to filter other slicers you have displayed, or repeat steps 2 through 4 in the previous section to add any others you want.

3. To remove a filter, click **Remove Filter** in the upper-right corner of the slicer (if you have one slicer that controls the filtering of other slicers, remove the filter from the controlling slicer to remove filtering from all the dependent slicers).

4. To remove a slicer, right-click the slicer and click **Remove Slicer**.

CUSTOMIZE SLICERS

Slicers, like shapes, pictures, and other graphics, can be modified from tools on the ribbon (see Figure 9-16) or within a dialog box.

Select the slicer you want to modify (select multiple slicers by using **CTRL+CLICK**). You have several groups on the Options tab (Slicer Tools) you can use to change the appearance of selected slicers.

- In the Slicer Styles group, apply one of the displayed styles; or click the **More** button, and click **New Slicer Styles** to create a new style by formatting each slicer element. Close the New Slicer Quick Style dialog box when you are done.

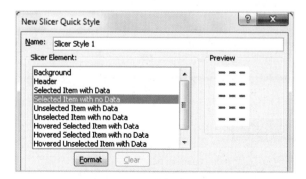

QUICKSTEPS

USING PIVOTTABLES (Continued)

to show values as what percentage they are of the grand total:

1. Right-click a value (for example, any of the Sum Of Per Year Revenue values shown in Figure 9-14) to display its context menu.

2. On the context menu, click **Show Values As**, and click **% Of Grand Total**. The column of values changes from its numerical values to percentages of the total.

APPLY CURRENCY FORMATS TO A VALUE FIELD

PivotTables don't extract the cell formatting from the table or range where the data originates. To add currency (or other numbering formats):

1. Select a cell in a value field to which you want to add currency formatting.

2. In the Options tab (PivotTable Tools) Active Field group, click **Field Settings**.

   –Or–

   Right-click a cell in the value field, and click **Value Field Settings**.

   Make any changes to how the field is calculated, and click **Number Format**.

3. In the Format Cells dialog box, click **Currency**, select the formatting you want, and click **OK**.

Row Labels ▼	Sum of Per Year Revenue
⊟ **Business**	**4.63%**
1996	0.38%
1999	0.27%
2001	0.67%
2003	0.60%
2004	0.32%
2005	2.04%
2006	0.36%
⊟ **Computers**	**84.66%**
1998	0.83%

Column Labels ▼		
	1990	1991
		$4,100
	$4,300	
		$6,150
	$4,300	**$10,250**

- In the Arrange group, rearrange the stacking of multiple slicers.
- In the Buttons group, change the size of buttons and the number of columns in which they appear.
- In the Size group, change the height and width of selected slicers.

–Or–

In the Slicer group, click **Slicer Settings** (or right-click a slicer and click **Slicer Settings**), and apply many of the same options that are available from the ribbon, as well as a few others, as shown in Figure 9-17.

Slicer Settings

Source Name: Category

Name: Category

Header

☑ Display header

Caption: Category

Layout

Number of columns: 1   Button height: 0.25"

Button width: 1.83"

Item Sorting and Filtering

◉ Descending (Z to A)   ☑ Show items with no data
○ Ascending (A to Z)   ☑ Visually indicate items with no data
☑ Show items with no data last

Position

Top: 2.54"   ☐ Disable resizing and moving

Left: 14.97"

OK   Cancel

*Figure 9-17: **Slicers have several functional and design options you can customize.***

Style a PivotTable

Excel offers a similar set of prebuilt styles for PivotTables as it does for standard tables, along with styling and layout options.

Category	Pub Date	Sum of Per Year Revenue
⊟Business	1996	$6,050
	1999	$4,250
	2001	$10,550
	2003	$9,400
	2004	$5,050
	2005	$32,150
	2006	$5,650
Business Total		**$73,100**
⊟Computers	1998	$13,150
	2000	$9,550
	2002	$41,500
	2003	$59,300
	2004	$181,100
	2005	$144,000
	2006	$214,900
	2007	$329,950
	2008	$323,450
	2009	$18,850
Computers Total		**$1,335,750**
⊟Education	1991	$4,100
	1995	$6,300
	1998	$4,150
	1999	$6,250
	2001	$4,350
	2003	$5,000
	2006	$5,700
Education Total		**$35,850**
⊟Medicine	1994	$6,200
	1996	$4,200
	2000	$4,400

*Figure 9-18: **You're just a few mouse clicks away from transforming your staid data into something you can use in presentations and other documents.***

SELECT A STYLE

1. Click a cell in the PivotTable.

   –Or–

   In the Options tab (PivotTable Tools) Actions group, click **Select** and click **Entire Table**.

2. In the Design tab (PivotTable Tools) PivotTable Styles group, point to the style examples on the ribbon.

   –Or–

   Click the row-by-row buttons.

   –Or–

   Click the **More** button to see the complete gallery.

   In all cases, pointing to a Quick Style icon will change the PivotTable to reflect the style attributes. (For more information on applying styles to PivotTables, see the discussion in Chapter 8 on applying styles to tables.)

3. Select one or more options in the Design tab PivotTable Style Options group.

CHANGE THE PIVOTTABLE'S LAYOUT

You can add some readability to a PivotTable by choosing a more expanded layout. For example, you can display the table in an outline or tabular layout.

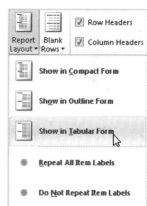

1. Click a cell in the PivotTable.

2. In the Design tab (PivotTable Tools) Layout group, click **Report Layout**.

3. Click each of the layout options to see which one presents your data in the best form for your purposes. One example combining layout and styling options is shown in Figure 9-18.

Create a PivotTable Chart

1. Click a cell in the PivotTable.

2. In the Options tab (PivotTables Tools) Tools group, click **PivotChart**. The Insert Chart dialog box displays chart types (see Chapter 6 for information on building and working with charts). Double-click the type you want. A chart area displays on the worksheet, and additional PivotChart Tools tabs display on the ribbon to support charting (Design, Layout, Format, and Analyze), as shown in Figure 9-19.

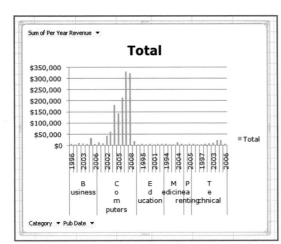

Figure 9-19: Don't be concerned with how a PivotChart first displays—you can easily modify it to meet your needs.

3. Make any changes to the PivotTable using the PivotTable tools (for example, collapse fields by clicking the minus signs next to them), and then click the PivotChart to return to charting tabs and tools. The chart will change to reflect changes made to the PivotTable.

4. Use slicers (see "Use Slicers" earlier in the chapter) to filter your active fields (first select a cell in the PivotTable to activate slicer functionality). When finished, you can get your chart to display only the data you want, an example of which is shown in Figure 9-20.

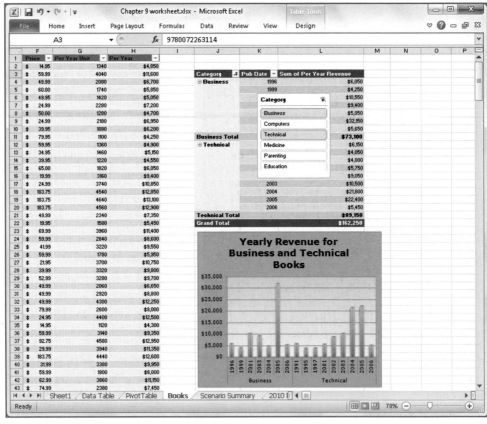

Figure 9-20: PivotTables and PivotCharts change dynamically as you modify layout and other options.

Work with Other Users

There are several ways to let others work with your data. One way is to control total access to the workbook file, choosing whether to allow others to open the file and/or make modifications. Another way is to provide access to the workbook and *protect* certain elements of the workbook and individual worksheets. You can also *share* the workbook so that all users can edit the same data, even simultaneously, while exercising limited protection.

Protect Workbooks with Passwords

The first level of security Excel offers is simple. If you know the correct password(s), you can open and/or modify the file when prompted.

ADD PASSWORD PROTECTION TO OPEN A WORKBOOK

1. With an Excel workbook open, click the **File** tab. In the Info view, click **Protect Workbooks** and then click **Encrypt With Password**.

2. In the Encrypt Document dialog box, type a password and click **OK**.

3. In the Confirm Password dialog box, retype your password and click **OK**.

ADD PASSWORD PROTECTION TO MODIFY A WORKBOOK

With an Excel workbook open, click the **File** tab, and click **Save As**.

In the Save As dialog box, click the **Tools** down arrow (at the bottom of the dialog box next to Save), and click **General Options**.

1. In the General Options dialog box, in the File Sharing area:

   ● Type a password in the **Password To Open** text box to control who can open the workbook if you haven't already done so (see the previous section).

   ● Type a password in the **Password To Modify** text box to control who can modify contents. (Leaving this password blank allows everyone to make changes; adding a password effectively provides read-only access to those who do not have the password.)

   ● Select **Read-Only Recommended** to prevent changes without requiring a password.

2. Click **OK**. Type the password a second time (or third time if you select both password options), and click **OK**.

3. Click **Save**. If you are working with an existing workbook, click **Yes** to replace the current file.

CHANGE OR REMOVE A PASSWORD

Only the originator of a file can remove its passwords and thereby turn off access controls.

With an Excel workbook open, click the **File** tab, click **Save As**, and repeat the steps in the previous section to display the General Options dialog box and delete or change the password(s). Click **OK**, click **Save** to close the Save As dialog box, and click **Yes** to replace the file.

Share a Workbook

Shared workbooks are particularly useful for users on a network when multiple people are adding and viewing data in tables (see Chapter 8 for more information on creating and using tables). However, Excel does impose several limitations on what can be accomplished in a shared workbook. Before the workbook is shared by you or the originator, much of the "design work" of a worksheet

TIP

When you apply password protection at the file level to a *shared* workbook, the Password To Open text box is unavailable. You can only choose to allow modifications or not.

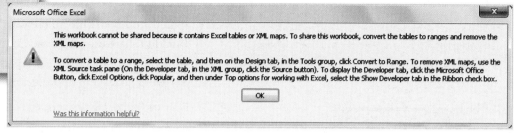

Microsoft Office Excel

⚠ This workbook cannot be shared because it contains Excel tables or XML maps. To share this workbook, convert the tables to ranges and remove the XML maps.

To convert a table to a range, select the table, and then on the Design tab, in the Tools group, click Convert to Range. To remove XML maps, use the XML Source task pane (On the Developer tab, in the XML group, click the Source button). To display the Developer tab, click the Microsoft Office Button, click Excel Options, click Popular, and then under Top options for working with Excel, select the Show Developer tab in the Ribbon check box.

OK

Was this information helpful?

CAUTION

If you want to password-protect a shared workbook against the possibility of someone removing the tracked changes history, create the password before you share the workbook. To do this, see "Protect a Shared Workbook" rather than use the information in this section.

CAUTION

Prior to sharing a workbook, you will need to convert tables to a standard data range (in the Design tab (Table Tools) Tools group, click **Convert To Range**). Advanced users might also need to remove some XML elements.

should be completed. Shared workbooks are best used for entering and editing data, not making major structural changes.

1. In the Review tab Changes group, click **Share Workbook**.

2. In the Share Workbook dialog box, select the **Allow Changes By More Than One User At The Same Time** check box. Click **OK**.

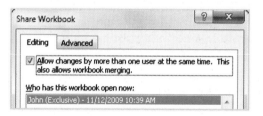

3. You might see a warning dialog box related to replacing external structured references (cell names) with errors. Click **Yes** or **No** to continue, depending on whether that is acceptable to you. If Yes is clicked, the workbook is shared and is so indicated by the word *Shared* added next to the workbook name in the Excel window title bar.

Chapter4 worksheet.xlsx [Shared] – Microsoft Excel

Review   View

NOTE

Not all changes are tracked. Tracked changes include changes to cell contents created by editing, moving and copying, and inserting and removing rows and columns.

QUICKSTEPS

WORKING WITH CHANGES IN A SHARED WORKBOOK

When sharing a workbook, you can adjust how often changes are kept, when they're updated, and how to resolve conflicts.

ENABLE TRACK CHANGES (IN UNSHARED WORKBOOKS)

When you enable Track Changes, you will also share the workbook.

1. In the Review tab Changes group, click **Track Changes** and click **Highlight Changes**.

2. If it isn't already checked, click **Track Changes While Editing**. Accept the default settings (the next section explains how to change these). Click **OK** to close the Highlight Changes dialog box. Click **OK** again to acknowledge that no changes were found meeting the default settings (assuming you didn't make any); or in the case of a new workbook, name and save the file in the Save As dialog box that appears.

MODIFY CHANGE ATTRIBUTES

In the Review tab Changes group, click **Track Changes** and click **Highlight Changes**.

- To highlight all changes, deselect the **When**, **Who**, and **Where** check boxes.

Continued . . .

Protect a Shared Workbook

Shared workbooks are inherently not secure. (If you wanted them secure, you wouldn't share them.) However, you can protect against other users removing the shared workbook's Track Changes feature and history, and require that a password be used to unprotect it.

1. In the Review tab Changes group, click **Protect And Share Workbook**.

2. In the Protect Shared Workbook dialog box, click **Sharing With Track Changes**.

3. Click **OK**.

–Or–

If the workbook is not shared at this time, type a password and click **OK**. In the Confirm Password dialog box, type the password a second time, and click **OK**. Click **OK** a third time to save the workbook. (If you are using a new workbook that hasn't yet been saved with a file name, you will be given that opportunity.)

Discontinue Sharing a Workbook

To stop sharing a workbook, you must first remove all users who may have the shared workbook open (contact any users and make sure they save any recent changes). In addition, if you need to keep a record of changes, save the data in the History worksheet (see Figure 9-21) to another workbook or other location before you stop sharing.

1. Open the shared workbook, and remove workbook protection by clicking **Unprotect Shared Workbook** in the Review tab Changes group, if enabled (see "Protect a Shared Workbook").

2. In the Review tab Changes group, click **Share Workbook**.

WORKING WITH CHANGES IN A SHARED WORKBOOK (Continued)

- To selectively highlight changes, select options from the When and/or Who drop-down list boxes, and/or click the **Where** text box, and select the range where you want changes highlighted.

- To view changes on-screen, select **Highlight Changes On Screen**.

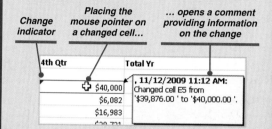

| Change indicator | Placing the mouse pointer on a changed cell... | ... opens a comment providing information on the change |

- To view changes on a separate worksheet, select **List Changes On A New Sheet**. Save your workbook. A History worksheet is added to the workbook, as shown in Figure 9-21.

WORK WITH CHANGES IN A SHARED WORKBOOK

1. In the Review tab Changes group, click **Share Workbook** and click **Advanced**.

2. To change whether and for how long changes are tracked, change the settings in the Track Changes area.

3. To determine when changes are updated and whether to view changes by others, change the settings in the Update Changes area.

4. To determine how conflicting changes are handled, in the Conflicting Changes Between Users area, determine how conflicts will be resolved.

5. Click **OK** when finished.

Continued ...

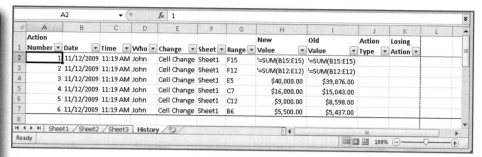

Figure 9-21: In shared workbooks, you can opt to have changes recorded on a separate History worksheet.

3. On the Editing tab, select any users other than yourself, and click **Remove User**.

4. Deselect the **Allow Changes By More Than One User At The Same Time** check box.

5. Click **OK**. Click **Yes** to accept losing the change history and any unsaved changes by other users.

Work with Views

Although you can create custom views at any time, not just when working in a shared environment, the feature is especially useful when sharing a workbook. Each user's view can be saved with many personalized display settings, so the next time each user opens the workbook, the same worksheet that he or she was last working on will be displayed with the same print settings, filter settings, and other settings. Users can create other views and switch to them as well.

CREATE A CUSTOM VIEW

Set up any filters, print settings (including print areas), zoom magnifications, and other settings as you want them saved.

1. In the View tab Workbook views group, click **Custom Views**. The Custom Views dialog box lists your default *personal* view that appears when you open the workbook.

QUICKSTEPS

WORKING WITH CHANGES IN A SHARED WORKBOOK *(Continued)*

ACCEPT OR REJECT CHANGES

1. In the Review tab Changes group, click **Track Changes** and click **Accept Or Reject Changes**.

2. In the Select Changes To Accept Or Reject dialog box, select options from the When and/or Who drop-down list boxes, and/or click the **Where** text box, and select the range where you want changes highlighted. Click **OK**.

3. When a conflict arises due to different users changing the same data, accept either your own (click **Accept**) or the change(s) made by the other user(s) (click **Reject**) in the Accept Or Reject Changes dialog box. Continue clicking **Accept** or **Reject** to view subsequent changes, or click **Accept All** or **Reject All** to finish the review.

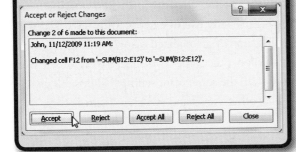

NOTE

If the workbook is shared, both Protect Sheet and Protect Workbook are disabled.

2. Click **Add**. In the Add View dialog box, type a descriptive name, and choose whether to include print settings, filter settings, and hidden rows and columns. Click **OK**.

3. Set up and add any other views. Click **OK** when done.

CHANGE VIEWS

In the View tab Workbook views group, click **Custom Views**. In the Custom Views dialog box, select the view you want to display, and click **Show**. To remove a view, select it and click **Delete**.

Protect Worksheet and Workbook Elements

If you generally "share" workbooks with others without formally creating a shared workbook, you can control whether several elements of both worksheets and workbooks can be changed.

PROTECT WORKSHEET ELEMENTS

Worksheet protection applies only to the currently active worksheet.

1. In the Review tab Changes group, click **Protect Sheet**.

2. Ensure that the **Protect Worksheet And Contents Of Locked Cells** check box is selected (see Figure 9-22). Optionally, type a password that will be needed to unprotect the worksheet.

3. Select the check boxes in the Allow All Users Of This Worksheet To list box for only those actions you want others to be able to perform. Click **OK**. If necessary, confirm the password and click **OK**.

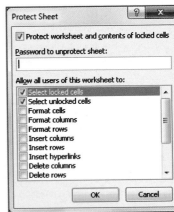

Figure 9-22: **You can protect worksheet elements selectively without sharing a workbook.**

MERGING WORKBOOKS

Let's say you e-mail a workbook you have shared to three college-attending children and instruct each to update their spending according to the worksheet you provide. You get back three workbooks and want to merge the changes on your master copy. You would think Excel would provide a mechanism to do that—and as it turns out it does, but not without some effort on your part. The command is not available on the ribbon, so a little sleuthing is required to find it, but first ensure you have the Allow Changes check box selected in the Share Workbook dialog box (see "Share a Workbook"). Click the **File** tab, click **Options**, and click **Quick Access Toolbar**. Click the **Choose Commands From** down arrow, and select **All Commands**. Scroll through the list of commands, and double-click **Compare And Merge Workbooks**. Click **OK** to close the Excel Options dialog box and add the command to the Quick Access toolbar. Place all four copies of the workbook in a folder, and open the master copy. Click **Compare And Merge Workbooks** on the Quick Access toolbar. Select the three other workbooks (click one file and hold down **CTRL** while clicking the other two), and click **OK**. Data in the master copy is updated according to any changes in the other files.

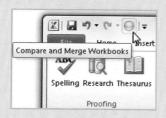

PROTECT WORKBOOK ELEMENTS

1. In the Review tab Changes group, click **Protect Workbook**. In the Protect Structure And Windows dialog box:

- Select **Structure** to prevent changes to noncontent aspects of the workbook, which include viewing hidden worksheets; inserting, moving, deleting, renaming, or hiding worksheets; moving and copying worksheets; and creating a scenario summary report.

- Select **Windows** to prevent resizing and repositioning workbook windows.

2. Optionally, enter a password. Click **OK**. If necessary, confirm the password and click **OK**.

Chapter 10
Extending Excel

In the final chapter of this book, you will learn several techniques that you can use to extend Excel beyond the desktop. Chapter 8 described how you could manage data of your own. In this chapter you will have to connect to data from several disparate sources, including Web pages from the Internet. Excel maintains a record of these connections, which you will see how to manage. You will also learn how to publish data to Web pages for use on Web sites of your own, and will be introduced to Excel Services, a server product for distributing your work to anyone, anywhere, with an Internet connection and a Web browser. Finally, you'll see how to automate steps you take in Excel by creating macros.

Acquire Data

In addition to typing data directly onto a worksheet or entering data by using a form—both of which are time-consuming and prone to error—you can import data from an external source into Excel. Once the data is "safely" on an Excel worksheet, you have all the tools and features this book describes to format, organize, analyze, or otherwise whip the data into the shape you want. You can import data from several *data sources*, including text files, the Web, and databases. Data sources include the *connections* to source data, and comprise the information needed to locate the data (or database server), as well as information needed to access the data, such as user names and passwords.

Convert Text to Data

Text files are files with file extensions such as TXT and CSV (comma-separated values) that can be formatted using commas, spaces, tabs, and other separators to organize data. Though the data might not appear to be structured, as shown in Figure 10-1, Excel can correctly place the data into columns and rows as long as it is separated in a consistent and recognizable format.

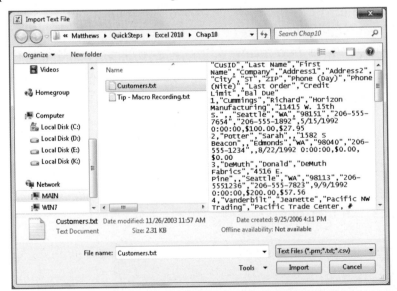

Figure 10-1: Text files might look like a jumble of unrelated data, but Excel can "see through" the clutter to properly format files.

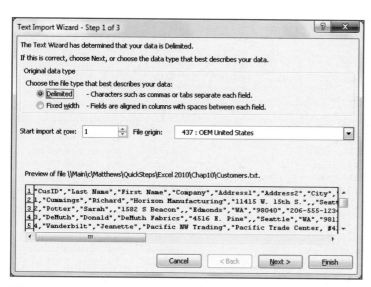

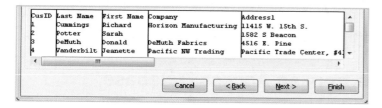

Figure 10-2: Excel provides an educated guess as to how the data in a text file should be divided.

1. Select the cell into which you want to place the beginning of the range of imported data.

2. On the Data tab Get External Data group, click **From Text**. In the Import Text File dialog box, locate the text file you want, select it, and click **Import**. Step 1 of the Text Import Wizard opens.

3. Preview the file in the lower half of the dialog box. If all appears to be in order, Excel has done a good job so far. If needed, make the following choices or decisions (see Figure 10-2), which immediately change the preview:

   ● Determine if the file is delimited (separated) by characters or if it is a fixed width. You can further refine your choice in Step 2 of the wizard.

   ● Decide from where in the text file you want to start importing data. You may not want the headers row if the worksheet already contains one. In that case, you would change the Start Import At Row spinner to 2.

   ● Choose a file origin that matches the text language used in the worksheet.

4. Click **Next** or—if you feel "lucky"—click **Finish**. (You can always delete and start over again.)

5. Step 2 of the wizard lets you fine-tune the delimiter used or set field widths (depending on your choice in Step 1) and preview how the changes align the data. Experiment with the delimiter option or column widths, and see which makes the preview most representative of how you want the data organized. Click **Next** or **Finish**.

6. Step 3 of the wizard lets you apply data formats on a column-by-column basis. You can also format the columns in the worksheet. Click **Finish**.

7. Verify where you want the data placed—either in the current worksheet or in a new worksheet. Make your choice and click **OK**. The data is displayed in Excel, as shown in Figure 10-3.

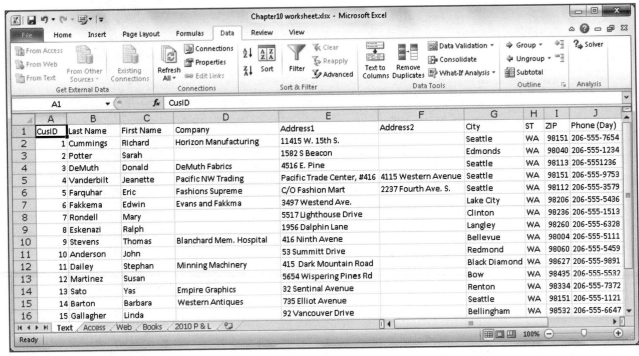

Figure 10-3: *Correctly delimited data imported from a text file is indistinguishable from other data in a worksheet.*

TIP

After you have imported data from a data source, such as an Access database, a data source *connection* is created and saved in a folder under your user Documents folder, titled My Data Sources. The next time you want to import data from that source, it will appear in the Select Data Source dialog box, along with other default connections.

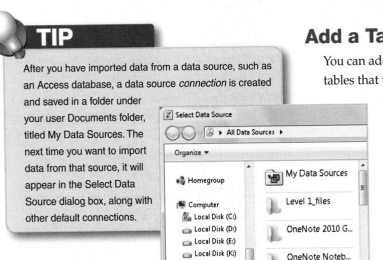

Add a Table from an Access Database

You can add data from a Microsoft Access database by choosing from a list of tables that the database contains.

1. Select the cell into which you want to place the beginning of the range of imported data.

2. On the Data tab Get External Data group, click **From Access**. In the Select Data Source dialog box, locate and select the Access database that contains the table of data you want. Click **Open**.

3. In the Select Table dialog box, select the table you want, and click **OK**.

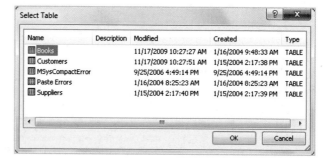

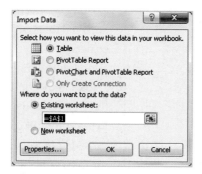

4. In the Import Data dialog box, select in which form you want the data and where you want the data placed—either in the current worksheet or in a new worksheet. Make your selections and click **OK**. The data will appear in the format you selected.

Get Data from the Web

More and more data is being offered on the Web sites of companies and individuals. Excel lets you select what pieces of data you want from a Web page and import them in a few clicks.

1. Select the cell into which you want to place the beginning of the range of imported data.

2. On the Data tab Get External Data group, click **From Web**. The New Web Query dialog box appears.

3. Type the address of the Web site from which you want to retrieve data, click **Go**, and then navigate to the page where the data is located (expand the dialog box by dragging a corner).

4. Click the table selection arrow in the upper-leftmost corner of each table whose data you want. The arrow changes to a check mark when selected (see Figure 10-4).

5. Click **Options** on the toolbar to open the Web Query Options dialog box. Make any formatting or other importing changes, and click **OK**.

6. Click **Import**. Verify where you want the data placed—either in the current worksheet or in a new worksheet. Make your choice and click **OK**. The data is displayed in Excel.

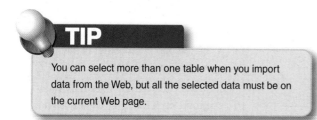

TIP

You can select more than one table when you import data from the Web, but all the selected data must be on the current Web page.

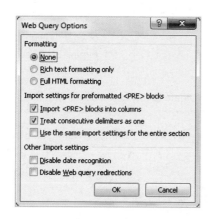

Add External Data from Existing Connections

You can import data from any existing connection files that are available on your computer or network. If you have not yet added data connections (see "Add Connections" later in the chapter), you might be able to add prebuilt connections provided by others. Excel provides sample connections you can use to download information from Microsoft Web sites.

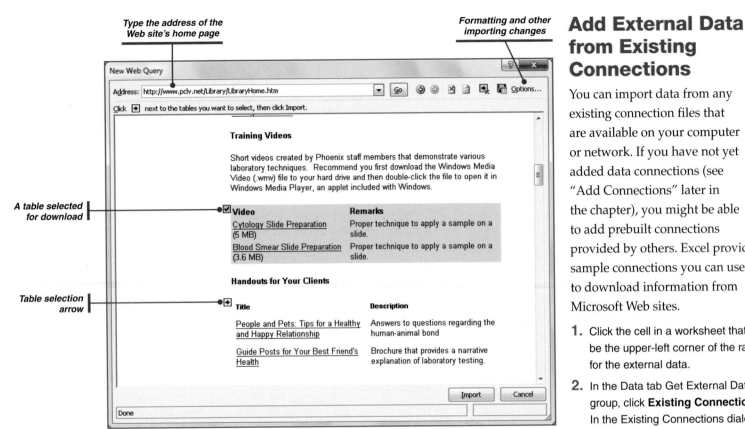

Type the address of the Web site's home page

Formatting and other importing changes

A table selected for download

Table selection arrow

Figure 10-4: Capturing data from the Internet is simply a matter of selecting table indicators.

1. Click the cell in a worksheet that will be the upper-left corner of the range for the external data.

2. In the Data tab Get External Data group, click **Existing Connections**. In the Existing Connections dialog box, select the connection you want from the current workbook, or your network or computer (see Figure 10-5), and click **Open**.

–Or–

Click **Browse For More** to navigate to any connections that are not listed in the dialog box.

3. Verify where you want the data placed in the Import Data dialog box, and click **OK**. The data is imported.

NOTE

When you open a workbook that contains data connections, by default, the connections are disabled. Click **Enable Content** on the Security Warning bar to enable connections that you are sure are safe. If the file is on a network, you may also be asked if you want to make the workbook a trusted document, that is, one that you will no longer be asked to verify its trustworthiness. Click **Yes** or **No**, depending on your security situation.

| ⚠ Security Warning | Data connections have been disabled | Enable Content |

10

QUICKSTEPS

SETTING EXTERNAL DATA RANGE PROPERTIES

You can change several parameters that affect an *external data range* (external data not in an Excel table). You can change when the data is refreshed, the name of the connection, and formatting properties. (A similar, but less detailed, dialog box, External Data Properties, appears when external data is within an Excel table, since many of the options are covered by table properties.)

Click a cell in an external data range. In the Data tab Connections group, click **Properties**. The External Data Range Properties dialog box appears, shown in Figure 10-6.

SET WHEN TO REFRESH

In the Refresh Control area, select whether you want to enable background (automatic) refreshes and when you want them, by time and/or when the workbook is opened.

DETERMINE HOW IMPORTED DATA APPEARS

In the Data Formatting And Layout area, select the formatting and layout options that you want. Avoid including row numbers, unless you absolutely need them. It only tends to confuse things with the row numbering provided by Excel.

CONTROL HOW NEW ROWS ARE ADDED

In the If The Number Of Rows area, decide if, when refreshing, you want to add new cells or new rows, or overwrite existing cells when there are more rows in the source data than in the worksheet.

Figure 10-5: Connections can be found locally in a workbook or computer, or on a network.

Figure 10-6: Control refresh and formatting options for imported data in the External Data Range Properties dialog box.

Workbook Connections

Name	Description	Last Refreshed
Acme Books		
Connection		
Customers		

Add...
Remove
Properties...
Refresh
Manage Sets...

Locations where connections are used in this workbook

Click here to see where the selected connections are used

Close

Figure 10-7: You can view and manage data connections within a workbook.

Manage Connections

Connections information—such as the path to source data and what form the data is in—is typically stored in connection files, such as Office Database Connections (.odc), or queries, such as Web Queries (.iqy) and Database Queries (.dqy). You can modify the parameters of these connections, refresh data in the workbook from these sources, and add or remove them, as well as use other features.

VIEW CONNECTIONS

1. In the Data tab Connections group, click **Connections**. The Workbook Connections dialog box, shown in Figure 10-7, shows any connections in the workbook.

2. To quickly locate where a connection is used within the workbook, click a connection to select it, and click **Click Here To See**. The sheet and range where the data is located in the workbook is displayed, along with other details, as applicable.

Locations where connections are used in this workbook		
Sheet	Name	Location
Access	Table_Acme_Books.accdb	$A$1:$J$30

REMOVE CONNECTIONS

1. In the Data tab Connections group, click **Connections**.

2. Select the connection and click **Remove**. Read the message that tells you removing the connection will separate the data from its source (the data itself is not removed from the workbook or source) and that refreshes will no longer work. Click **OK** to remove the connection.

Microsoft Excel

Removing connection(s) will separate this workbook from its data source(s), and data refresh operations in the workbook will no longer succeed. Click Cancel to keep connection(s), or click OK to proceed with connection removal.

OK   Cancel

ADD CONNECTIONS

1. In the Data tab Connections group, click **Connections** and click **Add**. The Existing Connections dialog box shows any connection files it finds on your computer or network (see Figure 10-5).

2. Click a connection you want to add, and click **Open**. The connection is added to your workbook.

NOTE

Adding a connection to your workbook does not import data from the source defined in the connection. To add data from a connection, see "Add External Data from Existing Connections" earlier in the chapter.

REFRESH DATA

External data can be updated, or *refreshed*, to transfer any changes in the source data to the data you imported into Excel. You can refresh an individual connection or all connections in the workbook in sequence.

- Refresh options include:
  - **Refresh** connects to the source data and updates it in Excel.
  - **Refresh All** updates all external data ranges in the workbook (it doesn't matter which cells are selected).
  - **Refresh Status** displays the External Data Refresh Status dialog box and the status of in-progress refreshes.
  - **Cancel Refresh** interrupts the updating of your original data with the changes in the source data.

- To refresh an individual connection, in the Data tab Connections group, click **Connections**, select the connection you want to refresh, and click **Refresh**.

  –Or–

  Click a cell in the external data range, and in the Data tab Connections group, click the top half of **Refresh All**.

- To refresh all connections in the workbook, click the **Refresh** down arrow in the Workbook Connections dialog box.

  –Or–

  Click the **Refresh All** down arrow in the Connections group.

  In either case, click **Refresh All**. A connection dialog box will appear for each connection and allow you to update the external data.

EDIT A QUERY

You may be able to change the specifics of the data you are requesting from a source, depending on how you acquired the data. For example, when selecting tables on a Web page, you are setting up a *query* that tells Excel which of the available tables you want. (When connecting to an entire Access table, you are not establishing a query.)

1. In the Data tab Connections group, click **Connections**, select the connection whose query you want to change, and click **Properties**.

2. In the Connection Properties dialog box, click the **Definition** tab. At the bottom of the tab, click **Edit Query**. The dialog box that appears depends on the type of connection you are editing. For example, when changing a query from a text file, the Text Import Wizard opens (see Figure 10-2).

3. Make changes to the data you want imported, click **Import**, and close the connections dialog boxes.

Use Excel with Web Technology

The work you do in Excel is not confined to your computer. You can share workbooks, as described in Chapter 9, but you can extend well beyond that in breadth, as well as in capabilities, by making your work available to be displayed in Web browsers such as Microsoft Internet Explorer. You can save or publish to Web pages what you create in Excel—from entire workbooks to individual elements—such as worksheets, charts, ranges, and PivotTable reports. Excel converts your work to *HTML*, the *Hypertext Markup Language* used to display text, graphics, and other items on the Internet and intranets. In addition, you can choose to publish many elements to Web pages with *interactive* capabilities, allowing users to not only view your work, but also to *use* your work to enter, change, sort, filter, and otherwise manipulate data. (This capability requires that you transfer workbooks to an Excel Services–enabled server, which is introduced later in this section.)

Save a Workbook as a Web Page

Workbooks can be saved for use on the Internet or within a local intranet (see the "Understanding the Difference Between Save and Publish" QuickFacts for more information on the meaning of *save* and *publish*).

1. Open the workbook you want to put on a Web page.

2. Click **File** and click **Save As**.

3. In the Save As dialog box, click the **Save As Type** down arrow, and click **Single File Web Page** to save the workbook data and all elements (such as illustrations and tables) within one file.

–Or–

Click **Web Page** to save the workbook as a "mapping" Web page that links to an associated folder containing workbook elements.

In either case, a few options for saving are added to the dialog box.

4. In the Save area of the Save As dialog box, verify that **Entire Workbook** is selected. (You can also save parts of a workbook by clicking Selection, as discussed later in the chapter.)

5. Click **Change Title**. In the Set Page Title dialog box, type a descriptive title for the Web page. This title appears in the title bar of the user's browser and helps to quickly identify the nature of the material on the page. Click **OK**.

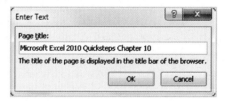

6. Browse to where you want the Web page located, type the file name, and click **Save**. A dialog box informs you that incompatible features will not be retained. Click **Yes** to continue. The workbook version in Excel is now in the Web page format. Figure 10-8 shows a worksheet saved as a Web page in Internet Explorer version 8.

Publish Workbook Items as a Web Page

You can choose to publish the entire workbook, individual worksheets, or just selected objects and cells.

1. Open the workbook you want to put on a Web page, and select the item or range you want placed on the Web page (you'll have the opportunity to fine-tune your choice later).

2. Click **File** and click **Save As**.

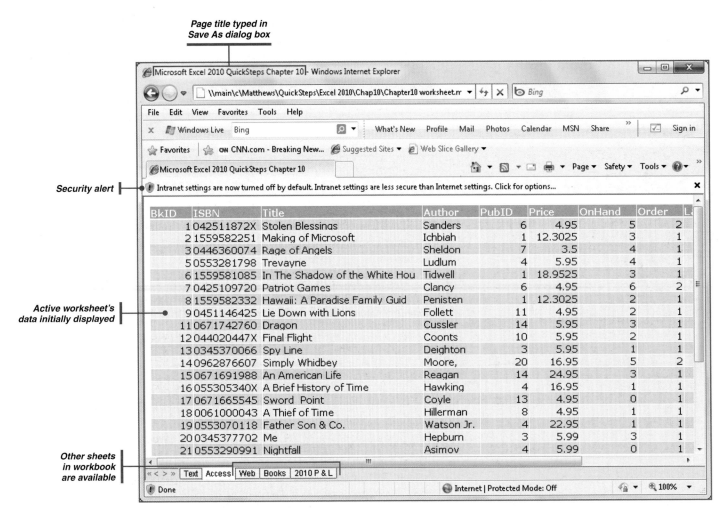

Page title typed in Save As dialog box

Security alert

Active worksheet's data initially displayed

Other sheets in workbook are available

BkID	ISBN	Title	Author	PubID	Price	OnHand	Order	L
1	042511872X	Stolen Blessings	Sanders	6	4.95	5	2	
2	1559582251	Making of Microsoft	Ichbiah	1	12.3025	3	1	
3	0446360074	Rage of Angels	Sheldon	7	3.5	4	1	
5	0553281798	Trevayne	Ludlum	4	5.95	4	1	
6	1559581085	In The Shadow of the White Hou	Tidwell	1	18.9525	3	1	
7	0425109720	Patriot Games	Clancy	6	4.95	6	2	
8	1559582332	Hawaii: A Paradise Family Guid	Penisten	1	12.3025	2	1	
9	0451146425	Lie Down with Lions	Follett	11	4.95	2	1	
11	0671742760	Dragon	Cussler	14	5.95	3	1	
12	044020447X	Final Flight	Coonts	10	5.95	2	1	
13	0345370066	Spy Line	Deighton	3	5.95	1	1	
14	0962876607	Simply Whidbey	Moore,	20	16.95	5	2	
15	0671691988	An American Life	Reagan	14	24.95	3	1	
16	055305340X	A Brief History of Time	Hawking	4	16.95	1	1	
17	0671665545	Sword Point	Coyle	13	4.95	0	1	
18	0061000043	A Thief of Time	Hillerman	8	4.95	1	1	
19	0553070118	Father Son & Co.	Watson Jr.	4	22.95	1	1	
20	0345377702	Me	Hepburn	3	5.99	3	1	
21	0553290991	Nightfall	Asimov	4	5.99	0	1	

Figure 10-8: A worksheet displays well in a Web browser, although it does not include any interactive elements, such as AutoFilter buttons.

3. In the Save As dialog box, click the **Save As Type** down arrow, and click **Single File Web Page** to save the workbook data and all elements (such as shapes and tables) within one file.

–Or–

Click **Web Page** to save the workbook as a "mapping" Web page that links to an associated folder that contains workbook elements.

NOTE

While there are benefits to saving or publishing your Excel work in HTML, you do run the risk that your worksheets will not display as fully intended. This is especially true for many of the latest Excel 2010 features. To provide the closest representation of your original work, your best option is simply to provide a copy of the workbook by disk, e-mail, or other means. For broader access, publish a copy to an Excel Services–enabled Web site, though, again, there are limitations to using only a Web browser (see the "Understanding SkyDrive, SharePoint, and Excel Services" QuickFacts later in the chapter). Perhaps the best compromise of true representation and broad access is to save the content as a PDF (Portable Document Format) or XPS (XML Paper Specification) file. Anyone with a reader program (such as the free Acrobat Adobe Reader) can view the more popular PDF file in whatever venue it is delivered to them, as shown in Figure 10-9. You can save workbooks, tables, sheets, and selected cells as a PDF or XPS file from Save As on the File menu.

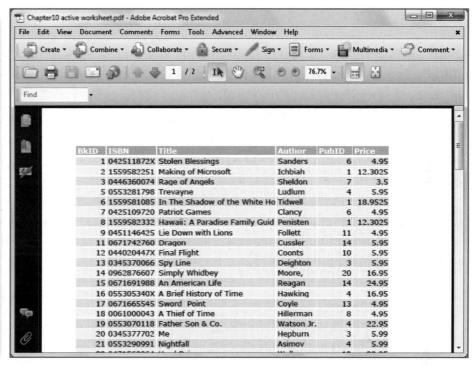

Figure 10-9: The PDF format is a universally recognized way to transmit just about any information you want to share.

4. In the Save area of the Save As dialog box, click **Entire Workbook**.

   –Or–

   Click **Selection: *your selected element***. (Don't worry if the element you want published isn't displayed—you will get a chance to choose it.)

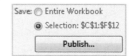

5. Click **Change Title**. In the Set Page Title dialog box, type a descriptive title for the Web page. This title appears in the title bar of the user's Web browser and helps to quickly identify the nature of the material on the page. Click **OK**.

TIP

You can modify several aspects of a saved or published Web page to improve how it appears in users' browsers. In the Save As dialog box, click **Tools** and click **Web Options**. In the dialog box of the same name, you can change options that deal with the users' anticipated browser and monitor resolution, fonts, and how files are named and located.

QUICK**FACTS**

UNDERSTANDING SKYDRIVE, SHAREPOINT, AND EXCEL SERVICES

You can upload an Excel Web page to any Internet server for public or private use, but Microsoft, through its Microsoft Live and Microsoft Office products, makes uploading easier and more integrated with Excel.

- **SkyDrive**, a part of Windows Live (see Figure 10-11), is a form of "cloud computing" similar to Google Docs whereby you can store documents on a Microsoft server located in the "cloud" of the Web for your own private access, or you can share them with others as you choose. All you need to view and work on documents of your own or those shared by others is a free Microsoft Live account and a browser.

- **SharePoint** is a platform for Web sites that supports team collaboration and document sharing using a server-based product (Microsoft SharePoint Server 2010 and associated tools) to host the data

Continued . . .

6. Browse to where you want the Web page located, type the file name, and click **Publish**. The Publish As Web Page dialog box appears, as shown in Figure 10-10.

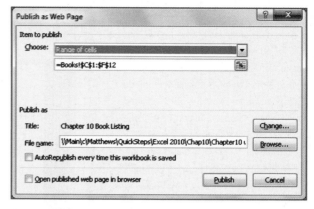

Figure 10-10: You can select what workbook item you want to publish, as well as other publishing parameters.

7. Verify that the item or range you want saved to a Web page is displayed in the Choose text box. If it is not correct, click the down arrow to select another worksheet and see the individual items on each sheet.

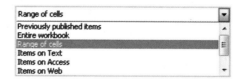

8. Select the **AutoRepublish Every Time This Workbook Is Saved** check box to automatically update the published range or item when the workbook is saved.

9. Select the **Open Published Web Page In Browser** check box to view the page in your default browser.

10. Click **Publish** when finished. A Web page of the selected range, worksheet, or entire workbook is placed in the folder specified in the Save As dialog box while the Excel workbook file remains the same.

Use Hyperlinks

Hyperlinks (or *links*) are items in documents that, when clicked, take you to other documents, different locations in the same document, other programs,

UNDERSTANDING SKYDRIVE, SHAREPOINT, AND EXCEL SERVICES *(Continued)*

and a desktop-based product (Microsoft SharePoint Workspace 2010) to connect with the server, upload content, and synchronize information. Excel provides an option to connect to SharePoint servers and save workbooks to them without the need to install the desktop component. See *SharePoint 2010 QuickSteps*, published by McGraw-Hill.

- **Excel Services** is the gold standard for sharing Excel information using Internet technology. This technology allows Excel 2010 to publish data to the server-based SharePoint Server 2010 (SPS) and provides interactive access to workbooks using only a Web browser. When a user clicks the workbook in a SPS document library, Excel Services loads the sheets and items you made available, refreshes any external data, recalculates, and returns the data to the user's Web browser. The user can edit the data within the browser. Security is paramount. Access to the file is protected by a logon password, and any interaction with the workbook can be logged and an audit trail established to satisfy regulatory rules.

The process for each of these features starts in Excel 2010 using the Save & Send command on the File menu. Select the service you want to save or publish to, and follow the logon instructions.

Figure 10-11: **SkyDrive on Microsoft Live provides free storage for your Excel and other documents.**

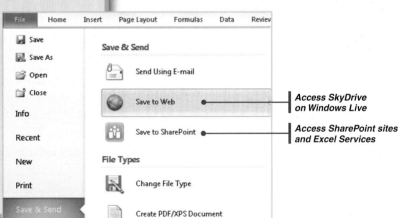

and other locations. The Internet has brought links to mainstream use ("surfing the Web" is really just following a trail of several links), but hyperlinking is not just confined to Web pages. For example, for each company in a table on a worksheet, you could create a hyperlink that would open Internet Explorer with that company's Web site home page (see Figure 10-12). In addition, you could create a link to a Microsoft Word document that provides narrative support for a value in a balance sheet, or you could create a bookmark to take you to a specific cell.

Figure 10-12: *Creating a hyperlink in a worksheet connects your data with other resources.*

Create a
hyperlink...

...to link to other
documents or
locations

CREATE A HYPERLINK

1. Select the cells, pictures, or other items you want to serve as the hyperlink.

2. In the Insert tab Links group, click **Hyperlink**.

   –Or–

   Right-click the selected item, and click **Hyperlink**.

3. In the Insert Hyperlink dialog box (shown in Figure 10-13), under Link To, select where the destination of the link will be.

   - **Existing File Or Web Page** opens a set of controls you can use to find a Web address or file. Click **Browse The Web** 🔍 to open your default browser to your home page. Click **Browse For File** 📂 to open a dialog box similar to the Open dialog box.

   - **Place In This Document** opens a text box where you can type a cell address and opens a list box where you can choose a cell reference or named reference.

   - **Create New Document** lets you name and locate a new Office document. It opens the blank document in its parent program if you select **Edit The New Document Now**.

   - **E-mail Address** displays text boxes that you use to enter e-mail address(es) and the subject of the message. When clicked, a new message dialog box appears in the default e-mail program with the address(es) displayed in the To box and the subject filled in. (You can send to multiple addressees by using a semicolon (;) to separate each address.)

4. Click **OK**.

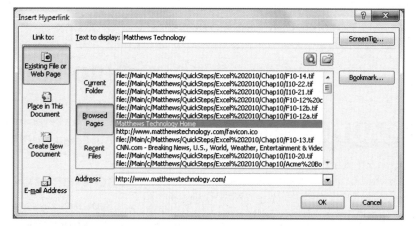

Figure 10-13: The Insert Hyperlink dialog box provides controls that allow you to tailor the destination of a hyperlink.

10

TIP

See Chapter 2 for information on defining locations in Excel by naming the cells.

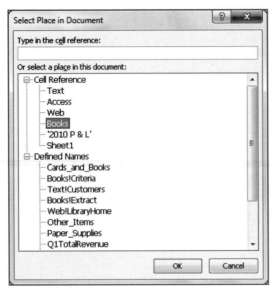

Figure 10-14: You can designate where in a workbook a hyperlink will land the user.

CAUTION

You can only save workbooks that contain macros using one of the two macro-enabled Save As Type formats that support them: Excel Macro-Enabled Workbook (.xlsm) or Excel Macro-Enabled Template (.xltm).

GO TO A BOOKMARK

Bookmarks are locations within the current workbook that you can use a hyperlink to "jump" to.

1. Select the cells, pictures, or other items you want to serve as the hyperlink.
2. In the Insert tab Links group, click **Hyperlink**.

   –Or–

   Right-click the selected item, and click **Hyperlink**.
3. In the Insert Hyperlink dialog box, under Link To, select **Existing File Or Web Page**, and click **Bookmark** (on the far right of the dialog box).
4. In the Select Place In Document dialog box, shown in Figure 10-14, type a cell reference or sheet, or select a named cell or range that you want as the hyperlink destination/bookmark.
5. Click **OK** twice.

EDIT A HYPERLINK

1. Right-click the cell that contains the hyperlink you want to change, and click **Edit Hyperlink**. The Edit Hyperlink dialog box appears, similar to the Insert Hyperlink dialog box (see Figure 10-13).
2. Make changes to the hyperlink destination (see "Create a Hyperlink").

   –Or–

   Click the **Remove Link** button to remove the hyperlink.
3. Click **OK**.

Automate Excel

You can automate repetitive tasks in Excel by using *macros*. Macros are recorded either by keyboard and mouse actions or by using Microsoft Visual Basic for Applications (VBA), a programming language.

Use Recorded Macros

Repetitive tasks you perform in Excel can be *recorded* as a macro and re-run at later times. For example, if you formatted a worksheet differently for each

NOTE

While working with macros, you might be interrupted and asked if you want to enable macros in the workbook (see Figure 10-15). By default, macros are disabled (as are data connections, described earlier in the chapter). Macro security is important, because macros are executable programs and can bring havoc to your system when used by hackers for malicious purposes. Though you can change the default settings in the Trust Center (see Chapter 4), it's a safer bet to go along with Excel and simply enable the actions as they are presented to you.

of your division heads, you could record the formatting sequence for each. For next quarter's report, simply run each macro in turn to quickly get the tailored results you want. Though macros are small programs written in the VBA programming language, you don't have to know VBA or be a programmer to record and run them.

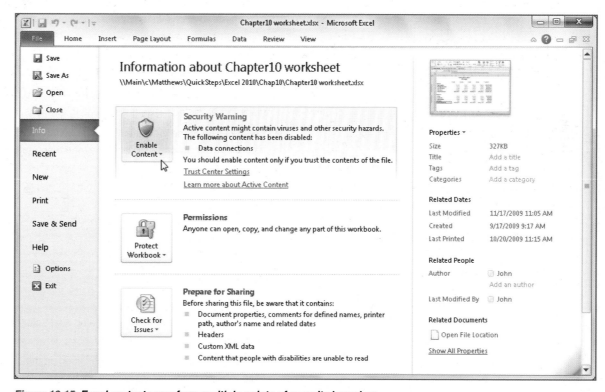

*Figure 10-15: **Excel protects you from multiple points of security breaches.***

TIP

If you record a step in the macro you don't want, you can open the macro in the Visual Basic Editor and remove the unwanted code. However, it might be easier to delete the macro and start over.

TIP

To use relative cell references in the cell addresses, click **Relative References** on the Macros menu before you start recording a macro (see Chapter 4 for information on relative and absolute references).

RECORD A MACRO

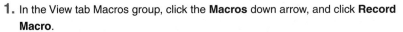

1. In the View tab Macros group, click the **Macros** down arrow, and click **Record Macro**.

2. In the Macro Name text box, create a name to identify the macro. Macro names must begin with a letter and must not contain spaces or be the same name as a cell reference.

3. In the Shortcut Key text box (creating a shortcut key is optional), type a letter (no numbers) to use in combination with **CTRL** that will run the macro. To use an uppercase letter, the key combination will be **CTRL+SHIFT+your letter**. (If you choose a shortcut key combination that Excel uses for other purposes, your shortcut will override Excel's when the workbook that contains the macro is open.) For example, in the last illustration, **CTRL+B** was used as the shortcut key; it is also used for bold type, so the bold shortcut will no longer work.

4. In the Store Macro In drop-down list box, choose whether you want to store the macro in the current workbook, in a new workbook, or in your Personal Macro Workbook, which makes the macro available to workbooks other than the workbook in which it was created.

5. In the Description text box (this step is optional), type a description that helps you identify the nature of the macro. Click **OK**.

6. Perform the steps involved to do the repetitive task. These steps might include opening dialog boxes, selecting settings, creating formulas, and applying formatting.

7. Click **Macros** in the View tab Macro group, and click **Stop Recording** to finish recording your actions as part of the macro and return to normal use.

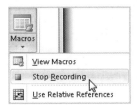

8. To test your macro, press your shortcut key.

   –Or–

   Press **ALT+F8** to open the Macro dialog box. Select the macro you want to test, and click **Run**.

9. If your macro doesn't function as designed, in the Macro dialog box, select it, and click **Step Into**. Each step of the macro will be executed in turn, allowing you to locate the place where there is an error.

DELETE A RECORDED MACRO

1. In the View tab Macros group, click **Macros** and click **View Macros**.

2. In the Macro dialog box, shown in Figure 10-16, select the macro you want deleted, and click **Delete**. Confirm the deletion by clicking **Yes**.

Figure 10-16: The Macro dialog box lists available macros and provides the tools to run, edit, configure, and remove them.

ADD A MACRO TO THE QUICK ACCESS TOOLBAR

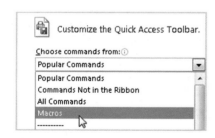

1. Open the workbook that contains the macro you want to add, unless the macro is stored in your Personal Macro Workbook.

2. Click **File**, click **Options**, and click **Quick Access Toolbar**. In the Customize The Quick Access Toolbar pane, click the **Choose Commands From** down arrow, and click **Macros**.

3. Click the macro you want to add to the toolbar, and click **Add**. The macro names appear in the right pane of the dialog box. Click **OK**. The macro is added to your Quick Access toolbar.

Edit a Macro

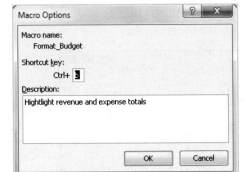

You can change minor attributes of a macro, such as its shortcut key, without using VBA. (To edit the code that defines the actions of the macro, you will have to use the Microsoft Visual Basic Editor, shown in Figure 10-17, a discussion of which is beyond the scope of this book. To access the Editor, click **Edit** in step 2 in the following procedure instead of clicking **Options**.)

1. In the View tab Macros group, click **Macros** and click **View Macros**.

2. Select the macro you want to change, and click **Options**.

3. In the Macro Options dialog box, change the shortcut key and/or the macro description.

4. Click **OK** when finished.

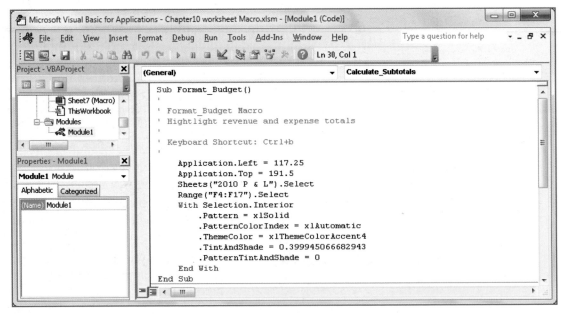

Figure 10-17: *The Microsoft Visual Basic Editor provides a graphical palette for working on macros and other VBA code.*

deleting in tables, 199
hiding, 55
identifying, 31
locking, 77–78
removing, 54
selecting, 42
selecting in tables, 199
unhiding, 55
unlocking, 79

S

Save As dialog box, displaying, 24
Save button, identifying on Quick Access
    toolbar, 24
Save Workspace feature, using, 79
saving
    AutoRecover information, 22–23
    copies of workbooks, 24–25
    legacy files, 25
    versus publishing, 260
    and viewing custom views, 136
    workbooks, 96
    workbooks automatically, 22–23
    workbooks manually, 24
scatter (XY) chart, function of, 140
scenarios
    comparing, 224
    creating, 222–223
    editing, 223–224
    running, 223
    saving Solver solutions as, 229
scientific notation, using to enter numbers,
    33–34
Scope down arrow, clicking, 88
screenshots, taking, 177–180
scroll bars
    function of, 5
    location of, 4
scrolling, controlling, 82
security. *See* Trust Center
security warnings, reading, 99
selections
    magnifying, 124
    printing, 127
shading, adding to cells, 74
shape fills, inserting pictures into, 191
shapes. *See also* SmartArt shapes
    adding, 168
    adding text to, 170
    changing, 175
    changing between, 169
    changing fill color of, 191

cropping to, 184
removing WordArt from, 193
resetting, 184
setting gradients and textures for,
    191–192
shared workbooks
    accepting changes to, 248
    discontinuing, 246–247
    protecting, 246
    rejecting changes to, 248
    using History worksheets with,
        246–247
    using passwords with, 245
    working with changes in, 246–248
SharePoint, 264–265
sheets. *See* worksheet
sheet navigator
    function of, 5
    location of, 4
short date setting, displaying, 34
shortcut, creating to start Excel, 2–3
Show/Hide Table of Contents tool, using
    with Help, 16
Shrink To Fit alignment, applying
    to text, 73
sizing handle
    function of, 4
    location of, 4
SkyDrive, 264–265
slicer filters, applying and removing, 239
slicers
    customizing, 239–249
    features of, 237–238
    inserting, 238–239
    removing, 240
Smart tags, using, 109
SmartArt shapes, 168. *See also* shapes
    changing, 174
    converting pictures to, 190
    inserting, 173–174
social security numbers, formatting, 37
Solver
    example, 227
    features of, 225–226
    installing, 227
    setting up, 228–229
Solver settings
    changing, 231
    saving, 229–230
Solver solutions, saving, 229–231
sorting data in tables, 206–209
sparklines
    creating, 162–165
    removing, 164

spelling, verifying, 48
splitting worksheets, 79–81
spreadsheets. *See* worksheets
stacked illustrations, reordering, 184
stacks, manipulating, 184
Start menu, using, 2
Starter 2010 version, described, 18
status bar
    function of, 5
    location of, 4
stock chart, function of, 140
Stop tool, using with Help, 16
styles. *See also* cell styles
    adding to outlines, 217–218
    applying to tables, 200–203
    basing on existing styles, 69
    customizing, 68–69
    place on formatting heap, 62–63
    removing from tables, 203
    selecting for PivotTables, 241
    using with illustrations, 187
subtotals, adding to tables, 217
SUM function, using, 108
summary rows, adding styles to, 218
surface chart, function of, 140
system date/time, caution about, 38

T

table data, referencing in formulas, 203
table elements, changing, 201
Table of Contents pane, displaying, 15
table styles, creating, 201–203
tables
    adding borders to, 197
    adding columns to, 198
    adding from Access databases, 254–255
    adding rows to, 198
    adding styles to summary rows, 218
    adding subtotals to, 217
    adding Total row to, 199–200
    applying styles to, 200–203
    column headers in, 31
    converting to standard data ranges, 245
    creating, 196–197
    creating data entry messages in, 205
    creating error messages in, 205
    creating from existing data, 198
    creating messages in, 206
    creating quickly, 199
    deleting columns in, 199
    deleting rows in, 199
    features of, 196

fields in, 196
filtering, 210–214
locating validation data in, 205
overview of, 196
performing functions in columns, 199
records in, 31, 196
removing duplicate values from, 202
removing filters from, 210
removing styling from, 203
reverting to ranges, 202
selecting columns in, 199
selecting rows in, 199
setting up criteria and extract ranges
    for, 213
setting up data validation in, 203
sorting data in, 206–209
summing last column in, 199
using AutoFilter with, 210–212
using wildcards in filtering
    criteria, 214
validating data in, 203–206
tabs
    creating, 10
    function of, 5
    locations of, 6
    rearranging, 9
    on ribbon, 7
task pane
    function of, 5
    location of, 4
    relocating and resizing, 176
templates. *See also* chart templates;
    Normal template
    creating charts from, 154
    creating workbooks from, 18–19
    saving themes as, 67
    saving workbooks as, 24
Templates folder, locating, 24
text. *See also* illustrations
    adding to shapes, 170
    adding WordArt styling to, 192–193
    aligning, 72
    alignment of, 30, 32
    applying formatting to, 70
    changing appearance of, 71
    composition of, 30
    constraining on multiple lines, 33
    converting to data, 252–254
    entering continuously, 31
    entering on one line, 31
    fitting into text boxes, 171
    interpreting numbers as, 33
    selecting for charts, 142
    wrapping on multiple lines, 32

text boxes
    adding, 171
    deleting, 183
themed colors, changing, 60, 62–64
themed fonts, changing, 64–65
themed graphic effects, changing, 66
themes
    changing, 60
    changing customizations of, 66
    examples of, 61
    fonts used with, 69
    identifying, 60
    locating and applying, 67–68
    place on formatting heap, 62
    saving as templates, 67
thousands separator, adding, 36
thumbnails, displaying for pictures, 175
time, adding to headers and footers, 120
times
    changing default display of, 37
    conventions for, 36
    entering, 36–38
    values assigned to, 37
times and dates, considering as
    numbers, 30
title bar
    function of, 5
    location of, 4
toner, conserving in printing, 126
tool tabs, appearance of, 7
tools. *See also* Quick Access toolbar
    adding and removing, 10–12
    hiding on ribbon, 13
    using with paste operations, 43–44
Top alignment, applying to text, 73
Total row, adding to tables, 199–200
Track Changes feature, enabling, 246–247
trendlines, using with charts, 159–160
Trust Center
    changing updating of links in, 101
    overview of, 98–99
typefaces, changing, 70–71

U

Undo feature
    using with deleted data, 39
    using with illustrations, 184
Unhide feature, using, 55
unions, referencing, 89
user name, changing in comments, 57

V

validation data, locating in tables, 205
Vertical alignment, applying
    to text, 73
View Side By Side feature, using, 82
views. *See also* custom views
    changing, 248
    customizing, 247–248
    switching between, 114
    types of, 114–116
Visual Basic Editor, accessing, 272

W

Watch Window, opening, 111
watches, removing, 111
Web, getting data from, 255–256
Web Apps version, described, 17
Web pages
    publishing workbook items on,
      261–264
    saving workbooks as, 260–261
what-if problems. *See* Solver
wildcards, using to filter tables, 214
windows
    arranging, 81
    controlling scrolling of, 82
    saving arrangements of, 79
Word, using charts in, 157–159

WordArt
    adding, 172
    removing from shapes, 193
WordArt styling, adding to text,, 192–193
workbook items, publishing on Web
    pages, 261–264
workbook name
    function of, 5
    location of, 4
workbook path, adding to headers and
    footers, 120
workbook views, accessing, 4–5
workbooks
    adding identifying information to,
      25–27
    browsing, 20
    closing, 4, 28
    comparing, 82–83
    creating, 18–19
    customizing, 21
    discontinuing sharing of, 246–247
    merging, 249
    opening, 19–21
    opening in Protected View, 21
    preparing for sharing of, 243
    protecting with passwords, 243–244
    saving, 96
    saving as templates, 24
    saving as Web pages, 260–261
    saving automatically, 22–23
    saving copies of, 24–25
    saving manually, 24
    sharing, 244–245
    source versus destination, 96
    splitting, 79–81
worksheet elements, protecting, 248–249
worksheet grid
    function of, 5
    location of, 4
worksheet name, adding to headers and
    footers, 120
Worksheet tabs, coloring, 82

worksheet window
    function of, 5
    location of, 4
    maximizing, 4
    minimizing, 4
    restoring, 4
worksheets
    adding, 81
    changing default number of, 82
    copying, 81
    defined, 3
    deleting, 81
    features of, 3
    grid layout of, 30–31
    moving, 81
    moving through, 82
    printing, 127–128
    printing in lieu or print areas, 127–128
    renaming, 82
    scaling data for printing, 134
    seeing more of, 115
    viewing from multiple workbooks,
      81–82
Wrap Text alignment, applying to text, 73
Wrap Text button, clicking, 32

X

"x," appearance in file extension, 22
.xls file format, saving files to, 25
.xltx files, saving, 24–25
XML files, benefit of, 22–23
XY (scatter) chart, function of, 140

Z

zip codes, formatting, 37
Zoom, selecting magnification, 124
Zoom percentage, selecting, 123